Acknowledgements

Because the FES has been running continuously for 23 years, it would be impractical to name all the people who have contributed to the successful running of the survey since its beginning in 1957. However, the authors wish to acknowledge the efforts and dedication of a great number of contributors: first, the interviewers and informants who have worked together to produce the data arising from some 115,000 households since 1957; second, the excellent support for the FES by the Social Survey Division Field Branch, which has been particularly important to the success of the survey; third, the FES demands very detailed and sophisticated coding, and the authors would like to acknowledge the contributions of the Primary Analysis Branch, some members of which have spent most of their SSD careers on this survey.

The authors would also like to acknowledge the contributions to the Handbook of a number of individuals: Terry Kenney, who is responsible for the analysis of referrals from Primary Analysis Branch as well as for the production of the FES Coding Notes, and to Rita Garnett who assists in this work; Bob Butcher, who was responsible for a number of innovations to the sampling procedures on the FES; Joan Warwick, who is in charge of the FES unit in Primary Analysis Branch; Madge Brailsford, currently FES Field Officer and also Field Officer for the Family Budget Survey experiments; Margaret Jones, former Field Officer of the FES and also Field Officer for the Annual Income Feasibility Study; Patrick Heady who designed and analysed the Annual Income Feasibility Study, and who also carried out major revisions to FES coding procedures; Anne Milne, who worked on the Family Budget Survey Pilot, and who also carried out desk research into inter-week bias in the FES; Malcolm Smyth, who carried out the experiment into usual earnings.

Contents

Appendices

1 Introduction

Definition. Fes is a continuous inquiry into into expenditure and income of domestic households in great Britain.

The Family Expenditure Survey (FES) is a continuous inquiry into the expenditure and income of domestic households in Great Britain; the FES in Northern Ireland is carried out completely separately though the same questionnaires and coding instructions are used in both surveys*. The survey was started in January 1957 and has been in continuous operation ever since. Since 1967 the annual sample has been about 10,750 addresses, drawn so as to represent all private households in Great Britain.

The responsibility for the running of the Family Expenditure Survey (FES) in Great Britain is divided between the Social Survey Division (SSD) of the Office of Population Censuses and Surveys (OPCS) and the Department of Employment (DE); while the overall design and content are kept under review by an inter-departmental committee under the chairmanship of the Central Statistical Office (CSO).

SSD is responsible for all stages of the operation up to and including coding, namely sample design, all the sample selection procedures, detailed design of the questionnaires and other documents used in the day-to-day work of the FES, field-work, editing and coding of completed budgets, including any recall on informants for further information. SSD also carry out operational research into the day-to-day working of the survey with a view to improving the technique, as well as special experiments. The computer analysis, analysis of annual results, presentation of annual reports and the provision of further data in tabular and computer tape form are the responsibility of DE. Close liaison is maintained between the DE, CSO and SSD in the day-to-day running of the survey.

The purpose of the Family Expenditure Survey Handbook is to discuss the contributions of the Social Survey Division of OPCS to the Family Expenditure Survey at the time of writing in late 1979, although most tables are only current for figures up to 1978. The Handbook includes the 1979 FES questionnaires and other interview documents current in 1979; it is therefore mainly for the user of FES data as well as for the survey specialist. It is intended to complement the FES Information Pack, which includes the FES Field Instructions, Coding Notes, Master Schedules as well as base tape codes and other computing documents.

Information Packs[1] have been prepared annually since 1975 by DE.

This is a revised version of the Handbook which was first produced by the Government Social Survey in 1969[2]. Each chapter has been up-dated, and there are several new chapters. These deal with uses of the FES, the role of the FES Research Unit, major changes in the FES since its commencement in 1957, a summary of all experimental work on methodology since 1950 and the use of the FES as a sampling frame for further surveys. Chapter 15 in the first edition, 'Limitations to the Accuracy of the FES,' has been expanded and retitled 'Reliability of the FES' (Chapter 14).

One major change has been to omit Chapters 10 to 14 of the first edition, which gave detailed notes about each questionnaire; these topics have either been moved to the appendices or omitted entirely, as much of this information is now available in the Information Pack.

In addition to the Handbook, there are three other sources of information available from OPCS about the work done by SSD on the FES. First, copies of the analysis of FES annual response figures; second, copies of current questionnaires; third, copies of the detailed Clerical Officer Sampling Instructions.

The main findings of the FES are reported in the annual report produced by DE. In addition to the annual report and the Information Pack, DE supplies unpublished tables of FES results on request. Reference to published results by other government departments is made in the FES Annual Reports. Copies of FES tapes are supplied to government departments for their own specialised analyses. Further copies of the tapes for the years 1961 — 63 and 1968 onwards are also held by the Social Science Research Council Survey Archive at the University of Essex, Wivenhoe Park, Colchester, Essex CO4 3SQ. Information for these years is provided to inquirers at the SSRC Survey Archive on request and subject to undertakings on the use of the data and on the maintenance of confidentiality, even though all computer tape information has been anonymised so that it is virtually impossible to identify individual households.

---

*The results of the Family Expenditure Survey appear in the Family Expenditure Survey annual reports, published by Her Majesty's Stationery Office. The FES annual reports, issued for each year from 1962, include results drawn from a sample of the Northern Ireland FES which is carried out separately by the Policy, Planning and Research Unit of the Department of Finance, Stormont. It is possible to merge the results of the two surveys to provide United Kingdom results as the Northern Ireland FES uses the same questionnaires, field instructions and coding notes as the Great Britian FES. The results of the full Northern Ireland sample are published in a separate report by HMSO Belfast.

References
[1] Family Expenditure Survey Information Pack— available on request from the Department of Employment.
[2] Kemsley, W F F. *Family Expenditure Survey-Handbook on the Sample, Fieldwork and Coding Procedures,* HMSO, London 1969.

2 Uses of the FES

[handwritten note: Fes is multi purpose survey, however, it is use by different government departments for different purposes.]

The FES belongs to the genus of surveys called consumer expenditure or budget surveys. The methods of collecting family (or household) expenditure differ widely: strictly speaking, the main purpose of this type of survey is to collect information about expenditure patterns, usually for the weights of a price index. However, the FES also collects income details from household members as well; in fact, although the FES is essentially a survey of household expenditure, a number of government departments value the FES solely for its income data. Therefore the FES is a multi-purpose inquiry covering a wide variety of needs, and providing an invaluable source of economic and social data.

One of its main advantages is that expenditure and income details are collected from each member of the household aged 16 and over; quite often in other surveys this information is collected by proxy. Another value lies in the fact that the FES has been carried out continuously since January 1957. (Most countries carry out this type of survey periodically every 5 or 10 years.) This means that statisticians and other researchers are provided with trend data in household expenditure patterns as well as trends in household income over a continuous period of up to 23 years.

The following are some of the main uses of FES data by government departments; some are publications of FES data by the departments; other uses are cases where the FES has been used to answer Written or Oral questions in Parliament.

Department of Employment

(i) *Retail Price Indices* A major use of the survey is in calculating the weights for the General Index of Retail Prices[1] compiled and published monthly by the Department of Employment. Prior to 1975, the weights were based on a 3-year moving average, based on the latest 3 years of FES data. Since January 1975 these weights have been derived from results obtained from the FES over a twelve-month period (covering July to June), except for a few items of expenditure for which a three-year period is used. In addition to the General Index of Retail Prices, since June 1969 there have been two special quarterly price indices for one-person and two-person pensioner households.[2] These two indices use three-year expenditure data from the FES to determine weights. General index and pensioner households are defined and their average expenditure shown in the Department of Employment Gazette.

(ii) *FES annual reports* FES data are published annually in a report issued by the Department of Employment by the end of the calendar year following that to which they refer. In preparing the data for the annual reports some adjustments to the original data collected by SSD are made by DE to a few items; in particular, to housing costs of owner-occupied and rent-free accommodation and to the income of employees temporarily not working. In addition, a sub-sample from the corresponding inquiry in Northern Ireland is merged with the data collected by Social Survey in providing data for the United Kingdom in the annual reports and the computer base tapes. Otherwise these reports give straightforward tabulations of the basic data showing how expenditure patterns vary for different household types, and in particular with household income. The reports also include tables giving characteristics of cooperating households in the sample.

Central Statistical Office

There are four main uses of the FES by the Central Statistical Office:

(i) *National Accounts*: The FES is used directly to provide data on consumers' expenditure in the United Kingdom where no other suitable data exists[3]. It is also of interest as a check on other sources[4].

(ii) *Distribution of income:* FES data on income are used in conjunction with the Inland Revenue Survey of Personal Incomes and the New Earnings Survey to produce tables of the distribution of income in the UK published in the National Accounts.[5]

(iii) *Re-distribution of income:* The FES has been used as a basis for an annual study into the effects of taxes and benefits on household income for various types of households[6]. Data on expenditure is also used to determine payments of indirect taxes.

(iv) *Regional accounts:* The FES is used directly in the compilation of estimates of regional consumers' expenditure and also for regional estimates of indirect taxes and gross domestic product.

H M Treasury

FES data have been used to estimate the effects of budget proposals on different family types in order to assess the extent to which direct taxes are progressive, as well as the distributional effects of other indirect taxes and benefits. It has also been used to estimate the number of households whose earnings are insufficient to claim all or part of their tax allowances, as well as estimating savings ratios.

Department of Health and Social Security

FES data are used in conjunction with administrative statistics to estimate the take-up of various means-tested benefits such as Supplementary Benefit, Family Income Supplement and free welfare food. The FES is also used to estimate the numbers of low income families (the poverty level) and the impact of tax rates on these families. It is also used to show the proportion of average income of retirement pensioners taken up by various types of expenditure. The FES has been used to estimate equivalence scales, which adjust income for household size and composition to obtain an equivalent standard of living[7]. Finally it has been used to estimate the proportion of lone mothers in full-time and part-time employment.

Department of Energy

The Department of Energy uses the FES to measure changes in the percentage of households served by gas and electricity and to estimate expenditure on various types of fuel by region, by size of household and by tenure. FES data has been used in a booklet 'Energy Tariffs and the Poor'[8].

Department of the Environment

FES income data is used to estimate the take-up of income -related benefits, such as rent rebates, rent allowances and rates rebates.

Department of Transport

FES data has been used to determine the relationship between household income and vehicle ownership[9].

This list provides some examples of the uses of the FES by government departments; the reader is referred to Appendix 9 of the *1978 FES Annual Report* and to the *Guide to Official Statistics* for more detailed references.

During 1979 FES results will be combined with family budget survey results for the other eight EEC countries to provide a 'harmonised' EEC Family Budget Survey[10].

The FES is not only used by government departments. It is widely used by Government Committees reporting on social characteristics of special household groups such as one-parent families with low income in relation to their needs. Recently the FES has been used, with data from other sources, by the Royal Commission on the Distribution of Income and Wealth[11]. The Office of Fair Trading is a main user of the instalment credit data, monitoring trends in interest rates charged for various types of credit. Local authorities use the FES for local estimates of shopping and travel expenditure. Academics have access to anonymised FES tapes at the SSRC Archieve at Essex University; tapes have been given to other educational establishments. FES data is also used by market research firms, trade unions and by businesses.

Users are not uncritical of the FES[12]. The main criticisms, both from within government and by academic users, concentrate on biases due to the FES response rate, on the accuracy of certain components of expenditure (alcohol and tobacco expenditure), and income (self-employment and investment income); and finally, on the size of the sample, which is too small for certain uses.

International comparisons indicate that relative to most other budget surveys, response on the FES is high, particularly as cooperation is defined in terms of *all* members of a household aged 16 and over keeping 14 day diaries of expenditure and also providing details of their individual incomes.

As will be pointed out in Chapter 14, experimental work seems to indicate that the problems of apparent understatement of alcohol and tobacco expenditure and investment and self-employment income may be intractable. Certainly other countries carrying out budget surveys share these problems.

Finally, most criticisms levelled at the survey merely reflect its importance to users of many varieties and requirements. The FES originally was designed to provide the weights for the RPI. Over the years, it has attempted to satisfy more and more users. This poses a classic dilemma for the survey practitioner who is gratified that the survey is used widely, but knows that all needs cannot be completely met by the one survey apparatus.

References

1 Department of Employment. *Method of construction and calculation of the Index of Retail Prices*, HMSO, 1967.

2 Department of Employment. *A Report of the Cost of Living Advisory Committee*, CMND. 3677, H M Stationery Office 1968.

3 Maurice, R.(Ed) *National Accounts Statistics, Sources and Methods*, HMSO, 1968.

4 A FES/Blue Book expenditure comparison for 1970-75 is available on request from the Central Statistical Office.

5 Estimates of the Distribution of income in the United Kingdom. *Economic Trends*, February 1979. This is the latest in a series of articles using FES data on non-taxable income and on incomes below the tax deduction card limit to estimate the distribution of personal income for the whole of the United Kingdom.

6 The Effects of Taxes and Benefits on Household Income 1977. *Economic Trends*, February 1979. This is the latest in a series of annual articles appearing in Economic Trends.

7 McClements, L D. *The Economics of Social Security*, Heinemann, London 1978.

8 *Energy Tariffs and the Poor*, Department of Energy Information Directorate, 1976; available from the Library, Department of Energy, Thames House South, Millbank, London SW1P 4QJ. The Department of Energy also publishes another report, *The Family Expenditure Survey Expenditure on Fuels*.

9 Giles, G E and T E Worsley, Development of methods for forecasting car ownership and use, in CSO *Economic Trends*, No. 310, August 1979. HMSO 1979, pp.99-108.

[10] While there was an attempt to harmonise coding nomenclature, each EEC country retained its own survey methodology. A comparison of the methodologies of the nine countries will be published in 1980 in a booklet entitled *Eurostat-Methodology of surveys on family budgets 1980.* It will be possible to obtain copies from Her Majesty's Stationery Office, P.O. Box 519 London SE1 9NH.

[11] Stark, T. *'The Distribution of Income in Eight Countries', Background Paper No. 4 Royal Commission on the Distribution of Income and Wealth*, London HMSO 1977.

[12] See Abel-Smith, B and Towsend, P. *The Poor and the Poorest, a new analysis of the Ministry of Labour's Family Expenditure Surveys of 1953-54 and 1960*; Occasional Papers on Social Administration, Number 17, G. Bell and Sons Ltd London 1965. Also see Townsend, P (Ed). *The Concept of Poverty*, particularly Chapter 5; and Townsend P, *Poverty in the United Kingdom: a survey of household resources and standards of living*, Penguin Books, Harmondsworth, Middlesex 1979.

3 The Work of the Social Survey Division on the FES

3.1 Summary of procedure

In the course of work on the FES, SSD interviewers visit nearly 11,000 addresses over each period of 12 months. The sample is based on a four-stage, stratified, rotating design with a uniform overall sampling fraction. Administrative areas of Great Britain form the primary sampling units, and 168 are in use each quarter. Each area is used four times at intervals of three months and is then replaced. Sixteen addresses are selected from the Electoral Registers in an area each time the area is used. At each selected address the interviewer endeavours to persuade the household to provide information on both expenditure and income. In order to ensure as complete an account as possible, each member of the household aged 16 or over (known as a 'spender') is asked to provide information. Only households where cooperation is forthcoming from each spender are accepted, and about 70% of pre-selected households actually participate in the inquiry.

Expenditure information is collected partly by interview and partly in diaries kept for 14 days by each spender in a cooperating household. At the preliminary interview information is sought on household composition, on various household amenities, and retrospective questions are asked about expenditure of a regular character such as rent and other housing costs and payments for electricity, gas and telephone. Questions are also put about items such as life assurance, season tickets for travel, payments for goods bought on hire purchase and by other credit arrangements. Also at the preliminary interview, a detailed questionnaire covering all sources of income is put individually to each spender. At the end of the interview record diaries are left with each spender. Several calls are made during the following 14 days in order to ensure that the necessary records are being kept throughout the period. At present, a payment of £2 is made to each spender in the household if every member completes a diary.

At the final call on a houshold the interviewer collects the completed diaries and carries out any outstanding checking on the recorded information. A note is also made of the address of the household and the name of each spender. This is necessary in order to make the payment to each cooperating member; also because sometimes further details are needed from the household before coding can be completed. However, it must be emphasised that the identity of each household is confidential to the Social Survey and is never divulged to another government department or to anyone outside OPCS.

When all the documents containing the data reported by a household (known as a household budget) are complete, they are sent by the interviewer to SSD for the initial stages of processing. Arrangements are then made for the payment promised to each spender. This is sent as a postal order from the Accounts Branch of OPCS and is usually received by the household some six to eight weeks after the final call by the interviewer on that household.

The processing carried out by SSD on each completed budget falls into three major operations. First, the collected material is edited by SSD Primary Analysis Branch. Usually this is done by making use of special editing questions on the schedule; for example, expenses charged to a business by a self-employed person, or recovered by an employee from his employer, are removed from reported expenditure, because the FES is restricted to private expenditure. This editing is often assisted by comparisons made ad hoc between data obtained in different parts of the interview schedules or recorded in the diaries. Secondly, items appearing in the diaries which fall within the regular expenditure fields covered by the interview schedules are removed. Thirdly, the descriptions against the diary entries are translated into the appropriate numerical codes. Before these operations can be completed it may be necessary to seek further information from the individuals providing the data. This is usually done by correspondence, but very occasionally by an interviewer re-visiting the household.

3.2 Organisation of FES work within Social Survey Division

The operations described above are continuous and are carried out by three technical branches of SSD as part of their regular commitment, namely the Sampling Implementation Unit, Field and Primary Analysis Branches. Their work covers day to day operations such as selecting individual samples, interviewer selection and training, interviewing and manual processing. These operations are of considerable magnitude. Some idea of their size can be obtained from the number of items which are collected and processed during the course of a year. The average number of items reported to interviewers, recorded in the diaries and in the various interview schedules, including answers to dependent and editing questions, is about 95 per cooperating household, while the average number of entries in the diaries is about 210 per household. Around 7,000 households cooperate in a year, thus providing over two million items of information. In addition, there is a research unit within the Social Survey Division responsible for the control and development of the work within the Division.

4 The Sample Design as at 1979

4.1 Outline

A four-stage, stratified, rotating design with a uniform overall sampling faction is used in which the primary sampling units (PSUs) are the administrative areas of Great Britain. The secondary units are wards. The third stage units are addresses within chosen wards drawn from the Electoral Register — the registers maintained for Parliamentary and Local Government elections. Finally, the interviewer uses the selected addresses to obtain the desired sample of households in the manner described in Section 4.9.

The probability of selection of a PSU for all units within a stratum is proportional to size (PPS). A single secondary unit is chosen from each selected PSU also with PPS, while a constant number of addresses is taken from each selected secondary unit. The selection of a PSU is made at random and is independent of all other selections, so that the sampling is random with replacement. The design is intended, theoretically, to be self-weighting, but in practice this is not realised completely through deficiencies in the data available for units listed in the frame.

In each period of three months 168 PSUs are used, selected so as to be representative of the whole of Great Britain. Each PSU is used four times at intervals of three months, and then replaced. In each selected PSU 16 addresses are chosen from different wards each time an area is used, making a total sample of 2,688 a quarter, or 10,752 addresses in any period of 12 months. The overall design as described above has been in use since 1967. There have been a number of minor modifications in the strata since then. These changes, and the pre-1967 design, are described in Section 15.1. The details as given below refer to the design operating in 1979.

4.2 Stratification factors

The sampling frame consists of London boroughs, the four cities of Scotland — Edinburgh, Glasgow, Aberdeen and Dundee — and district councils. In all, a total of 455 out of 459 administrative areas in Great Britain are included in the sample frame. The Isles of Scilly and the three Scottish Island districts (Orkney, Shetland and Western Isles) are not included in the frame because of excessive travel costs and difficulty of accessibility. In addition, the island parts of Cunninghame, Argyll and Bute, Lochaber and Skye and Lochalsh districts are excluded for the same reason.

The frame is stratified by three factors:

I A regional factor forming 16 major strata, namely:

   (a) The eight standard regions of England and the Greater London Council area

   (b) Wales — divided into three groups of counties:
     i) Clywd, Gwynedd, Powys, Dyfed
     ii) Glamorgan — Mid, South and West
     iii) Gwent

   (c) Scotland, divided into four groups:
     i) Highland Grampian
     ii) Tayside, Central, Fife, Lothian
     iii) Strathclyde
     iv) Border, Dumfries, Galloway

II The second factor distinguishes the PSUs into four types of areas; one consists of London Boroughs and Metropolitan County Districts and the Clydeside Conurbation; the other three are formed by District Councils divided by population density into three bands, with boundaries at 3.2 persons per acre and 0.9 persons per acre. These boundaries were fixed so as to yield approximately equal numbers of PSUs in each band. In Tables 4.2.1, 4.2.2, and 10.5.1 and for purposes of analysis generally, the central Clydeside Conurbation is classified with Metropolitan Districts, while the other cities of Scotland, Edinburgh, Aberdeen and Dundee, are included with non-Metropolitan Districts of higher population density.

III The third factor is an economic indicator based in England and Wales on the proportion of domestic property with rateable value over £400 and in Scotland on the proportion of industrial rateable value to total rateable value.

The number of areas classified by the first two stratification factors with corresponding populations are shown in Table 4.2.1. The consecutive numbers in column O indicate the order of arrangement of the intermediate strata in the frame. Within each intermediate stratum PSUs are arranged in descending order of the third stratification factor. In order to facilitate selection of PSUs, the sampling frame has been divided into 168 minor strata of approximately equal size, one PSU being selected from each stratum. This division has been made in such a way as to ensure a correct regional representation in the final sample and, as far as possible, a correct distribution by area type. Table 4:2.2 will help to explain how this is achieved.

In the 'Expected' columns of Table 4.2.2, the populations of Table 4.2.1 are shown divided proportionately to give a total of 168, thus providing the expected number of strata in each cell. For sampling purposes this has to be an integral number, and to ensure that it is so the two marginal distributions have, after rounding, been taken as fixed and the number of strata in each cell adjusted to

Table 4.2.1 Distribution of sampling frame by the two main stratification factors

Standard region	Type of area												Regional factor totals	
	Metropolitan districts, London boroughs and Strathclyde conurbation			Non-metropolitan districts by population density — persons per acre										
				3.2 or greater inc. other Scottish cities			0.9 but less than 3.2			less than 0.9				
	O	Pop.	N	O	Pop.	N	O	Pop.	N	O	Pop.	N	Pop.	N
England														
Northern	1	1.20	5	2	0.62	6	3	0.67	7	4	0.64	11	3.13	29
Yorkshire & Humberside	5	3.40	9	6	0.55	4	7	0.18	2	8	0.77	11	4.89	26
North Western	9	4.35	15	10	1.04	9	11	1.04	11	12	0.18	2	6.61	37
East Midlands		—		13	1.66	12	14	0.81	10	15	1.23	18	3.70	40
West Midlands	16	2.79	7	17	0.67	7	18	0.77	8	19	0.94	14	5.16	36
East Anglia		—		20	0.35	3	21	0.28	3	22	1.11	14	1.74	20
Greater London Area	23	7.28	33		—			—			—		7.28	33
South Eastern (Exc. GLC)		—		24	3.91	38	25	3.79	38	26	2.04	22	9.74	98
South Western (Exc. Isles of Scilly)		—		27	1.53	11	28	0.50	5	29	2.14	30	4.17	46
England		19.01	69		10.31	90		8.04	84		9.05	122	46.42	365
Wales: Counties														
I Clwyed, Gwynedd, Powys, Dyfed		—			—		30	0.30	4	31	0.71	16	1.01	20
II Glamorgan — Mid/South/West		—		32	0.37	2	33	0.93	10		—		1.30	12
III Gwent		—			—		34	0.38	4	35	0.07	1	0.44	5
Wales		—			0.37	2		1.60	18		0.77	17	2.75	37
Scotland: Regions														
I Highland, Grampian		—		36	0.21	1		—		37	0.41	12	0.62	13
II Tayside, Central, Fife, Lothian		—		38	0.67	2	39	0.66	6	40	0.42	5	1.75	13
III Strathclyde	1	1.56	11		—		42	0.19	2	43	0.49	6	2.53	19
IV Borders, Dumfries, Galloway		—			—			-		44	0.24	8	0.24	8
Scotland		1.56	11		0.88	3		0.85	8		1.56	31	5.16	53
Great Britian		20.57	80		11.56	95		10.49	110		11.38	170	54.32	455

Population totals do not add because of rounding
O = Order of intermediate strata in frame
Pop. = Mid 1973 population estimate in millions
N = Number of district councils, London boroughs or Scottish cities

the nearest whole number consistent with these marginal totals. By this means the sample has a fixed composition by standard region and also, as far as possible, by area type. The final numbers for each cell are shown in the column headed 'Actual'. The slight differences between the Actual and Expected figures are inevitable and indicate the presence of slight distortions in the selection probabilities. While the overall regional distribution is reasonably close to what it should be, there is the possibility of greater divergence in the distribution by area type.

Further, in two cases, the expected number is too small to justify a whole PSU for the cell. In Wales the population of Gwent is insufficient to justify more than one PSU and thus can be of either medium or lower population density; this is indicated by the letter 'a' in Table 4.2.2. The relative probability of selecting a medium density area as compared with a low one is in the ratio 1.17 to 0.22, as can be seen from Table 4.2.2. The other case where there is some uncertainty is in the Strathclyde region of Scotland where two PSUs have been allocated to districts with population density of less than 3.2 persons per acre. These are treated as one stratum with the result that both PSUs could come from the medium density areas, or both from the low density areas, or one PSU from each. However, the relative probability of selecting a low density area, as shown in Table 4.2.2, is 1.50 to 0.59.

4.3 The first stage — selection of PSUs from sampling frame

In each period of three months the sample consists of one PSU from each of the 168 strata. Successive selections of PSUs are made from each stratum using random numbers; each selection from a stratum is independent of previous selections from that stratum and from selections from other strata. The actual selection of a PSU is thus made at random with replacement; PPS sampling is employed by using a random number within the interval defined by the total number of electors in a stratum. The measure of size in the PPS sampling is thus the population estimates on which Tables 4.2.1 and 4.2.2 are based, that is mid-1973 estimates.

The result of the division into 168 strata is that the selected PSUs are distributed according to column A in Table 4.2.2. Since sixteen addresses (a constant number) are selected from each PSU, the composition of the set of addresses follows closely the correct regional distribution.

The distribution by area type is not so clear cut. As explained in the preceding section, while the numbers of PSUs allocated to each group of Welsh counties and each group of Scottish regions are fixed, some random variations are possible in the distribution of PSUs as between medium and low density areas. From Table 4.2.2 it can be

Table 4.2.2 Distribution of strata by the two main stratification factors

Standard region	Type of area								Regional factor totals	
	Metropolitan districts, London boroughs and Strathclyde conurbation		Non-metropolitan districts by population density — persons per acre							
			3.2 or greater inc. other Scottish cities		0.9 but less than 3.2		less than 0.9			
	E	A	E	A	E	A	E	A	E	A
England										
Northern	3.71	4	1.92	2	2.07	2	1.98	2	9.68	10
Yorkshire & Humberside	10.52	10	1.70	2	0.56	1	2.38	2	15.12	15
North Western	13.45	13	3.22	3	3.22	3	0.56	1	20.44	20
East Midlands	—		5.13	5	2.51	2	3.80	4	11.44	11
West Midlands	8.63	9	2.07	2	2.38	2	2.91	3	15.96	16
East Anglia	—		1.08	1	0.87	1	3.43	4	5.38	6
Greater London Area	22.52	23	—		—		—		22.52	23
South Eastern (Exc. GLC)	—		12.09	12	11.72	12	6.31	6	30.12	30
South Western (Exc. Isles of Scilly)	—		4.73	5	1.55	2	6.62	6	12.90	13
England	58.79	59	31.89	32	24.87	25	27.99	28	143.57	144
Wales: Counties										
I Clwyed, Gwynedd, Powys, Dyfed	—		—		0.93	1	2.20	2	3.12	3
II Glamorgan — Mid/South/West	—		1.14	1	2.88	3	—		4.02	4
III Gwent	—		—		1.17	a	0.22	a	1.35	1
Wales	—		1.14	1	4.95	4 + a	2.38	2 + a	8.51	8
Scotland: Regions										
I Highland, Grampian	—		0.65	1	—		1.27	1	1.92	2
II Tayside, Central, Fife, Lothian	—		2.07	2	2.04	2	1.30	1	5.41	5
III Strathclyde	5.75	6	—		0.59	b	1.50	b	7.84	8
IV Borders, Dumfries, Galloway	-		—		—		0.74	1	0.74	1
Scotland	5.75	6	2.72	3	2.63	2 + b	4.81	3 + b	15.93	16
Great Britian	64.54	65	35.75	36	32.45	31 + a + b	35.18	33 + a + b	168.00	168

E = *Expected number*
A = *Actual number in final design*
a,b indicate two cells combined to form: a — 1 stratum
b — 2 strata

seen that the PSUs allocated to medium and lower density areas together in Non-Metropolitan Districts total 67. The most likely division of the 67 is into 33 medium and 34 lower density areas together in Non-Metropolitan Districts total 67. The most likely division of the 67 is into 33 medium and 34 lower density areas. There is, however, a possibility of the sample yeilding 31 and 36 respectively at one extreme and 34 and 33 at the other. The next point concerns the actual division of the sampling frame into 168 strata. As an example, there are 18 district councils in the East Midlands region with lower population density. (Table 4.2.1). These have been formed into four strata (Table 4.2.2) by first listing the areas in descending order of the economic indicator, namely the proportion of domestic property with a rateable value over £400. The 18 areas had a total population of 1.23 million, so that each of the four strata is equivalent to about 0.31 million. As can be expected, the boundaries between each pair of chosen strata fall within three of the 18 areas. In making a selection, each such area is therefore sampled twice, once in each of the chosen strata. Since PPS sampling is used the probability of selecting one of these is only proportional to the part of the area contained in each segment.

On the other hand, some of the administrative areas are so large that the whole of a minor stratum is included within one of these areas. Where this happens, that area will always occur in the PSUs selected for a quarter. Moreover, through the operation of the boundary feature just described, some areas may sometimes appear more than once in a quarter.

4.4 The rotating system at the first stage

The sample design incorporates a rotating system in which successive selections are made from the strata in the sampling frame in such a way as to provide a gradual replacement of PSUs quarter by quarter. Each selected PSU is used four times at intervals of three months and then, after the fourth time, replaced by another PSU selected from the same stratum. Each selection is made at random and independently of previous selections in that stratum and independently of selections in other strata.

In order to accommodate the rotating arrangement the 168 strata have been divided into four separate groups. They constitute four inter-penetrating groups of strata, each group being as alike as possible to the other groups but at the same time incorporating a random element. This has been done so that if there is a cyclical pattern in the sampling frame, there is little risk of it being confounded with quarterly changes in the sample, thus introducing spurious seasonal variations through the operation of the rotating system. This has been achieved by dividing the 168 strata into a random complex of 42 sets of four and then assigning each of the four at random to one of the four strata groups. Quite apart from this precaution, each sample of PSUs is balanced quarterly as each of the 168 strata contributes a PSU to the sample for the quarter. The arrangement of these four groups in the rotating system can be seen from Table 4.4.1.

Successive selections are made from the four strata groups in turn. In the diagram, A_i represents the ith selection of 42 PSUs from the strata group A; B_{i+1} the

$(i + 1)^{th}$ selection of 42 PSUs from strata group B, and so on.

Table 4.4.1

Successive calendar quarters	Strata groups			
j	A_i	B_i	C_i	D_i
j + 1	A_{i+1}	B_i	C_i	D_i
j + 2	A_{i+1}	B_{i+1}	C_i	D_i
j + 3	A_{i+1}	B_{i+1}	C_{i+1}	D_i
j + 4	A_{i+1}	B_{i+1}	C_{i+1}	D_{i+1}
j + 5	A_{i+2}	B_{i+1}	C_{i+1}	D_{i+1}

It will be seen that in any period of 12 months two sets of PSUs (B_i and D_{i+1} in the periods j + 1 to j + 4) are used once, two sets (C_i and C_{i+1}) are each used twice, two sets (B_{i+1} and D_1) are used three times, and one set namely A_{i+1}, four times; altogether seven different sets of PSUs are in use over a twelve month period, making 294 in all.

4.5 Introduction of a new sampling frame into the rotating system

The frame described in Sections 4.2 and 4.3 is based on the latest data available. With changes in the size and location of the population and in the boundaries of local authorities, this frame becomes out of date. The matter is kept under review by the Social Survey, and from time to time a new sampling frame is constructed on the same lines as the original one; that is, the procedure described in 4.2 is followed, but using the most up-to-date information available at the time of construction. The method of introduction of a new frame presents certain problems, which are described in the following paragraphs.

The simplest way of changing over from one frame to another is to introduce a new frame as soon as circumstances make it necessary by selecting one PSU from each stratum of the new frame, and dropping all selections from the old frame. This is impracticable because of the rotating system, since once an area has been introduced it cannot be replaced until it has been in use for four quarters. The new frame therefore cannot be introduced at once but has to be brought in gradually over a period of three quarters, during which there will be a mixture of old and new frames. It will not be until the fourth quarter that all the selected PSUs come from the new frame. This is illustrated by the diagram below, which reproduces the diagram in Table 4.4.1, but modified to show the introduction of a new sampling frame at quarter j + 1.

Table 4.5.1

Successive calendar quarters	Old frame				New frame			
j	A_i	B_i	C_i	D_i				
j + 1		B_i	C_i	D_i	A_{i+1}			
j + 2			C_i	D_i	A_{i+1}	B_{i+1}		
j + 3				D_i	A_{i+1}	B_{i+1}	C_{i+1}	
j + 4					A_{i+1}	B_{i+1}	C_{i+1}	D_{i+1}
j + 5					A_{i+2}	B_{i+1}	C_{i+1}	D_{i+1}

In the diagram the new frame is introduced at a quarter when areas selected from strata group A are due to be replaced by a new selection from the same strata. It will be seen that the new frame is introduced bit by bit in four successive quarters. If the new frame is introduced at a different quarter in the cycle, for instance when areas in strata group C are due to be replaced, the operation will still take four quarters to complete but will proceed by taking strata groups from the new frame in the order C, D A, B.

In so far as the 168 strata can be regarded as the basic elements and each strata group is an adequate representation of the whole, the method of introducing the new frame is satisfactory. There are, however, certain features about this which require comment. In any quarter during which all PSUs are drawn from the same sampling frame, whether old or new, the whole of the country can be regarded as being covered by the selection procedure. However, in the three transition quarters, where there is a mixture of selections from the old and new frames, the position is more complicated. All the strata into which the country has been divided figure in the selected sample, but because the content of a stratum may have changed between the old and new frames the relative position of a particular administrative area may have changed within the set of 168 strata. Consequently, a particular area which appeared in a certain stratum in the old frame may reappear in a different stratum in the new frame. In the transition period of three quarters where there is a mixture of selections from old and new frames there is thus a possibility that two different strata groups will both contain one and the same local authority area, while other areas may be omitted altogether from the samples of areas used in that quarter. For example, if an area had been listed originally in strata group B but in the new frame appeared in C (Table 4.5.1), this area will not feature in the lists of areas from which the final areas will be selected for quarter j + 2.

There is no easy way of avoiding this problem without losing some of the essential features of the present sample design. The 168 strata are organized as a random complex to provide four sets of 42, each representative of the whole. If, instead of taking these sets of 42 in sequence when replacing areas, a set of 42 were drawn at random from the whole 168 independently of other selections of 42 each time a replacement was required, the composition of the sample each quarter would consist of four sets of 42 random selections. There would then be no distinction in the composition of the selections each quarter as between those where all selections were made from one frame, or a quarter where selections were made from a mixture of two frames. Such an arrangement, however, would destroy one of the more important features of the present design, namely that in each quarter in which the selections are made from a single frame the whole 168 are represented equally. Another alternative is to quadruple the strata in each intermediate strata of Table 4.2.2 and replace each of the present groups A, B, C and D by a set of 168. This would require the selection of 672 PSU's each quarter instead of 168. On the assumption that the present total size of sample remain unchanged, this would mean that the quota in each area per month would be reduced to four, which is an uneconomic proposition. If the total number of PSU's in a quarter were less than this, that is less than 672, the distribution of the sample by standard regions and by type of area would suffer.

This difficulty can be avoided, at least theoretically, by reconsidering the concept of the sampling frame. Instead of treating local authority areas as the basic elements of the frame, the 168 strata and their partition into four groups of 42, can be regarded as the basic entities. The content of each stratum can be considered as being in a state of flux varying continuously with changes in size and location of the population, but discontinuously with changes in the boundaries of local authorities. Where an area has changed in type, relative size of population or in the relative value of its economic indicator, it can be argued that it has become something different, and the original area as such no longer exists. Although an area may physically be the same, if its characteristics have changed in the new frame it may be regarded for purposes of this argument as though it were a different area. Further, if it is argued that the actual content of a stratum at any time is a random selection from an infinite population of areas and that the contents of a stratum as listed in the old and new frames are equally random choices from the same infinite population the composition of the sample during the transition quarters can be considered a validly representative sample of the whole country.

4.6 Allocation of selected PSU's into the monthly samples

The 168 PSU's selected for a quarter are divided into three sets of 56 in order to provide monthly samples. This division is made through the medium of the four rotation groups described in the preceding section. For this purpose the 42 strata forming one of the four strata groups has been partitioned into 14 sets of three consecutive strata, while still retaining the sampling frame order. One out of each three PSU's is taken at random, thus forming three inter-penetrating sets of 14. This process is applied to each of the four strata groups separately, thus providing three inter-penetrating samples of 56. The three sets of 56 PSU's chosen for a quarter are then allocated to the three individual months of that quarter. In the following quarter the PSU's relating to the three unchanged strata groups are allocated to the same three relative months as they were in the preceding quarter, but the remaining 42 PSU's from the fourth strata group are replaced by a new random selection, but are themselves partitioned into three inter-penetrating samples of four independently of the previous choices. The object of this additional randomization is to prevent the creation of spurious monthly seasonal patterns in the final data which might otherwise be produced if the 168 PSU's were allocated systematically to the monthly sets.

4.7 The second stage — selection of wards

An intermediate stage is introduced into the sample design so that fieldwork can be confined to an area of reasonable size suitable for a single interviewer to handle. This requirement is particularly desirable in the FES where the survey procedure requires an interviewer to re-visit a cooperating household at least three times after diary records have been placed. For this purpose a ward is

taken as the secondary unit throughout the frame, but where a ward has fewer than 2,500 electors it is combined with others on a geographical basis. Four wards are chosen at the secondary stage from each selected PSU with PPS, using a fixed interval with a random start, the measure of size being the electorate at the time of the selection. The four selected wards are allocated at random to the four times that an area appears in the sample. This procedure usually results in the use of four different wards so that fieldwork in any one period is confined to a ward, but to different wards on each of the four occasions an area is used. Occasionally, however, the same ward appears more than once in the selection as an accident or the PPS sampling.

4.8 The third stage — selection of addresses

At this stage 16 addresses are chosen from each selected ward, thus providing a total sample of 2,688 addresses a quarter or 10,752 in any one period of 12 months. The addresses are obtained by random selection from the electoral registers maintained for Parliamentary and Local Government elections. An interval sample is then drawn using a random start. The procedure then varies according to the number of surnames at an address, and is described in Section 4.9. The number of addresses produced by this process may vary by a small random number from the exact 16 required. Adjustments are then made to bring this number exactly to 16 either by discarding some at random or by further random selections from that register.

It is unlikely that an address will re-appear in the sample within a short period. This follows from the fact that a fresh selection of areas is made after 12 months, and that normally four different wards are chosen. It is only comparatively rarely that the same ward will be selected, and even rarer if the procedure at the third stage then throws up an address which had already appeared. Precautions are taken by the Sampling Implementation Unit (SIU) to ensure that the same address is not repeated in the FES (and also in the General Household Survey) within a period of 13 months). When this does occur, the duplicated address is rejected and another random selection is made.

4.9 The fourth stage — selection of households

In about 97% of cases an address as listed in the electoral register contains only one household, but in the remaining cases the interviewer will find 2 or more households (see Table 4.10.2). An example is a complex of flats where the electoral register does not list each flat separately. Another example occurs in some rural areas where several houses may all be listed under one address such as 'The Street'. These cases require special multi-household procedures. At the third stage the procedure differs according to the number of different surnames listed in the register at the address. If the address as listed contains one, two or three surnames it is included by the SIU on the address list if the elector selected is also the first entry on the register at that address. Therefore a 'firsting' procedure is adopted so that all such cases have an equal chance of inclusion.

However, if the electoral register lists four or more different surnames at the address containing the selected elector, it is only included if the elector selected is the first at that address with that surname. Such addresses are called 'pre-sampled multi-household addresses' and are then sampled with probability proportional to the number of different surnames listed at the address. On making contact at such an address an interviewer has first to enumerate all the households there, (see front page, Appendix G11) and then consult the special table provided on the reverse side by the SIU for that address. But the number of households subsequently found by the interviewer may be different from that suggested by the number of surnames on the register. For this reason the interviewer has to carry out a sub-sampling procedure so as to give each household a constant probability of inclusion. For this purpose the SIU provide a special table for each address containing four or more different surnames (see Appendix G11). This additional information is in fact provided at the same time as the address list. If m households are found at the address the table indicates which household in the random l to m is to be included in the sample. These tables are structured in such a way that the choice of a particular household is at random but with probability inversely proportional to the number of different surnames listed on the register for that address. Usually this procedure results in only one household being chosen from an address, but sometimes it provides no household and sometimes more than one.

The procedure just described is applied with 'pre-sampled multi-households', ie where there are 4 or more different surnames on the Electoral Register. There are a few cases, however, where the interviewer finds that the address contains more than one household (but this was not detected at sampling stage as it had fewer than 4 surnames on the Electoral Register). Should there be more than 3, the interviewer lists the surnames in a systematic order and takes a random sample of 3 households (see Appendix G12). These will therefore provide extra cases of 'concealed multi-households' which will add slightly to the total sample. Ideally, the number of households selected should be determined by the total number of households at the address. For practical reasons, the total number of extra cases allowed in an interviewer's quota is limited to four, so that the maximum number of households interviewed is 20. This could result in slight under-representation of multi-households in areas like Glasgow, Dundee and the Inner London boroughs.

4.10 Exclusion of ineligible addresses from the sample
The pre-selected samples include ineligible addresses which do not yield households either because the dwelling is empty or because it is no longer in existence or because the establishment at the address is not within the coverage of the survey. The cases excluded are mostly establishments where the residents do not form domestic households in the usual sense, or where personal expenditure is so inter-mixed with that of a commercial undertaking that it is impossible to obtain satisfactory estimates of domestic expenditure only.

The main exclusions are hotels, guest houses, public houses, boarding houses and institutions of all kinds. Generally speaking, households living at a public house or an institution are excluded unless the living accommodation is entirely self-contained and the catering arrangements are independent of the rest of the establishment. Private households occasionally taking in boarders present a problem; a private household with less than 4 boarders at the time of call is included in the sample; domestic households with 4 or more boarders at the time of call and also commercial boarding houses are excluded. The numbers thus excluded in 1976 and 1977 and 1978 are given in Table 4.10.1.

Table 4.10.1 1976, 1977 and 1978 addresses analysed by eligibility of establishment

	1976	1977	1978
Establishment not a domestic household			
Hotel	13	16	15
Public house	31	29	25
Boarding house	15	17	11
Institution	16	31	30
Business and private expenditure not separable	*	*	14
Total	75	93	95
No residents at address			
Accomodation empty	328	324	329
Accomodation demolished	15	27	31
Other	72	62	39
Total	415	413	399
Deleted addresses	326	†	†
Addresses withdrawn on sub-sampling by interviewer	—	104	78
Addresses containing domestic households	9,936	10,142	10,180
Total set sample	10,752	10,752	10,752

Category not applied until 1978.
†*The deletion procedure was abandoned in 1977*

Two other groups in the table require explanation. Although most of the cases classified under 'Institutions' in 1976 and 1977 were, in fact, institutions, that category also included a few where it was not possible to distinguish personal from commercial expenses, eg cafe owners who took most of their meals in their own cafe. In 1978, these were separately distinguished and are shown in Table 4.10.1. The other category under 'No residents at address' covered a wide variety such as a holiday home, a flat above a shop used occasionally by a shopkeeper, and accommodation reserved by a firm for visiting employees. Comparison with the corresponding 1967 data (Table 4.8.1, first Handbook) shows little change over the ten years. The main differences are increases in empty accommodation, from 231 in 1967 to 328 in 1976, 324 in 1977 and 329 in 1978, with a decline in demolished property from 44 to 15, 27 and 31 respectively.

Table 4.10.2, Part A, shows that the 9,936 addresses containing domestic households in 1976 included 249 cases where more than one household was selected at the address; these led to the inclusion of 361 extra households in the sample. From Table 4.10.1 it will be seen that 326 deletions were made in 1976 to compensate for these additional cases. There was therefore a net addition to the sample of 35 households arising from the multi-households addresses contacted towards the end of the placing month and when there were no longer any uncalled-on addresses to delete. Comparison with Table

Table 4.10.2 Conversion of sample into a sample of households

	Addresses	Households
A 1976 sample		
Number of households selected at each *address*		
1	9,687	9,687
2	137	274
3	112	336
All addresses containing domestic households	**9,936**	**10,297**
B 1977 sample		
Number of households selected at each *address*		
1	9,993	9,993
2	121	242
3	28	85
All addresses containing domestic households	**10,142**	**10,320**
C 1978 sample		
Number of households selected at each *address*		
1	10,034	10,034
2	123	246
3	23	69
All addresses containing domestic households	**10,180**	**10,349**

	1976	1977	1978
D Samples after multi-household adjustment	10,297	10,320	10,349
Excluded because household:			
contained USA serviceman	2	1	2
contained a diplomat	2	3	3
away beyond end of placing period	171	127	159
about to move out of the area	42	44	50
Total excluded	217	175	214
Effective household sample	**10,080**	**10,145**	**10,135**

4.8.2 in the first Handbook indicates that the number of multi-household addresses had fallen very substantially over the period 1967 to 1976; from 437 to 249 — a reduction of 43 per cent. Presumably this was due to changes in housing, and to improvements in the description of addresses in Electoral Registers.

As explained in Section 15.1, procedures for selecting at multi-household addresses changed from the beginning of 1977. Prior to 1977, interviewers were asked to delete an address for every extra household found; 326 deletions were shown in Table 4.10.1 for 1976. Deletions have been eliminated under the new procedure so that there is no entry for 1977 or 1978 in Table 4.10.1, but this table does contain an item not appearing for 1976 or earlier years. This is a group of 104 and 78 addresses respectively preselected by the SIU each containing 4 or more surnames and issued by the SIU in the expectation that they would contain more than one household; however, when the appropriate sub-sampling procedure was applied by the interviewer no household emerged (see Section 4.9, penultimate paragraph). The new procedure continues to produce extra households, but fewer are selected at each address than under the previous arrangements. Table 4.10.2, Part B, shows that in 1977 there were 149 such addresses yielding 327 households and 146 such addresses in 1978, yielding 315 households (Part C). Therefore there were 178 extra households in 1977 and 169 in 1978. The address sample has therefore been increased by about 1.7 per cent, but against these extra households should be set the 104 addresses (1977) and 78 addresses (1978) withdrawn at the Field stage (See Table 4.10.1); this gives rise to net increases of 74 units in 1977 and 91 in 1978.

Strictly speaking, the final numbers of households given in Part D of Table 4.10.2 are approximate; included are cases where the interviewer was unable to make contact with anyone at the address. The interviewer continues to call until the end of the placing month before writing off an address as a non-contact. Cases where no contact can finally be made account for a very small part of the sample; around 1 per cent (Table 10.2.1). However, in the course of pursuing non-contacts the interviewer will sometimes obtain information from neighbours that there is no-one living at the selected address at the time. Such cases range from those away on holiday for a week or two to others who have left the district for good. Some can be eliminated forthwith as not containing a domestic household, classified as 'Accommodation empty' in Table 4.10.1; while at the other extreme are households away for only a short time. In between there is a whole range of cases varying from those where none of the neighbours knows whether anyone is really living at the address, to cases where it is known that a family will be away indefinitely. The compromise adopted is to exclude from the sample those about to move out of the district and those away beyond the end of the placing month; in 1978 these comprised 50 and 159 respectively (Part D, Table 4.10.2); forming about 2 per cent of the total sample. Where no information could be obtained, the case was retained in the effective sample as a non-contact.

The sample is further reduced by the exclusion of households containing a USA serviceman or a foreign diplomat; leading finally to samples of 10,080 households in 1976, 10,145 in 1977 and 10,135 in 1978.

4.11 Sampling errors and design factors

Estimates of sampling errors are published regularly in an appendix to each annual report (See Appendix 3 of the *1978 FES Annual Report*). Since the sample design is multi-stage and the PSU's are stratified by various factors, it is of interest to examine the design factor. This can be done for the FES because the annual reports publish two sets of estimates based on two methods of calculation. Formula 1 in the appendix to the annual report gives standard errors derived from the single stage random formula. Formula 2 is an approximation of the true value taking into account the main features of the sample, namely its multi-stage design and rotating nature. The effect of the multi-stage design is a tendency to increase the true standard error and offset any gain in efficiency derived from stratification. The situation is complicated by variations in the number of cooperating households so that in practice mean expenditure and income are both ratios of two random variables.

Data based on the two methods have been published from 1969 onwards. The ratio of formula 2 to formula 1 provides an estimate of the design factor, and the mean ratio derived from the eight years 1969 to 1976 are shown in Table 4.11.1. The table also gives corresponding data for 1961, the only earlier year for which estimates of the design factor are available[1].

Table 4.11.1 FES — Sample design factors

	1969-1976 (mean factor)	1961
Income	1.30	1.12
Expenditure group		
Housing	1.25	1.18
Fuel, light and power	1.13	1.07
Food	1.15	1.11
Alcoholic drink	1.14	1.11
Tobacco	1.15	1.03
Clothing and footwear	1.10	1.15
Durable household goods	1.02	0.99
Other goods	1.22	0.95
Transport and vehicles	1.16	0.98
Services	1.10	1.15
Miscellaneous	1.03	0.98
Total (all expenditure groups)	**1.24**	**1.08**
Other payments recorded	1.00 to 1.24	1.00 to 1.24

As can be seen, the design factor is quite small for the major expenditure group totals, all design factors falling below 1.31. The design factor for total expenditure is 1.24 (1969 — 76). A close examination of Table 4.11.1 shows that the majority of the 1961 factors lie below the corresponding values for 1969 — 1976. However, formula 2 referred to above and used in estimating the latter values, is an approximation derived by collapsing the basic sample strata of the 1969 — 1976 design into seven broad strata. Such a considerable reduction in the number of strata may possibly have led to the incorporation of some variance components in formula 2 which are actually excluded by the stratification of the sample design; if so, the 1969 — 1976 factors may be over-estimated. On the other hand, the 1961 data are based on a relatively small sample and are thus subject to relatively larger sampling variances than the later results. Such small differences as appear should therefore be ignored, and they should not be regarded as reflecting on the relative efficiency of the two sample designs.

Most of the separate items within the major groups also show low design factors, but there are some exceptions. All items with factors above 1.25 are given in Table 4.11.2.

Table 4.11.2 FES — Sample design factors: items with mean factor above 1.25 in 1969-1976

Ref. in App. 5* 1976		1969-1976
1-4	Housing: rent, rates etc.	1.98
7	Gas and hire of gas appliances	1.51
8	Electricity and hire of electric appliances	1.34
12	Bread, rolls etc.	1.31
31	Potatoes	1.30
34	Sugar	1.42
36	Sweets and chocolates	1.26
41	Icecream	1.52
70	Toys and stationery good etc.	1.35
80	Railway fares	1.34
81	Bus and coach fares	1.42
83	Postage, telephone, telegrams	1.43

*See FES 1976 Report, App.2

The higher factors arise where the variable is liable to geographic clusters; the outstanding example, as is to be expected, occurs in Housing where 'Payments such as rent, rates etc' has produced a factor of about 2. The corresponding factors by type of tenure, which, in itself, is clustered geographically, that constitute this category display considerable variation, as can be seen from the breakdown of the 1969 to 1976 data shown below:

	Housing sample design factors 1969-76
Rented unfurnished from:	
Local Authority	1.64
Other	1.27
Rented furnished	1.16
Rent free	1.07
Owner-occupied:	
in process of purchase	1.53
owned outright	1.40

On the other hand, the design factors for the other major category included in Housing, 'Repairs, maintenance and decorations', is small at 1.01 (1.11 in 1961). Apart from Housing the only other categories to show design factors above 1.50 in 1969 — 76 were 'Gas and hire of gas appliances' and 'Ice-cream'. However, in the case of ice cream, the estimates of the factor are of doubtful reliability; the ratio of formula 2 to formula 1 displays an exceptionally wide range, varying from 1.00 in one year to over 2.00 in another.

Reference

[1] Kemsley, W F F. Sampling errors in the Family Expenditure Survey, *Applied Statistics,* Vol. XV, No. 1, pp 11-13, 1966.

5 Spacing of fieldwork over time

5.1 The importance of a steady flow of data

Considerable care is taken to see that the fieldwork is spread evenly over time and that, as far as possible, there is a steady flow of completed budgets. This is important for two main reasons. First, expenditure is variable from day to day and week to week, and is subject to marked seasonal variations, especially in certain sectors such as heating, travel, purchases of clothing and meals out. Even food for domestic consumption, where total expenditure is likely to remain fairly constant in real terms, will show marked seasonal variations in, for example, purchases of fruit and vegetables. Second, there will be long term changes in the distribution of expenditure arising out of changes in price levels, in social customs and technical improvements in the goods available. Measurement of long-term changes might be met by periodic surveys, and indeed most of the EEC countries only carry out periodic budget surveys*. However, this would not fully cope with short-term fluctuations or seasonal patterns.

Furthermore, a household budget survey, if it is conducted properly, requires a well-trained staff. It is more efficient and likely to produce better results if, once staff have been recruited and trained, it is maintained and used on a continuous basis. There are clear advantages in organizing a survey as specialized as the FES on a continuing basis without breaks, rather than as a periodic survey conducted say two or three weeks at a time at three-monthly intervals. The argument about work load applies with particular force to fieldwork, but it is also relevant to the regular pre-selection of addresses and to the processing of completed budgets.

In practice, where a voluntary survey is based on random samples, refusals to cooperate will inevitably occur, and cause the number of completed budgets to display random variations over time. The next sections show how successful has been the organization of the survey in producing a steady flow of data.

5.2 Constancy of number of budgets month by month

As explained in Section 4.6, a constant number of PSUs are allocated to each month and in each, 16 addresses are selected from a ward in the PSU. There is thus a constant set sample of 896 addresses each month, and this produced on average 570 budgets a month in 1978. There is slight

variation from this figure month by month arising from short-term variations in the response rate; however, the numbers cooperating in December, are generally lower because the non-contact rate increases. Figures for 1978 are given below in Table 5.2.1.

Table 5.2.1 Monthly variation in number of cooperating households 1978

January	610
February	587
March	554
April	567
May	568
June	578
July	585
August	583
September	583
October	572
November	560
December	525
	6,872

5.3 Distribution of cooperating households within a month

As a further means of obtaining an even flow of budgets the initial fieldwork for each quota of 16 is spread over each calendar month by taking four addresses in each of the four placing weeks in the month. The placing weeks are defined by dividing each calendar month into four placing periods of seven or eight days; week 1 runs from 1st to 7th day; week 2 from 8th to 15th; week 3 from 16th to 23rd and week 4 from 24th to the end of the month. This applies to all months except February, where the last two placing weeks begin on 15th and 22nd respectively.

Interviewers are asked to work through their address lists in order, but some flexibility is essential. It could be argued that since the FES is based on a continuous sample it should be random over time as well as geographically. While there is some force in this argument, too rigid a programme could lead to an achieved sample more biassed than it need be by the unnecessary loss of some households. The flexibility built into the programme described in Section 6.1 avoids this danger. For similar reasons (see Section 6.5(i)) the weekly quota of four includes ineligible and unproductive cases arising in the placing week. Table 5.3.1 illustrates how this programme has worked out in 1976. For this analysis the 7,051 households cooperating in 1976 have been classified according to their position on the relevant address list. Budgets from the first four addresses have been classified to the first row; those from 5 to 8 to the second row; and so on. The four rows then relate to the situation as it would have been if there has been no delays and each

---

* For details about the periodicity of European budget surveys, the reader is referred to the Eurostat booklet described in reference 10 of Chapter 2. Another source is U.S. Bureau of the Census *Methodology of Consumer Expenditure Surveys, Working Paper No. 27,* (by Robert Pearl), Bureau of the Census, Washington D.C.

household had started record keeping in the week assigned by the position of the address on the list. The columns in the table show the actual outcome.

Table 5.3.1 Distribution of budgets within a month 1976

| Week to which orginally assigned | Week of month in which budget started | | | | | |
	1st	2nd	3rd	4th	Next month	Total
1st	1163	363	117	79	17	1739
2nd	545	848	249	150	20	1812
3rd	88	611	751	269	42	1761
4th	22	154	653	805	105	1739
Whole month	1818	1976	1770	1303	184	7051
Percentage of total in week originally assigned						
1st	**66.9**	20.9	6.7	4.5	1.0	100.0
2nd	30.1	**46.8**	13.7	8.3	1.1	100.0
3rd	5.0	34.7	**42.6**	15.3	2.4	100.0
4th	1.3	8.8	37.6	**46.3**	6.0	100.0
Whole month	25.8	28.0	25.1	18.5	2.6	100.0

It is clear that not all budgets are placed in the week originally assigned; however, the main aim of ensuring that a fairly even number of budgets is placed each week was achieved. The bottom row of Table 5.3.1 shows that there is a slight excess in the second week over an even 25 per cent; the extra 3 per cent in that week and the 2.6 per cent carried forward into the next month are counterbalanced by the short-fall in the fourth week. Of the households assigned to the first week, 67 per cent actually started their records in that week; the remaining 33 per cent who were unable to start until later were replaced by those originally assigned to later weeks. Most of these, in fact two-thirds, began record keeping in the second week, so that the average delay was not very marked; the delay by those originally assigned to the second and later weeks is even less.

The table also shows a slight bias towards the first and second weeks. This reflects the tendency for non-contacts and more difficult cases to gravitate towards the end of the placing month. It is a consequence of the interviewers re-visiting addresses week after week until a decision is reached. If interviewers had been free to continue calling for a week or so longer it is probable that a few more households would have been contacted and there might ultimately have been a few more cooperating cases.

Examination of regional placing patterns showed little variation: in each region the proportion starting record keeping was between 21 and 31 per cent in the first week, 25 and 31 per cent in the second, 22 and 28 in the third and 19 and 22 per cent in the remaining period.

Moreover, there has been little change in this pattern since 1967. This can be seen by comparing Table 5.3.1 above with the corresponding table in the first edition of this Handbook[1]. The main difference is that 1976 shows a slightly more even distribution of cooperating cases over the first three weeks of the month. This has been achieved by bringing forward more cases originally assigned to a later week into an earlier week, thus leaving the fourth week with slightly fewer cases.

The earlier Handbook also contained some remarks about the characteristics of 'delay' households taken from an earlier study made in 1961 and 1962[2]. In almost all cases the delay was unavoidable and outside the interviewer's control. Delay households tended to be over-represented very slightly with those from the London area, the higher income groups and smaller families. Furthermore, the average expenditure of delay households, both in total and in the main expenditure categories was above the corresponding amount for households which started in the assigned week. This confirms that it is essential to include these delay households, since without them the achieved sample and final results would be biassed. This finding justifies the need for a placing period of four to five weeks which enables the non-contact rate to be kept to a minimum of 1 per cent (See Table 10.2.1).

5.4 Day of week on which records started
Flexibility in the field programme is essential if the interviewer is to obtain the best response. The interviewer is left free to call on any day in the assigned week that is convenient provided it fits into the programme as described in the previous section. On agreeing to take part, a household usually begins record-keeping on the same day as the interview or on the day following. However, since diaries cover 14 days it is not very material on which day of the week they are actually started. As a matter of interest Table 5.4.1 has been included to show the distribution by days of the week. The main starting days are Tuesday and Wednesday with Monday and Thursday being only slightly less popular. A similar pattern was observed in 1967[3].

Table 5.4.1 Day of week on which record started 1976

	Number	Percentage
Monday	1249	17.7
Tuesday	1610	22.8
Wednesday	1564	22.2
Thursday	1278	18.1
Friday	863	12.2
Saturday	375	5.3
Sunday	112	1.6
	7051	99.9

There was remarkably little variation in this pattern quarter by quarter; the largest deviations occur in the third quarter when the earlier part of the week was slightly less popular, with Wednesday accounting for 20.8 per cent of the 'starts' while Thursday and Friday increased their shares to 19.9 per cent and 13.4 per cent respectively.

References
[1] Kemsley, WFF. *Family Expenditure Survey—Handbook on the Sample, Fieldwork and Coding Procedures*, HMSO, London 1969. Table 5.2.1. p 23.
[2] Ibid p 24.
[3] Ibid p 25.

6 The interviewer's work

6.1 Programme of work on each quota of 16 addresses

Each interviewer is given an address list (blank form in Appendix G1) for the area in which she is working during a particular placing month. This address list has been drawn up by the Sampling Implementation Unit (SIU) and contains the 16 pre-selected addresses from the relevant Electoral Register. The addresses are as described in the Register; in particular, if the address refers to a specific flat in a large block, only that specified flat is visited. On the other hand, an address may contain several households in the same building, or even several distinct dwellings each with its own household. In these cases the rules governing multi-household addresses apply (4.9).

The address list also gives the various surnames registered at an address, and against each surname the number of males and females appearing on the register. This information is given for the convenience of the interviewer and is of some assistance in contacting the correct address or in recognising the potential existence of a multihousehold address. However, if a registered household has moved since the register was compiled, it is the household living at the address at the time of the interviewer's first effective call which is required. If the accommodation is empty at the time of the first call, no other household is taken even if someone moves into the accommodation shortly after the interviewer's call.

The interviewer takes the address in the order listed by the SIU and works as far as possible to the following programme:

Placing weeks of sample month

1st	First four addresses called on; preliminary interviews taken with those promising to cooperate, and record books left.
2nd	Second set of four addresses dealt with; interviews with those promising cooperation and record books left; intermediate calls on those who had started records in the first week.
3rd	Third set of four addresses dealt with interviews with those promising cooperation and record books left; intermediate calls on those who had started in first and second weeks; final calls on those cooperating households who had completed 14 day records.
4th	Fourth set of four addresses dealt with; interviews with those promising cooperation and record books left; intermediate calls on those who had

started in the second and third weeks; final calls on all completing 14 day records in this week.

Following month

1st week	Intermediate calls on those who started in the third and fourth weeks; final calls on all completing 14 day records.
2nd week	Intermediate and final calls on those starting in fourth week.

In practice, the programme may turn out to be more complex than this. It may happen that in the first placing week there is no reply at an address after several attempts, or it may not be possible to get a definite decision on whether or not cooperation will be forthcoming. In such case the interviewer proceeds to the 5th address, and if necessary to subsequent addresses, until four have been dealt with in the first placing week. The second placing week begins first with calls on those who were visited in the first week but from whom no definite decision had been obtained. Further addresses are then called on in the order of the address list until a further four addresses have been dealt with. Similarly, the third placing week begins with visits to those left undecided at the end of the second placing week, and then further addresses are taken in order until a third group of four addresses have been dealt with. The fourth placing week begins with visits to those left undecided at the end of the previous week and then all the remainder are covered.

Where an address contains concealed multi-households the extra households are dealt with in the same placing week so that, in practice, the weekly quota of four may extend to five or more. A further variation in the programme can occur where one of the last four addresses was visited for the first time in the fourth placing week but could not be contacted in that week. With the agreement of Field Branch the interviewer may be allowed to continue calling in the week following the end of the placing month. This, of course, leads to corresponding delays in the intermediate and final calls. In general, fieldwork extends over six calendar weeks and sometimes even to seven, although this applies to only about 2 per cent of the sample. As will be seen from this description, the fieldwork in any one area 'tails' in and out; it is heaviest in the third and fourth placing weeks when calls on households started in different weeks overlap.

6.2 The preliminary interview and placing of diaries

At each selected address calls are first made to find out how many people are living at the address, and how many are aged 16 or over (spenders) and whether the occupants constitute more than one household. Should there be more than one household at an address, the interviewer has to apply the rules described earlier (4.9) and decide which household to include in the sample.

In each selected household the interviewer then has to try to arrange an appointment to see all spenders together in order to explain the purpose of the survey and what co-operation involves. This is because cooperation is defined as all members of a household 16 years and over keeping diaries (see section 7.4). At this point it is usual to mention the payment sent to each spender if all cooperate. If, as is often the case, only one person is seen when contact is first made, only a brief explanation is usually given. This is done to avoid the risk of misunderstanding, particularly by other members, since this might lead to a refusal by one of them, a situation which would mean the loss of the whole household since partial cooperation is not accepted. For the same reason these initial contacts are always made in person, never by letter.

When cooperation appears to be forthcoming the interviewer goes through the Household Interview Schedule (see Appendix C2) followed by the Income Schedule (see Appendix D2) with each spender. In most cases these questionnaires are dealt with when the whole household is together. In a small proportion of cases one or more household members are seen separately from the rest of the household; usually this is for the convenience of informants. Perhaps a spender is not at home when the rest of the family are available, or an adolescent is going out for the evening before the main interviews are finished. Very occasionally someone considers his earnings and income so confidential that he does not want other members of the household to overhear his answers. Interviewers are trained to check before embarking on the main interview whether everybody is willing to be interviewed together; only in a few cases, estimated at 2 per cent of cooperating households, does someone ask specifically for an interview to be completed separately from the rest of the household. In some cases he or she may be content to write down the details on the questionnaire in the presence of the interviewer; these interview schedules are never left with informants. Wherever possible, informants are asked to produce records or bills which help provide accurate answers to interview questions. When such records are not available at the initial interview, interviewers make notes asking informants to search for the documents during the next 14 days.

When all spenders have been interviewed, but not until then, a schedule D, that is a seven-day diary, is left with each spender. Each person is asked to begin record keeping on the same day as other members of the household, either on the day of interview or the following day. If the former is chosen, the first day's record should contain all payments made on that day, including any prior to the interviewer's visit. Each page of the diary is dated by the interviewer before it is handed to the spender to try to avoid the possibility of including in the record payments made after the end of the record keeping period. While introducing the diary records the interviewer also deals with the checking schedule on Regular Commitments Ques-

tions (Appendix G3). This form covers the whole household, and provides an advance warning to the interviewer that certain items may need special attention when she re-visits the household. For example, if it appears from the answers to these questions that the housewife usually pays the milkman weekly, the interviewer has to check that such payment appears once in each of the two seven day diaries. If the housewife says she will be paying a grocery bill within the 14 days, the interviewer asks whether the bill can be itemised on the day when it is paid; if not, then she asks the housewife to record the total bill and all items acquired on account during the record period from the same shop.

At some stage during the main contact with the household a Purpose Leaflet is left (Appendix G2). This is done in order to leave with the household some documentary evidence of the interviewer's call, to explain briefly why the survey is being made and for which department. Usually the leaflet is handed over after all the spenders have been interviewed, but occasionally it is used at an earlier contact when, for instance, it proves impossible for all spenders to be seen together.

In all cases an interviewer completes a Calls and Contact sheet, which records the outcome of each call. (see Appendix G10).

6.3 Intermediate calls on cooperating households

At least two intermediate calls are made after the start of records and before the end of the 14 days record keeping period. Additional calls are at the discretion of the interviewer and are made when necessary to avoid losing cooperation; for instance, where a spender is living on his or her own and has difficulty in keeping the record. The first intermediate call is made on or before the 5th of the 14 days, and the second on or soon after the 8th day. Before the first intermediate call the interviewer:

i)   looks through the interview schedules for completeness and consistency;

ii) looks through the 'Regular commitments' questions to see whether there are likely to be entries in the diary records which require special attention;

iii) makes up the main checking sheet; this contains a check on gross pay on the Income schedule, and on the reverse a reminder about the regular items on the Household schedule which are likely to occur during the record keeping;

iv) makes up the 'consistency checks' sheet; this is obligatory for all trainee interviews (Appendix G4).

At the first intermediate call the interviewer is expected to deal with outstanding queries arising from these checks, and to cross-check diary entries against details on the 'Regular commitments' form and on the two checking sheets. She also 'probes' for missing detail in the diaries. Finally, the interviewer leaves dated diaries for the second seven days for each spender.

At the second intermediate call the interview collects in diaries for the first seven days and checks that the second set have been started correctly. At the same time, all entries made since the first intermediate call are checked through making use of the various checking sheets.

6.4 The final call

The final call is made by the interviewer as soon as possible after the end of the 14 day period. At this visit all the diaries for the second set of seven days are collected, together with any relating to the first seven days which were not collected at the previous call. The checking operations based on the 'Regular commitments' sheet and the main checking schedule are applied to all entries made since the previous visit.

Before actually leaving each household the interviewer has to complete an E form (Appendix G6). In order to ensure the payment to each cooperating person, this form has to contain the correct postal address of the household and the surname and initials of each household member keeping records. Care is taken over this since errors lead to delays in payment, particularly as sometimes Electoral Registers do not give the full postal address. Finally, interviewers tell informants that SSD coders may possibly write back for further information for coding purposes.

6.5 Returns made by interviewers to Field Branch

Copies of the various forms will be found in the Appendix. They are:

i) Form H (Appendix G8) Weekly Progress Return. This form shows the progress of work during an interviewer's quota and is made week by week until the whole quota has been dealt with. The form contains details of addresses dealt with in a particular placing week (6.1). Normally there will be 4 entries, but provision is made for two extra cases should these occur at a multi-household address. Households are not entered on these forms until a definite decision has been obtained, either a promise to cooperate or a refusal. The weekly quota of four include:
   a) household interviewed and promising to keep records that week;
   b) household refusing cooperation;
   c) address not containing any household; accommodation empty or demolished;
   d) household contacted, but excluded because it will be moving more than 30 miles away during the 14 day record-keeping period; household not contacted but found to be away until after the end of the placing month;
   e) household known to be in residence but failing to reply;
   f) no contact could be made at address and no information available as to whether occupiers were away. This category, and (e), only apply in the last placing period;
   g) no residential accommodation at address, or catering arrangements could not be separated from a business or institution;

h) pre-selected address subsequently excluded following the operation of the multi-household rules (Section 4.9).

ii) Form E (Appendix G6)—Record of spenders in co-operating households. This is completed in duplicate for each cooperating household. It contains the postal address of the household together with the surname and initials of each spender, that is each household member aged 16 or over. These forms provide the only accurate source of identity of those taking part in the FES. They are used in making the payments and whenever it is necessary to re-contact the household.

iii) Form F (Appendix G7)—Record of outcome at each household other than cooperating cases. This provides basic data for the non-response analyses.

iv) Form J (Appendix G9)
   —Despatch Note
v) Calls and Contact sheet
   (Appendix G10)

Like the H form, both are used by Field Branch to control field operations.

For a fully cooperating household the documents have to be returned no later than two working days after the final call. These documents are:
1 Calls and contact sheet
2 Two E forms
3 Household Schedule
4 The check sheets
5 Income Schedule and diaries in person number order, with the D schedules following each B schedule.

For all other cases the documents are returned as soon as possible. For each such household they comprise:
i) Calls and contact sheet
ii) F form
iii) Any other documents (Household, Income Schedule or Diary) partly or wholly completed.

6.6 Selection, training and supervision of interviewers

All new interviewers are recruited and trained in the same way irrespective of whether eventually they work on the FES or not. Potential recruits are invited to an initial interview at which their manner, availability, understanding and interest in the job are assessed. They also take a clerical test designed to indicate whether they are capable of following instructions and can record accurately. If successful at this stage they then attend a three-day training course run by the Field Branch. This covers interviewing techniques used by Social Survey Division, methods of approach to the public, and the basic ideas of sampling.* If successful at this stage, potential interviewers are offered probationary training. When new interviewers are working on their first survey a training officer always accompanies each one to demonstrate and train in interviewing as well as to assess the new interviewer. After

---

* For a discussion of SSD field techniques, see Atkinson, J. *A Handbook for Interviewers*. A manual for government Social Survey interviewing staff describing practice and procedures for structured interviewing, M 136, HMSO 1967. (This book is currently being revised.)

about three months new interviewers take a further test in the office involving taped interviews and also a written paper. If both fieldwork and test results are satisfactory they are accepted and placed on the regular panel of interviewers.

Most Social Survey Division ad hoc projects involve a personal briefing of interviewers before fieldwork commences. With the FES, there are monthly briefings for new or inexperienced interviewers. Currently, there are one and one half day conferences for FES briefings. When first offered an FES quota all interviewers have to attend one of these personal briefings before they are allowed to begin work. Prior to the briefing they are given a learning pack with examples of difficult cases and they are also expected to study the schedules and field instructions. Following the briefing, they are also given personal training by training officers on the FES during their first quota of addresses; this is irrespective of whether they have already worked on other surveys and have already some field training. For experienced FES interviewers there are periodical refresher briefings at which the survey is discussed and ways of improving performance are considered. In recent years, interviewers have spent time in Primary Analysis Branch in order to familiarise themselves with coding requirements.

Response rates achieved on each quota and the quality of data obtained are monitored and interviewers are graded according to a combination of factors. Ideally only those interviewers with a high grade are given quotas, although it is not always possible as other surveys have equal demands on the same interviewing force. A great deal depends on the personality and training of the interviewer. For most informarts the keeping of a record is an unusual activity and one in which they would not normally take part. To be successful an interviewer has to be able to make the explanation of record-keeping clear and accurate. In many cases informants only agree to keep and maintain records as a personal commitment to the interviewer, and not in pursuit of some ideal purpose which the survey is intended to fulfil.

During the three year period 1977-79 the number of interviewers who had carried out at least one quota of FES addresses was in a range from 270-290 each year. These were not the same interviewers as inevitably there is wastage and from time to time new interviewers have to be brought in to keep the field force up to strength. In recent years the demand for FES-trained interviewers has increased because there has been an increase in requests for financial surveys to be carried out by the SSD.

Interviewers can only be fully trained by actually working on the FES in the field; however to ensure that new interviewers' lack of experience does not unduly affect the survey results, the number of trainees in any month is kept as small as possible.

The role of the Field Branch in charge of the FES is not only educational. Maintaining morale is an important function and contact is made by telephone with interviewers who often are working in difficult conditions and are usually isolated. Furthermore the Field Branch monitors response of individual interviewers and attempts to answer queries about why response is fluctuating. It is true that the FES is an extremely complex survey covering a wide variety of matters that need clarification. Field instructions cannot be expected to cope with all possible situations and the Field Officer acts as a liaison between the Research Unit and the individual interviewer when queries arise.

On completing fieldwork at a cooperating household, the interviewer returns all field documents for that household to Field Branch. This is done within a few days of the final call. A preliminary check is then made in Field Branch to ensure that a complete set of documents has been returned having regard to the size and composition of the household. In particular, there has to be an income schedule and two diary records for each spender in addition to the household schedule. Each set of documents is then passed to Primary Analysis Branch for editing and coding.

7 Subsequent operations in SSD

7.1 The work of Primary Analysis Branch (PAB)

The staff working on the editing and coding of the FES are divided into three teams consisting of about fifteen coding staff in all, with a supervisor in charge of each team and a higher grade supervisor who has overall responsibility for the work of the three teams. Preliminary coding takes place; all the more straightforward items are coded, but more complicated coding is not tackled at this stage. Queries arising from entries in the documents, omissions and inconsistencies between two or more entries are 'flagged up'. The second team checks the coding carried out by the first team and codes the more complex areas which are not undertaken by the first team. The second team also examines the queries raised by the first team coders. The types of queries that arise from inadequacies in the data are identified and referred to the Research Unit, who decide whether or not to write a letter to an informant requesting further information. When replies to letters are received the second team amend and code the entries according to the information given. The third team check the coding of the second team, and review problem cases. Matters of principle relating to new data that are not covered by existing instructions, such as entries reflecting changes in the National Insurance Benefits system, new legislation or practices relating to income or spending, expenditure items which are new on the market etc are also referred to the Research Unit, and this leads to new procedures for coding.

Coding instructions written by PAB are based on the Research Unit's Coding Notes. Coding instructions cover procedures in greater detail; they give guidance on how to deal with special cases, and instruct coders on how to carry out the more complex arithmetical calculations. Instructions of this kind are required to avoid any inconsistencies of treatment that could arise over time if coders worked directly from the more general Coding Notes. Coding Instructions are up-dated completely every year.

In the course of coding, consistency checks are carried out into the accuracy of the information reported by each household, eg benefits received are checked against age and family circumstances; education grants against income and parental contributions; rates against rateable values and poundages; and all business expenditure, refunds and allowances against business expenses are edited out of the survey. When carrying out checks and editing, coding staff are required to refer to various documents in order to check the data and resolve queries. For these purposes staff are issued with a number of lists covering such information as current Social Security benefits, rate poundages, private pensions sources, etc.

In addition they have available for reference purposes a full range of government leaflets on benefits and pensions; new leaflets are inserted in the collection as soon as they are available. It takes about six months to a year for a coder to reach the stage when he is considered to be trained and fully conversant with FES procedure, but coders are not considered for the third team until they have had at least two years' experience of the work.

The total volume of coding and editing work is very considerable. In 1967 it was estimated that nearly 95 items of information were collected from a household by interview, and nearly 210 items were recorded in the diaries; in all, about 300 items per budget. Based on these figures, interviewers and coders handle over two million items a year. Since 1967 the interview schedules have increased in length, so that the number of items requiring attention may also have increased.

Although the Handbook only discusses SSD operations, it is perhaps relevant to mention that the Department of Employment carries out a one in thirty check of budgets. The 'error rate' is less than 1 per cent.

7.2 Referrals to Research Unit

As mentioned in the previous section, Primary Analysis Branch are sometimes not able to take coding action at a question because there is insufficient information recorded on the questionnaires or in a diary. This is because (i) a question has not been asked; or (ii) an answer has not been recorded by an interviewer; or (iii) further information is needed; or (iv) informants have said they cannot answer the question; and (v) some situations fall outside the scope of the Coding Notes and coders need to seek advice. All of these cases are referred to the FES Research Unit.

Table 7.2.1 below gives an indication of the incidence of referrals, comparing the proportions of household budget referred to the Research Unit for additional information in 1969 and in 1978.

Table 7.2.1 Proportion of household budgets referred to Research Unit

		1969	1970
(i)	Total number of household budgets per year	6834	6872
(ii)	No. of household budgets with at least one query referred to Research	4088	2048
(iii)	$\frac{(ii)}{(i)}$ x 100	60%	30%
(iv)	No. of household budgets referred per working day (base = 250 days)	16.35	8.19

20

In 1969, the first year for which figures are available, 60 per cent of all households in the sample had at least one query which needed to be resolved by referral to the FES Research Unit. There were, on average, 16 budgets referred per working day. The proportion and number of budgets referred per working day have been halved, indicating that the addition of editing questions to the questionnaires and improved training of coders and improvements to coding instructions have had some beneficial effect; however, it is also true that, currently, more decisions are made to impute rather than to refer back to informants for further information.

Referrals are now dealt with in several ways, although in the early years all cases found at the coding stage to require further information were dealt with by an interviewer revisiting the household. In 1968 an experiment attempting to obtain missing information by post proved successful and, in 1969, the option of writing back was adopted. A third possibility is to impute a missing amount without further contact with the informant. Imputation is usually based on FES results from the previous year, particularly where there is a relationship between household income and an expenditure variable such as gas or electricity expenditure. Imputation tables are provided by the Department of Employment.

The Research Officer's decision on which action to adopt depends very much on the circumstances of the individual household; for example, elderly people are not sent letters in case they become unduly worried. Often he will consult the Field Branch before deciding to ask the interviewer to return. Cost considerations play a role, as referral by interview is obviously costly; generally this type of referral can be justified if a return visit has educational benefit for an interviewer or where there are a number of queries or where the query is about a sensitive topic, like missing investment income, that is best sought by face-to-face contact.

Postal queries have an obvious advantage of cost savings over interviewer re-visit; however there are disadvantages as well. There can be long delays in receiving a reply, even though a self-addressed, pre-stamped reply envelope is provided. Delays can affect the timetable (see next section). Also, a letter received from a government department can raise suspicions in informants' minds that confidentiality pledges are not being observed; they become aware that coders are scrutinising the information given to the interviewer. (This is the reason why interviewers are briefed to remind informants at the final call that they may receive a letter from OPCS asking for further information.) Finally, there is a problem of non-response to postal queries.

Table 7.2.2 below shows how the pattern of obtaining missing information has changed between 1969 and 1978.

Clearly there has been a shift towards decisions to impute either from the outset or because of non-response to letters. Postal non-reponse (or an unacceptable delay in responding) has increased from 10 per cent in 1969 to 20 per cent in 1978.

The pattern of referred queries by schedule is illuminating and is shown in Table 7.2.3 below. Again figures for 1969 and 1978 are provided.

The average number of queries has almost doubled for the Income Schedule and has increased slightly for the Household Schedule. The queries on the Household Schedule are mainly concerned with rates and rates poundage figures. In fact, rates poundages are often confirmed by telephoning the rating authority. Queries on the Income Schedule are predominantly about informants' estimates of their usual earnings (Q.15 in Appendix D2) and result from a number of consistency checks carried out by coders. The main finding from the table is that the number of queries arising in diary records has dropped considerably since 1969; this is mainly due to improved field training methods.

7.3 Timetable

On the completion of the work in Primary Analysis Branch the coded and edited documents forming each budget are sent to DE for computer analysis and reporting. Each budget contains a Household Schedule A, and Income Schedule B, and a credit card payments sheet for each spender, and two diary records D for each spender. These documents do not contain any information on personal identity nor the address of the household. This information appears only on the E forms, and these are never passed outside OPCS.

The progress of each budget through SSD is monitored by the FES Research Unit in order to ensure that the completed and coded documents reach DE in time for all the processing operations to be carried out prior to using the data for the RPI weights. On average, a budget reaches DE some six to seven weeks after the 14 day diaries are

Table 7.2.2 Means of obtaining missing information (1969 and 1978)

Missing information obtained by:	1969		1978	
	No.	%	No.	%
(i) interviewer re-visit	571	14	55	3
(ii) letter	2593	63	623	30
(iii) Decision to inpute; a) without futher contact of informant	640	16	1211	59
b) after non-response to letter	284	7	159	8
Total household budgets referred	4088	100	2048	100

Table 7.2.3 Referral queries per sample household by FES Schedule (1969 and 1978)

FES Schedule	1969		1978	
	No. of queries	Queries per sample household*	No. of queries	Queries per sample household*
Household	2269	0.33	1672	0.24
Income	1976	0.29	2329	0.34
Diary	2284	0.33	270	0.04
	6529	0.96	4271	

*total sample (1969) = 6834
total sample (1978) = 6872

completed. This breaks down approximately into:

	Weeks
Time between end of diaries and documents reaching Primary Analysis	1
Time in PAB in coding and editing	4 — 5
Extra time if reference is made back to a household	1

Completed documents are sent to DE usually every other week in batches of 260 budgets. The critical cases are those where the diaries begin towards the end of the third month of a quarter. This is especially true of those who on account of difficulties of contact, did not begin the diaries until after the end of the third placing month. Such cases are usually not available in the office for coding until at least a month later, particularly if there have been further difficulties in contacting a household to collect the completed diaries, or inspection leads to a reference back to the household. In spite of problem cases such as these, the last batch of completed budgets placed in a quarter reaches DE within 9 to 10 weeks of the end of that quarter.

Despite the decline in the number of cases referred back to informants for further information, there has been an increase in coding and editing as the interview schedules have continued to grow in size and complexity. In spite of this increasing complexity, the mean time before completed budgets can be passed to DE has remained fairly constant at between 6 and 8 weeks.

7.4 Payments to each household

Since the very beginning of the FES a small payment has been made to each person who cooperates in the inquiry. Section 17.1 gives the background as to why payments are offered. The payment was £1 per person from 1957 to June 1971; since July 1971 it has been £2. (At the time of writing, a higher payment is being considered.) The payment is only made provided each household member aged 16 or over cooperates. Cooperation means keeping a diary of expenditure over 14 days and, in the words of the Purpose Leaflet "…..answering questions about payments over longer periods, and giving details of your incomes and other money coming into the household". A refusal by one member either to keep diaries or to give income details will prevent a complete assessment of the total expenditure of the whole household. For this reason it is essential, if full use is to be made of the survey results, to get cooperation from each household member, and interviewers are trained to drop the case if any one individual refuses to be persuaded. In practice, most people who agree to provide income details will also agree to keep records for 14 days; however, as pointed out in Section 14 informants often do not know the answers to all questions. Obviously, payment is not withheld in these cases.

These payments are made by a separate postal order sent to each cooperating individual. One purpose of the preliminary check made by Field Branch when the completed documents are first received from an interviewer is to see that all the required documents are available so that payment can be made. The postal orders and covering letters are issued by the Accounts Branch of OPCS on the basis of the personal details and address contained on the E form (see Appendix G6).

8 Role of the FES Research Unit

The FES Research Unit has four main functions:

(i) to liaise with government departments who use the FES;

(ii) to carry out desk research or field experiments relevant to the FES;

(iii) to maintain contact with the public, including queries from FES informants, users other than government departments and general queries.

(iv) to carry out overall administration of, and responsibility for, the survey operations.

8.1 Liaison with Government users

There are eleven government departments which attend the FES Sub-Committee, which is chaired by the Central Statistical Office. A working group, the FES Technical Group, serves the Sub-Committee. The FES Research Unit regularly contributes technical papers on various aspects of the survey to both committees. Additionally, a considerable amount of time is spent servicing departmental needs, either by helping departments formulate their requirements or by carrying out desk research to answer queries about FES computer tapes. Contact with Department of Employment (DE) is almost on a day-to-day basis as new coding principles are agreed with the main sponsors. Policy about proposed additions to the FES is determined in the first instance by the FES Research Unit, after consultation with both Field and Primary Analysis branches. Ultimately, decisions rest with the FES Technical Group. Although the FES has remained remarkably unchanged in its main components of income and expenditure, there is continued pressure to add questions by government users. This presents a problem in that it is generally recognised that the FES has been fully stretched in terms of tasks demanded of interviewer and informant alike. There is always the danger that adding too many new questions can depress response or affect interviewer morale. Field Branch monitors interview time and public reaction and individual questions and layout; Primary Analysis Branch tests the working of questions at coding stage. Often new questions are piloted. Both branches submit reports to the Research Unit and on the basis of their advice proposals are made to the Technical Group. The Research Unit can advise rewording of questions or, where there are very few mentions in a code, deleting a question. Suggestions for deletions also arise where there is poor quality data or where response to the whole survey is threatened. Often new questions are taken on experimentally for a year and then reviewed. Therefore, the FES Research Unit keeps a continuous scrutiny of how individual questions are working.

Another function performed by the Research Unit is to try to resolve queries from government departments about apparent anomalies in FES tapes. Often these anomalies cannot be resolved without resort to the original field documents. These documents are inaccessible to all client departments except for DE because of confidentiality pledges to respondents. Often such investigations result in improvements to coding procedures.

8.2 Experimental research

The FES research unit also carries out special desk research projects either to determine the incidence of certain cases or else as ad hoc projects. DE often provides special computer tables. Recent examples are: an investigation into inter-week bias (the difference in recording of expenditure between recording weeks); a study of instalment credit methodology; a study of the characteristics of informants who cannot give income from investment and selfemployment income; and the quality of data count carried out on 4th quarter 1978 household budgets.

Finally, the Research Unit designs and analyses special methodological experiments. These experiments are described more fully in a later section; however some recent examples are the Family Budget Survey experiments and the Annual Income Feasibility Study. (Section 17.7).

8.3 Contact with the public

All queries from the public concerning the SSD operations of the Family Expenditure Survey are dealt with by the Research Unit. (DE receives queries about special unpublished tabulations, the annual reports, computer tapes and the main purposes of the survey). Queries often arise from potential FES respondents who either wish to know more about the purposes of the survey or who seek reassurance about matters such as confidentiality. People who have cooperated sometimes write to say that they have not received £2 postal orders. Most queries are usually formally answered by letter from the Research Officer, as maintaining good public relations is vital to the continued success of the survey. Increasingly, requests for information about the survey come from local government, academics and even other countries who seek advice about expenditure surveys. The FES Research Unit also contributes to the seminars on the FES held by the SSRC Survey Archive, at Essex University which holds copies of FES tapes.

8.4 Administration of the FES

The FES Research Unit is responsible for updating and re-issuing Field Instructions and Coding Notes each year. However there also is a need to initiate new coding notes during the year, as new situations arise, eg new benefits like the electricity discount scheme, the £10 Christmas payment to pensioners, new credit arrangements, etc. The FES Research Unit attempts to keep in touch with the new developments in a variety of ways by receiving departmental leaflets, by reading Hansard daily, etc. Often the need for changes in procedure arise from Field and Primary Analysis branch

The role of the Research Unit in making decisions about 'referrals' from Primary Analysis Branch has already been discussed in Section 7.2. Analysis of referrals by question, is carried out and this helps identify problem areas.

One major role of the Research Unit is to carry out an annual analysis of response which is presented to the FES Sub-Committee. Response is analysed by quarter, by region and by type of area. (Copies of this analysis are available on request.)

The Research Unit 'progress-chases', keeping records of time elapsed between the time when a household budget arrives and when it is despatched to the Department of Employment for punching.

Decisions are occasionally required about including certain households in the sample; other cases occur where diary records are not complete, or where only partial co-operation is achieved.

Finally, although briefings are mainly conducted by Field trainers, the Research Unit also contributes to the briefings, explaining the uses of the FES, giving confidentiality undertakings and describing what happens to the data, as well as the need to maintain good public relations.

9 Confidentiality

9.1 The importance of the confidentiality undertaking

There are two distinct aspects of obtaining cooperation from the public. First, those who take part in the FES have to be assured that the information they provide will be of value. But, secondly, and more importantly to the individual, interviewers must be able to persuade potential informants that any information they provide will not be used in any way to their detriment. A failure to provide the necessary assurances to safeguard the confidentiality of the data is likely to make the interviewer's task more difficult when attempting to persuade people to co-operate, particularly as the FES collects highly sensitive data about income and expenditure. It might also put the interviewer in an awkward and weak position in discussion with possible participants. Adequate arrangements for confidentiality are essential not only to safeguard informants, but also to maintain the morale of interviewers and secure a good response rate.

While some people provide information without querying what will happen to it afterwards, others will be reluctant to cooperate in case an interviewer should disclose details about them to neighbours, while others may assume that information given to one government department will automatically find its way to other departments, to their personal disadvantage. Recent government reports have confirmed the public's concern about transfers of data between departments and central data banks[1,2]. In a small community someone may even have misgivings over neighbours knowing that he or she has taken part in the survey at all. To a large extent problems of this kind can only be overcome by the personality of the interviewer and her conviction that the data she collects will be jealously safeguarded by OPCS. Concern by informants that information they provide might adversely affect their tax position, their Social Security benefits or their dealings with another government department is taken seriously. It is not sufficient to explain that the results of the FES are required in connection with the weighting of the Index of Retail Prices and only for statistical purposes. It is also essential that interviewers explain convincingly the safeguards on confidentiality, and how information can not be misused in such a way as to affect those who provide the information. This is particularly important at a time when FES data tapes are disseminated more widely than ever before. A considerable portion of the FES interviewer briefings is taken up with an explanation of what happens to field documents, and how anonymity is safeguarded when tapes are passed to government and academic users.

9.2 Arrangements to ensure confidentiality

The confidentiality undertaking is set out in the Purpose Leaflet (see Appendix G2) and it contains the following;
"We ensure that information given by individual households and members is kept confidential. Names and addresses of people who cooperate in the survey are removed from the original documents on which data is recorded and are known only by OPCS. They are never passed to any other government department, nor to members of the public or Press.

Access to questionnaires on which data is recorded is restricted to the staff in the Social Survey Division of OPCS who collect and code the data and to the staff of the Department of Employment who process the data and retain the documents. Data collected during the survey are sent to other government departments only in such a form that no individual can be identified from them.

In published reports the identity of an individual is never revealed either directly or by implication from the details of results released."

The pledge therefore covers the Department of Employment as well as SSD, because the former process the data on the DE computer at Runcorn. All interviewers, coders and research workers are obliged to sign the Official Secrets Act, and any divulgence of details would be punishable under this Act.

As already explained, the identity of each person cooperating in the FES is recorded on an E form. This is essential to ensure the payment of £2 to each participant, and to enable reference back to households for further details when necessary, and sometimes to provide a sampling frame for a follow-up survey. Details of identity do not appear on any documents containing the statistical data, but only on these E forms. The interviewers return all documents, including these forms, to Field Branch at the end of the 14 days record-keeping period; as a safeguard against loss in the post they are sent by recorded delivery. In Social Survey the E forms are removed from each budget as soon as there is no longer any possibility of a need to refer back to household members. These forms are stored separately in Social Survey Division and retained for sometime before being destroyed at the end of three years.

The interview schedules and diaries which are passed to DE when coding is completed do not, therefore, contain names and addresses. Neither does DE have access to personal identity information which is stored in Social Survey Division. Apart from DE, no government department has access to the field documents. When computer tapes are passed on to other government departments it is highly unlikely that households can be identified, as sampling areas are not identified. Tapes held by the SSRC Survey Archive do not contain the household reference numbers.

Should further work by a department necessitate additional visits to households, the department requiring this has to provide OPCS with the household serial numbers from its copy of the computer tape, so that Social Survey Division can then arrange for interviewers to re-visit the particular households under the same kind of confidentiality undertaking as in the standard FES. Since the coded documents do not contain details of personal identity there is little possibility that anyone examining them will be able to identify a cooperating household. But as a further safeguard the original documents and certain coding frames are not released. As regards the results, there is little risk that any item in the statistical analyses or reports will lead to identification because the FES is based on a sample with a sampling fraction less than 1 in 2,500 in any period of 12 months.

9.3 Data linkage
Data linkage is not a subject which is likely to give rise to any serious problem. In the first place, it should be clear from the arrangements described that a user department cannot link data on the FES computer tape with personal data already in that department. Secondly, a linkage

cannot be effected without the prior cooperation of Social Survey Division. If a department has a good reason to link its own data with material from the FES, Social Survey Division will only agree after each cooperating household has been contacted by Social Survey Division and an explanation given as to what is involved and its purpose and the household's agreement requested; a refusal would exclude an individual from any linkage arrangements.

The exercise described elsewhere in this Handbook on differential response (10.7) is not an example of data linkage. No data from the FES was merged or linked with the 1971 Census. As explained later, The Census Offices did not see the FES documents, nor did Social Survey Division see the Census forms. The exercise carried out by the Census Office identified the whole 1971 FES sample among the Census forms and then provided tabulations of census data broken by whether or not households had cooperated in the 1971 FES.

References
[1] Younger Committee. *Report of the Committee on Privacy*. Cmnd 5012. HMSO, London 1972.
[2] Lindop Committee. *Report of the Committee on Data Protection*. Cmnd 7341. HMSO, London 1978. Chapter 26.

10 Response rates

10.1 Problems in securing adequate response

The collection of data on expenditure and income from members of the public presents many problems. First, the FES asks about income in great detail and also asks people to keep diary records for 14 days. Certain people feel that income details are too private to reveal and refuse at the outset. Keeping diaries for 14 days may present a problem for some people, notably the elderly. Another factor which affects the response rate is the requirements that each household member aged 16 and over must co-operate. Cooperation is more difficult to secure where a household consists of several adults, or where a member is elderly or illiterate. The self-employed constitute a special problem as it is often difficult for someone running his own business to disentangle his personal affairs from those of the business. Also up-to-date figures are often not available and finally, self-employed informants often complain about the number of government forms they already fill out.

Inquiries whose main purpose is statistical are not likely to attract a high degree of co-operation of themselves. The FES is no exception to this generalisation. It provides no direct benefit to anyone who takes part other than receipt of the small payment, and there is little in the FES which is of such personal interest as to induce people to cooperate out of concern with the subject. The main feature which an interviewer uses in presenting the FES to an intended cooperator is its use in providing data for the weights of the three indices of retail prices. Even here, the appeal is indirect; public concern is not with the indices themselves, but with the effect of rising prices; the measurement of change in price levels is carried out quite separately by the DE.

Furthermore, it is useless for an interviewer to pretend that the FES will take up only a small of the informant's time, as can sometimes be said of other social inquiries. The very opposite is the case; the preliminary interview may take an hour or more, while the diary records if kept conscientiously, will certainly take further time during the following 14 days. The interviewer is therefore asking people to do a great deal for the survey but is not in any position to offer much in return. It is true that each cooperating individual is given a small payment and this no doubt improves the situation, although the actual effect on response is ambiguous. The evidence from the 1950/51 experiments (Section 17.1) is that making payments will increase response by possibly one-third, while doubling the payment leads to a further but smaller improvement. On the other hand, when payment was doubled to £2 in 1971 after the FES had been running for over 14 years there was virtually no improvement in

response rate. The conclusion would seem to be that probably some payment is advantageous but that within limits the exact amount of the payment may not matter.

Offering incentives to people keeping diaries is common practice in most European budget surveys. However, the general feeling is that payment mainly has a beneficial effect on interviewer morale and confidence, rather than on those informants, who have set their minds against cooperation and are not likely to be dissuaded by the offer of an incentive; in fact, this can further aggravate the situation. Also, most interviewers prefer not to think of payment as a 'bribe'. There may be some evidence that payment prevents drop-outs, ie those people who initially agree to keep diaries, then do not complete full diaries.

Research work carried out in the early years of the survey (Section 17.2) confirmed that when two interviewers were working under virtually the same conditions, the difference between their two response rates was greater than could be expected by chance. This result implied that to some extent response was dependent on the interviewer, thus suggesting that there was scope for improvement by selection and training; a conclusion which was confirmed subsequently as the response was gradually improved from just under 60 per cent at the beginning of the FES to about 70 per cent by the time the survey was in its fourth year. Interviewer training is undoubtedly an important factor in the continued success of the survey. The length of the preliminary interview is probably not an important deterrent to cooperation, but the length and complexity of the interview schedules may well have an adverse effect indirectly on interviewer morale, particularly of newly recruited interviewers.

To sum up, the continued success of the FES depends very much on the individual interviewer who must be able to give an explanation to record-keepers which is clear and relevant, and must also be able to spend sufficient time with each informant as to be accepted as someone the informant wishes to please. In practice, many informants probably agree to keep and maintain records more to please the interviewer personally than in pursuit of some ideal statistical purpose.

10.2 Response rates 1957-1978

As shown in Tables 4.10.1 and 4.10.2, the calculation of response begins by first excluding from the set sample those addresses which do not contain any domestic households, and then allowing for the multi-household procedure. This results in the effective samples for 1976-78 of 10,080, 10,145 and 10,135 respectively, as shown in Table 10.2.1 below. During these three years,

Family Expenditure Survey   Quarterly Response Rates

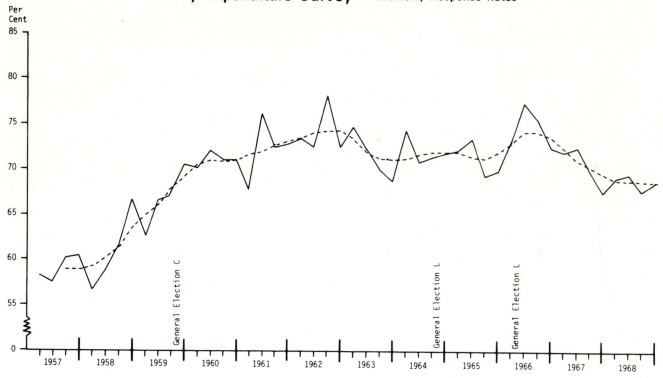

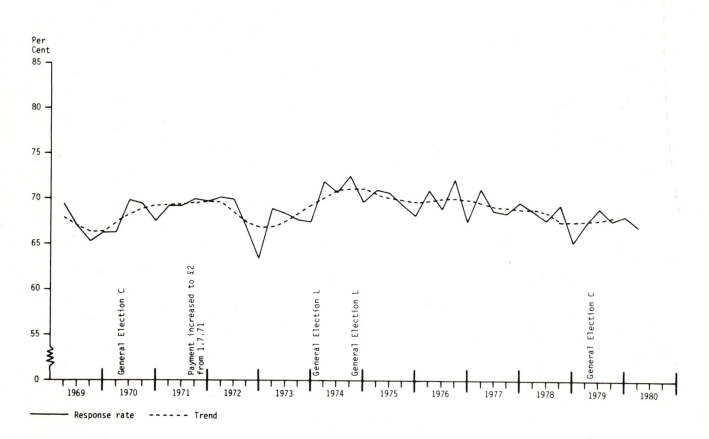

Response rate   ----- Trend

Table 10.2.1 Response in 1976, 1977 and 1978

	1976		1977		1978	
	No.	%	No.	%	No.	%
Cooperating households	7,051	69.95	7,055	69.54	6,872	67.80
Records promised but no completed	278	2.76	328	3.23	389	3.84
Other refusals	2,644	26.23	2,637	26.00	2,747	27.11
Non contacts	107	1.06	125	1.23	127	1.25
Effective sample	10,080	100.00	10,145	100.00	10,135	100.00

Table 10.2.2 Response rates by year 1957 to 1978

Year	Cooperating households	Response rate %	Year	Cooperating households	Response rate %
1957	2839	59.1	1968	7023	69.0
1958	2915	61.0	1969	6834	66.9
1959	3010*	66.7	1970	6230*	68.3
1960	3421	71.1	1971	7087	69.5
1961	3422	72.4	1972	6867	67.7
1962	3527	74.1	1973	6971	68.3
1963	3357	71.5	1974	6549*	71.2
1964	3168*	72.3	1975	7058	69.9
1965	3341	71.2	1976	7051	70.0
1966	3223*	74.8	1977	7055	69.5
1967	7201	70.5	1978	6872	67.8

Reduction in numbers consequent on suspension of fieldwork over period of General Election.

these effective samples yielded 7,051, 7,055 and 6,872 cooperating households. Most of those not cooperating were refusals, and most households who promise to cooperate in fact complete the survey. Roughly 3-4 per cent failed to complete the 14-day records, a slightly higher proportion than in 1967[1]. Where there is any difficulty in contacting the household the interviewer continues to re-visit until the end of the placing month. This persistence is justified, and the proportion not contacted eventually had fallen by 1976/77 to about 1 per cent, half the figure in 1967.

The number of cooperating households with the corresponding response rates are given in Table 10.2.2 for each year from 1957.

To begin with, the response was rather low, slightly under 60 per cent. During the first few years it rose fairly steadily to reach 70 per cent by the end of 1959. From 1960 to mid-1967 the trend as measured by a five-point centred moving average of quarterly rates varied little, lying within the range 71 to 74 per cent (see Chart). There was then a temporary setback to response of about five years following the enlargement of the sample introduced in 1967. These changes necessitated the employment of more than three times as many interviewers compared with the pre-1967 position, and at the same time there was a consequential rise in the number of supervisory staff. This expansion was only made possible by a considerable recruitment and training programme. The trend values gradually fell throughout 1967 to 1969, and reached their lowest level of 66.9 per cent at the end of that year. Thereafter the response rates showed some improvement, and from 1974 to 1977 they were more stable around the 70% level. Since 1978 response has been in slight decline for a number of reasons. First, comparisons with response rates of other continuous surveys showed a decline in 1978, indicating that external factors may have

played a part. Second, SSD carried out a number of ad hoc surveys requiring FES-trained interviewers during 1978 and 1979 and this may have had a depressing effect on response.

Summing up, it is clear that the FES has undergone several phases in response trend. During the first three years, response increased sharply while intensive field training was having dramatic effects. During the next seven years, FES response was consistently above 70 per cent and almost reached 75 per cent on several occasions. Following the doubling of the sample, annual response dropped below 70 per cent and remained at this level until 1974. The change of almost 4 per cent in average annual response between the 1960-66 period (average response of 72.5 per cent) and the 1967-73 period (average response of 68.6 per cent) may be indicative of the sacrifice to response when a sample is enlarged.

10.3 Variations over quarters
Quarterly response rates for the years 1957 to 1968 appeared in the first Handbook[2] and for 1969 to 1974 in the comparison of the 1971 FES sample with the Census[3]. Similar data for 1975 onwards are given in Table 10.3.1.

Table 10.3.1 Response by Quarters 1975-1978

	Quarters			
	I	II	III	IV
	%	%	%	%
1975	71.1	70.8	69.4	68.3
1976	71.1	69.0	72.3	67.4
1977	71.2	68.7	68.4	69.8
1978	68.7	67.8	69.6	65.2

Quarterly deviations from the trend are generally quite small. There is little evidence of any seasonal patterns except in the deviations of the 4th quarter from the trend. For each year from 1961 to 1976, except 1968, the deviation for the 4th quarter has been below the trend as measured by a five-point, centred, moving average, the mean negative deviation over these 16 years being 1.3 per cent. For the first three years, however, the deviation was in the opposite direction, averaging 2.0 per cent above the trend; 1960 was a year of transition with zero deviation in the 4th quarter; the other quarters displayed no pronounced tendency either above or below the trend except that for each of the years 1972 to 1976 the first quarter was above the trend by an average of 1 per cent. Taking all quarters together, the root mean square deviation in the period 1960 to 1966 was 1.9 per cent and for 1967 to 1976 was 1.3 per cent. The reduction in size of the deviations is a consequence of the expansion of the sample in 1967. Considering only the ten years 1967 to 1976, the root mean square deviation was about 1% for each of the first three calendar quarters, but about 1.7 per cent for the 4th quarter.

10.4 Regional variations
The response for each standard region is shown below in Table 10.4.1 for the years 1975 to 1978.

Response by region for 1966 and 1967 are shown in the

Table 10.4.1 Response by Standard Region *percentages*

	1975	1976	1977	1978
Northern	75.9	80.2	74.3	73.4
Yorkshire & Humberside	75.0	77.2	74.2	71.8
North Western	69.0	67.6	69.8	65.7
East Midlands	74.3	74.1	72.9	69.9
West Midlands	66.4	68.2	71.2	66.8
East Anglia	72.8	71.6	67.6	68.9
Greater London Area	61.8	60.6	61.0	60.9
South East (Excl. GL Area)	70.1	69.6	68.3	67.4
South Western	70.5	68.7	69.4	69.3
Wales	73.6	77.9	78.0	76.3
Scotland	70.6	69.2	68.9	67.9
All regions	69.9	70.0	69.5	67.8

first Handbook[4]; regional results for 1969 — 1974 appear in the 1971 Census comparison article[5].

The rates for 1975 to 1978 confirm previous experience that the GL Area consistently produces the lowest response rate, rarely rising above 60%. The highest response tended to come from the Northern region and Wales. Regional differences of this nature must, however, be treated with caution. Response is to a great extent dependent on the skill and experience of the interviewer, and some of the consistency of response from a region probably arises from the tendency of interviewers to work in neighbouring areas year after year. On the other hand, in a small region where only a few interviewers are employed, for example East Anglia, there may be considerable variations in response due to changes in interviewers.

10.5 Variations by type of area
In an earlier analysis of response by type of area in 1967[6] there was a steady increase in response from the GLA, through provincial conurbations, other urban areas, semi-rural areas, to reach its highest level of nearly 80 per cent in rural areas during the years 1973 to 1974. This area type breakdown was based on the second stratifying factor but with the re-organization of local government in 1974, this factor was changed. Areas other than the GLA were divided for stratification purposes into four groups defined as Metropolitan Districts and Clydeside conurbation; then with non-Metropolitan districts divided into 3 by density of population. Table 10.5.1 is based on this new factor. It continues to display some increase in response with type of area, but the increase is not as marked as in the breakdowns for 1969 to 1974 quoted above.

Table 10.5.1 Response by Type of Area *percentages*

	1975	1976	1977	1978
Greater London Area	61.8	60.6	61.0	60.8
Metropolitan districts and Clydeside conurbation	69.3	71.1	70.0	66.2
Other areas by density: Higher (3.2 persons per acre or greater)	69.8	69.7	69.4	68.6
Medium (below 3.2 but 0.9 or greater)	72.5	71.3	72.1	69.2
Lower (less than 0.9 persons per acre)	73.5	73.8	72.3	72.4

10.6 Differential response — studies before 1971
With a response rate of about 70 per cent there is ample scope for the appearance of differential response, so that the composition of the final sample may differ from the

sample as originally selected. Until the 1971 Census check, reported in the next section, very little was available on differential response. There was data on variation by region and by type of area which has been referred to in the previous section; otherwise, the only information was restricted to that given in the first Handbook which showed variation in response with rateable value and rates paid and size of household[7].

These tables were based on information obtained in the three years 1964 to 1966, and indicated that response tended to fall with rateable value and rates paid, but to increase with size of household. These earlier results were dependent on data from non-cooperating cases and were subject to certain qualifications especially as regards the size of household. These qualifications do not apply to the study described in the next section.

10.7 Differential response — 1971 Census check
This study is more fully reported by Kemsley[3] and Harris[8]. The Census check was made possible by supplying the Census Offices with a list of the responding and non-responding households drawn in the 1971 FES sample. The Census Offices identified the 1971 Population Census returns for these households and from these produced statistical tables for the Social Survey Division. In the course of this exercise great care was taken to ensure the confidentiality of the various documents; the Census Offices did not see the FES field documents recording the data reported by cooperating households, nor did the Social Survey see the Census returns.

Identification by the Census Offices of the lists of names and addresses provided by the Social Survey was successful in about 94 per cent of cases. In a further 3 per cent the address, but not the household, could be identified; in these cases there would have been a removal between the Census and survey dates leading to one household being replaced by another. The results are based on these 97 per cent. In the remaining 3 per cent the address could not be identified.

This matching produced two sets of distributions; one of cooperating households and the other of non-cooperating cases, each pair of distributions classifying FES households by a Census variable. Since the FES is a household survey all the variables, 17 in all, refer to an attribute of the household or the head of the household or the housewife. Each pair of distributions was compared using the Chi Square test as a measure of association. Many of the values were high, well above any conventional level of significance. The paper quoted gives response rates for separate categories defined by those variables displaying a substantial degree of differential response. Much the most striking result was the variation of response with age of HOH or of the housewife; there was a regular decline in response of about 2 per cent for each increase of 5 years of age, ranging from a response over 80 per cent for persons under 30 years to below 65 per cent for those above 70 years. Households without children produced a response rate of about 66 per cent while those with children had a rate of 75 per cent or more. Another breakdown displaying considerable variation was that of employment status of HOH; employees other than managers showed a response of 72 per cent or over, while for self-employed those with employees produced an average rate of only 56 per cent, and those working on their own a rate of 63 per cent.

As in the 1964 to 1966 analysis, there was an increasing response with household size; comparative data for the two studies are shown in Table 10.7.1.

Table 10.7.1 Response by household size

Number of persons	1964-1966	1971
1	66	67
2	68	68
3	72	69
4	79	74
5+	81	75
All	72	70

Both agree in the direction of regression on household size but the slope of the regression in the earlier study is considerably greater than in 1971. To some extent this may be misleading in that the non-response data for the earlier study depends on information obtained by an interviewer from non-cooperating cases and, as pointed out in the first Handbook, this 'will sometimes be incomplete and will therefore appear in the table as of a smaller size than it really is. The effect of this will be to decrease response rates in the smaller households and increase them in the larger'[9]. Since the data for 1971 was obtained independently of the FES, the 1971 study does not suffer from this bias.

It seems likely, therefore, that the difference in the regression of response rate on size of household as between the two studies is spurious. It has arisen from the difficulty in collecting complete data even about household size from households that do not cooperate fully.

References
1. Kemsley, WFF. *Family Expenditure Survey Handbook*. HMSO, London 1967. Table 7.1, p28.
2. *Ibid*. Table 7.2, p28.
3. Kemsley, WFF. Family Expenditure Survey: a study of differential response based on a comparison of the 1971 sample with the Census. *Statistical News 31*, HMSO, November 1975. Table 1, pp31.3—31.21.
4. Kemsley, WFF. *Family Expenditure Survey Handbook, Op cit*. Table 7.3, p29.
5. Kemsley, WFF. Family Expenditure Survey: a study of differential response. *Op cit*. Table 2, p31.17
6. Kemsley, WFF. *Family Expenditure Survey Handbook. Op cit*. Table 7.4, p30.
   Ibid. Tables 15.2.1 and 15.2.2, pp89—90.
8. Harris, RP. Differential response in the Family Expenditure Survey: the effect on estimates of the redistribution of income. *Statistical News 39*. HMSO. November 1977. pp 39.7 — 39.11.
9. Kemsley, WFF. *Family Expenditure Survey Handbook. Op cit*. p90.

11 Some design aspects

11.1 Continuous nature of the FES

The question might be raised as to why the FES is conducted on a continuous basis rather than as a series of ad hoc surveys as and when data are required. There are two main reasons; first, the constantly changing nature of the data and second, the collection processes. Under the economic conditions prevailing for many years it is impossible to find a sub-period sufficiently stable to be representative of a longer period. Measurement of long-term changes might be met by periodic surveys, however, there will still be short-term fluctuations in food, clothing and holiday expenditures. The only reasonable alternative to a continuous operation is a survey conducted several times a year at regular intervals, say, two or three weeks at a time, at three-monthly intervals. The argument in favour of continuous working is strengthened by considerations arising out of the fieldwork. As pointed out in Section 6.6, the FES requires staff, particularly interviewers, who need special training and experience in order to handle each case successfully and accurately. Continuous working enables expertise to be built up gradually, and this experience would be lost if the survey were carried out on an ad hoc basis, or at infrequent intervals. This argument also applies to the supervisory staff in the Field Branch, and to some extent to those concerned with the subsequent work on the completed budgets, including the managerial staff. Finally, of course, there is the point that the FES is used for a wide variety of government requirements and it is particularly valuable as a time series.

11.2 Limitation to domestic households

One of the basic limitations of the FES sample for certain purposes is that it excludes residents of hotels, hostels, hospitals and other institutions. A survey to obtain data from establishments thus excluded would involve multi-stage sampling using institutions as one of the stages, and even then the survey could be expected to provide only personal expenditure. Such a survey would give rise to problems in the selection of institutions if due regard is to be had to size and type of institution, and in some cases to problems in gaining access to the individual resident. Even when these difficulties could be surmounted, the resulting data would exclude substantial parts of consumers' expenditure, namely housing, fuel and light and catering.

An alternative approach might be to sample the population as individuals using the Electoral Register as the sampling frame. This would take in some residents in many institutions, but not all, since it would exclude temporary residents. The main objection to such a survey is that it would make it more difficult to collect data on

expenditures such as food covering households as a whole. Nor is there any simple means of allocating the appropriate proportion of such expenditures to the selected individuals. On the whole it is more convenient, and probably safer to confine the survey to domestic households. Even so, there will be problems over certain fringe cases such as those occupying separate accommodation but being provided with meals by a different establishment.

11.3 Electoral Register as a sampling frame

The Electoral Register is used as a sampling frame in preference to any other list of addresses. There are various reasons for this; a single copy of the register for England, Wales and Scotland is available within OPCS; secondly, these registers enable an intermediate stage of sampling, namely wards, to be employed; and thirdly, they contain the names of most adults resident at a listed address. Against these advantages must be set certain drawbacks; the registers are up-dated only once a year, and then they are not available for sampling purposes until they are four or five months out of date. Also, they do not contain all those entitled to vote, but only those who have actually registered. It also does not include aliens resident in Great Britain who are not entitled to vote. Furthermore, the registers provide a list of individual electors but do not give actual households, although sampling problems arising from this defect have largely been resolved by the adoption of the sampling procedure described in Section 4.9. The effect of other shortcomings is probably not as serious as might be thought, particularly, as the lists are used as a sampling frame of addresses and not of individuals. Provided at least one person at the address has registered at the most recent qualifying date, that address will be within the coverage of the sample.

Exclusions will consist of addresses at which no-one registered at the latest registration, together with addresses of new buildings occupied for the first time since the register was compiled. However, with the reduction of the age of majority to 18, very few households will consist entirely of persons ineligible for the Register.

At the time of writing, the only alternative worth considering is the use of local authority rating lists. (For the future, the post-code address file may be considered). Their main advantage over the Electoral Register is that new property usually appears on a rating list with little delay, and furthermore, the lists provide complete coverage for an area. The main disadvantage of rating lists as a sampling frame is that they cover the whole of a local authority area without any convenient sub-divisions. The lists therefore do not enable households to be clustered into intermediate sampling units, a most important requirement in the FES where re-visiting households during the 14-day recording period makes it imperative to confine an interviewer's work into a small and compact area. Furthermore, individual names are not available; at the best, only the surname of a rate payer is given on the list. One minor advantage possessed by rating lists over electoral registers is that housing estates are usually separated from other property. To be of value, however, stratification of individual households would require prior knowledge of household income and composition. The small additional stratification that might be introduced through the rating lists therefore would not be justified for the FES. Failing this, the present rudimentary stratification at the primary stage is probably all that is worthwhile.

11.4 Sample size

In a survey as complex as the FES it will probably always be possible to produce arguments for a sample larger than the one actually available. Since the doubling of the sample in 1967 the sample has usually produced between 6,800 and 7,200 cooperating households a year except in the year of a General Election. This is adequate for some of the purposes served by the FES; that is for estimating weights for the RPI and providing quarterly patterns of expenditure. However, in some detailed breakdowns the number of relevant households may be so small as to lead to suggestions for a further increase in sample size. Even with annual samples of 7,000 or so, the number with expenditure in a narrow field, for example a specific consumer durable, may be so small as to cast doubts on the statistical reliability of the results. Similar difficulties will arise over the estimation of expenditure patterns for households of a particular composition in a narrow income range; in particular, it is not entirely adequate for exercises into the redistribution of income. The temptation then is to say that the sample size should be increased, but to be of value the increase would need to be considerable, probably by a factor of several times. Any expansion, even a small one, can only be achieved by increasing the number of interviewers working on the survey at one time, and at the same time adopting a sample design to accommodate the increased number.

Expansion of the field force is not to be undertaken lightly. The doubling of the sample size in 1967 was followed by a slight fall in response rate (Section 10.2); a trend which was only partially reversed after several years. To achieve the enlarged sample in 1967, a considerable effort was necessary in recruiting and training extra interviewers and in expanding supervisory staff. In practice, the number of budgets available for any analysis is the resultant of three factors; the size of an interviewer's work load, the number of PSUs in use at any one time and the period over which it is reasonable to accummulate the data. With a continuous survey the period can be made as long or as short as one wishes. The major objection to increasing the time period indefinitely is that this will include in a single aggregate cases where prices differ substantially through the changing value of

money. Providing there are no objections to making corrections for changes in price levels, there is no barrier to securing large samples simply by accummulating data for several years. The other two factors, an interviewer's work load and the number of PSUs in use at any one time, are not so easily adjusted.

11.5 The interviewer's work load

This is a critical factor in any decision about sample size and the number of PSUs in the sample design. In each week the present design requires an interviewer to contact 4 new addresses, interview and persuade the households to cooperate.

Up to 1967 the interviewers' work load was based on six new households each week. The reduction from six to four was made partly to ensure that the interviewer had adequate time to make all the necessary recalls, and partly to enable the number of PSUs in the sample design to be increased. Re-visiting each cooperating household is essential in order to give maximum support to people, most of whom will have had no previous experience in keeping records of spending. It does imply, however, that the area covered by a quota has to be compact otherwise some interviewers might not be able to complete their whole programme of work, particularly in the third and fourth weeks of a quota.

11.6 Number of primary sampling units in the sample design

The fact that one interviewer can cover only a limited area rules out any possibility of using a single-stage design. On the other hand, a multi-stage design makes it more difficult to produce representative samples for subdivisions of the country. A further disadvantage of a multi-stage design is that any gain in efficiency from stratification tends to be offset by the clustering effect of the compact areas covered by each interviewer's quota; although judging from the design factors (Section 4.11) this is of no great importance in the FES. For fixed field resources the representativeness of the sample design can be improved by maximising the number of PSUs and making an interviewer's quota as small as is reasonably possible.

It was pressure to improve regional representativeness that led to the increase in sample size in 1967, and the reduction of each interviewer's quota to 16; before that each quota was 36 or 42 spread over 6 or 7 weeks. A quota size as small as 16 is only practicable provided the area is compact, that fieldwork is completed in a short time, and that there is a reasonable prospect that the same area or an adjacent one is used again after a short interval. A calendar month was taken as a minimum placing period. A period of this length was chosen partly for operational convenience and partly to give sufficient time for an interviewer to deal with a whole quota of 16. Even so, the placing period has sometimes to be extended beyond the end of a calendar month if there has been difficulty in contacting at an address due to be visited for the first time in the last week of a month. In any case, fieldwork must continue for a further 14 days after the last set of diaries has been placed. This means that fieldwork invariably overlaps work in other areas nearing completion from the previous month. An interviewer working in one area in one month cannot therefore be working the next month on another quota unless the latter is an adjacent area or within reasonable travelling distance.

Furthermore, the number of PSUs must be well within the capacity of the SSD Field organization. The sample must not be set so large that there is a risk that the selected PSUs cannot all be worked in the month to which they are allocated. With many ad hoc surveys the data are such that short falls of this nature can be overcome by extending the period of fieldwork so that a quota not covered in the main fieldwork period can be dealt with later by an interviewer who has already completed an allotted quota. This is not practicable in the FES where it is essential to spread the fieldwork evenly over each placing period.

The next consideration in deciding the number of PSUs in the sample design is the minimum time period over which representative data are required. Something longer than a month is desirable in order to obtain as many PSUs as possible in the design. On the other hand, something shorter than a year is needed when changes in expenditure are likely to occur within a period of 12 months. The compromise adopted in the FES is to base the design on calendar quarters. The number of PSUs chosen when the sample was re-designed for 1967 was fixed at 168 in order to satisfy the following requirements. It had to be:

(a) divisible by 3 to allow for each quarterly selection of PSUs to be split into three separate months;
(b) divisible by 4 to permit of quarterly rotation;
(c) divisible by a further 2 so that each monthly rotational stratum could, if required for experimental purposes, be divided into two parallel samples;

This implied that the number of PSUs in use in any one quarter had to be a multiple of 24. Since each quota consisted of 16 the choice of sample size was finally determined by taking that multiple of 384 which gave a quarterly sample nearest to the required 2,500. The nearest such number is 2,688 (obtained by taking a multiple of 7 times 384), thus leading to 168 PSUs.

11.7 Data for regions and sub-regions

Annual income and expenditure data are published in each FES annual report for some standard regions as defined for statistical purposes; for certain regions, two years are combined. The question is sometimes raised as to whether data can be provided for any sub-regions. The answer really turns on the sample design and is equivalent to asking for what sub-regional area representative data can be obtained having regard to the randomisation process, subject of course to adequate sample size. Randomisation occurs at three stages. First, in the selection of PSUs from a cell formed by a group of local authorities within a region. Second, in the selection of a ward from each chosen PSU; and third in the selection of households from a chosen ward. Theoretically then the

smallest 'area' for which representative data can be obtained is each cell defined by the first two stratification factors in Section 4.2. Reference to that section and Table 4.2.1 will show that there are 44 such cells. Table 4.2.2. indicates that there are a number of cases where the cell contains several PSUs, particularly those based on Metropolitan Districts. Remembering that over 12 months each PSU will have a set quota of 64 addresses, or with an average response rate of 70% will produce about 45 cooperating households, any cell with 9 or more PSUs should provide a sample of about 400 households in the course of 12 months. This would seem an adequate sample for many purposes.

At the other extreme are the cells containing only one or two PSUs. Samples based on such cells, even for 12 months, will be completely inadequate for two reasons. First, one or two local authority areas taken by themselves cannot be regarded as representative of the whole area covered by a cell. Theoretically, the difficulty might be overcome in the FES by increasing the total number of PSUs in the sample design, but for a fixed sample this will entail a substantial reduction of an interviewer's quota, that is below 4 addresses a week, something which would be uneconomic and almost certainly would have other consequences as regards organisation and training of field staff. The second objection is that with only one or two PSUs, the sample size even for twelve months would be less than 100 and totally inadequate.

Precisely where the line is drawn as to how many PSUs constitute a reliable sample is a matter of opinion. One solution is to use samples covering two or more years. This will both increase sample numbers and improve representativeness since the longer the period the more local authorities there will be in the sample due to the operation of the rotating design. What is not possible, however, is to secure an adequate sample of any one specified local authority; at the most, any one area only appears four times before a fresh selection is made under the rotating system from the areas in any particular stratification cell.

11.8 Time periods associated with a budget

Since a major part of expenditure and income relates to a relatively short period of time, either following or preceding the interview, it is possible to regard the data provided by a budget as giving a spot estimate of current expenditure and income. The FES can then be looked upon as a continuous succession of up-to-date snap shots of expenditure and income patterns. This is a useful concept, particularly in a period of rapid change so that data for a long period, say one year, can be obtained by taking all the budgets sampled in that year.

Alternatively, the transactions obtained in the course of a year's work on the FES can be regarded as a sample of all possible transactions and selected, not directly by choosing individual transactions at random, but by taking clusters arising from a series of households. This concept is only slightly distorted by collecting data on some topics by means of interview questions. In general, this technique is restricted to topics which involve payments made at regular intervals; the resulting data are then reduced to a weekly equivalent and merged into the expenditure and income patterns as though they had actually occurred during the budget period. During a time of rising prices this has the disadvantage that there will be a slight understatement of the current rate of expenditure in certain sectors.

With income the corresponding distortion from the current situation is confined to the self-employed and to income from investments, where the relevant interview questions cover twelve months retrospectively. This technique is also applied to the earnings of employees and to pensioners, but little distortion, if any, can arise since most payments are weekly or monthly.

While this is a convenient concept for many purposes when looking at the FES as a whole, the subject deserves further consideration for two reasons. First, both income and expenditure are flow variables and cannot be defined fully without making some statement as to the period of time to which they relate. Second, because the budget must relate to a period of time there is always the chance that the composition of a household will change during the interval, and this is a matter which is dealt with in the next section.

A more basic issue is the reference period of an individual budget. The FES is designed to produce an even flow of data indefinitely, and with as little trouble as possible to cooperating households. This has led to the adoption of a mixed technique based partly on interviews and partly on diaries, so that the household information comes from a complex of moving time periods generated by sets of households as they enter the FES week by week. The resulting hybrid arrangement means that information for any one household does not relate to a single time period.

This is not a serious drawback if the main interest lies in information about mean expenditure and mean income of groups of households. Since there is an even flow, the data for each expenditure or income sector will produce a valid estimate of these means. The only minor disadvantage is one already mentioned, namely that all interview data will be lagged behind the diary data by an amount which will vary with a particular expenditure or income sector. For example, the mean payment for electricity supplied by account meter relates to a time preceding any mean data derived from diaries by approximately seven and a half weeks. Where a whole year's sample is aggregated to produce the means this does not seem to be a particularly serious matter, but it may be more important if quarterly data are under examination. The foregoing is on the assumption that different sets of data are obtained from the same households. However, the question of lag might sometimes be avoided by making time periods more comparable by basing the interview data on a later set of budgets than those used for diary data. Exact comparability of time periods is impossible unless the interview data relate to retrospective periods of two weeks, and in general this is not the case.

For many purposes served by the FES lack of a standard reference period does not matter. On the other hand, it may be important where attention is focussed on single budgets, as will be the case with frequency distributions of amounts, and the shape of this distribution will depend, to some extent, on the length of the reference period. The situation becomes even more complicated when different sectors are added together to form data covering a broader sector. A further example where the hybrid nature of the data gives rise to problems is in the relationship between income and expenditure. The lack of any standard period implies that it is not reasonable to compare the two variables for separate households.

11.9 Length of diary records

There is no simple answer as to what constitutes the optimum length of an individual diary record, and practice varies widely between countries. For example, the French and Italian budget surveys in 1979 had 11 day record-keeping periods. At the other extreme, the Belgian budget survey asks informants to balance outgoings against incomings over an entire year[1]. Some of the Eastern European budget surveys ask people to keep records for more than a year. Throughout its history, the FES has used a 14 day diary. What can be suggested is that a compromise is necessary between the ideal length of time, which could be a year or longer (from the statistical standpoint) and practical considerations such as response obtained and quality of data.

A long period, has the great merit that it provides a better estimate of individual 'normal' spending patterns than does a diary lasting only a few days or weeks. The longer period will also provide more mentions of infrequent items and thus facilitate more detailed analysis. But the argument in favour of a longer period has force only if there is a need to consider each individual or household separately.

There are so many practical objections to a long recording period that there seems little point in regarding it as the ultimate ideal. Even in theory this seems an unnecessary refinement. If the spending pattern recorded for the chosen period is regarded as a multi-variate vector, this will approximate to the variate representing some postulated normal spending behaviour. The deviation of the observed vector from the normal vector can be regarded as dependent on individual characteristics but with a random element, the relative variance of which is likely to be reduced as the recording period is increased. From this point of view the length of the recording period is unimportant provided there is no great interest in individual records per se, and also that the sample is sufficiently large to permit of reasonably accurate mean estimates of the spending patterns.

There are several practical considerations favouring a short period. First, there is the probable effect of a long period on the response rate. While there is no evidence that substantial variations in response appear between recording periods of different lengths if they are all less than a few weeks, such indications as there are suggest that extending the records beyond a month will meet with diminishing enthusiasm by both informants and field staff[2].

Second, problems will arise if changes in household composition occur during the period a household is under survey, and the risk of this happening is naturally greater the longer the period. Some changes, for instance the coming and going of visitors, are unlikely to affect adversely cooperation or the analysis of the data; others, such as the death or removal of a member to hospital or the inclusion of a new household member, may lead at the least to problems in analysis and at the worst to the loss of the household from the survey.

Third, while the volume of data is proportional to the length of individual diaries, the intrinsic value of the information is not. Infrequent items will be better reported the longer the recording period, but other categories may recur more or less identically week after week, as with some food purchases, or may conform to a fairly regular pattern. Increasing the period, therefore, does not improve the reliability of the data evenly over the whole expenditure field.

Fourth, the cost of obtaining the data tends to increase with the length of the recording period. The gain in reliability is thus limited to certain sectors, and may be achieved only at the expense of a dis-proportionate amount of resources. The cost itself is made up of several components; a substantial part is incurred in making the initial contacts and preliminary interviews. But to this must be added the cost of further calls on a household during and at the end of the record-keeping period. The need to maintain contact by a series of intermediate calls if reasonable and accurate cooperation is to be secured, means that the cost will increase as the recording period is extended. Furthermore, the manual work on the budgets in coding and preparing the diary data for the computer will increase nearly in proportion to the recording period. In the early experiments an exercise was carried out comparing cost and quantity of information[3]. The results suggested that a short period of two or three weeks made the most efficient use of resources. It is true that this result rests on certain simplifying assumptions and that the basic data are now rather old. Nevertheless, the results support the view that a short recording period has certain financial advantages.

Fifth, a short period has great operational advantages because its flexibility enables a more efficient sample design to be employed. The present survey design, using 14-day diaries and allowing a minimum of two weeks for contact, requires a field period of six or seven weeks in each area. If, instead of 14 days, each diary were to last 28 days and interviewers were to have the same time for contact as now, fieldwork would continue for 8 or 9 weeks in each area. The result inevitably would be that for a fixed field force, fewer areas could be worked at one and the same time, and there would be fewer PSUs in the basic time period over which representativeness was achieved, thus resulting in poorer regional representation.

On the other hand, there are objections to very short periods. There is evidence from earlier studies[3,4,5] that where a diary covers two or more weeks there are small differences in the level of expenditure between weeks, thus suggesting that it is unwise to rely on a single week as the records could be biased temporarily by the mere novelty of keeping a record. In fact, there is evidence of a 'first three days' effect where expenditure on the first three days of record-keeping is higher than during the remainder of the week. Furthermore, the notion of participating in a nationwide sample of 14 day units may be difficult for most informants to grasp. Consequently, informants may make purchases within the period that they would have normally delayed in order to satisfy themselves that their own household's expenditure is 'typical', despite interviewer assurances that they are taking part in a nationwide sample over time.

Records shorter than 7 days have the serious drawback that they are difficult to organize so as to produce an even flow of data over the entire time period. This is principally because it is unrealistic to consider interviewing on every one of the seven days of the week as a regular and routine operation.

As a matter of fact the Social Survey has carried out budget surveys incorporating at different times 7, 21 and 28 days before adopting 14 days for the FES as a compromise solution to the problem.

11.10 Balance between interview and diary data
One means of overcoming the problems posed by extending diary records is to collect certain information retrospectively. This way infrequently purchased items are better represented; in the case of commitments that require regular but infrequent payments, a substantial proportion of short-period diaries will be without any of the relevant entries. Examples are payments of gas, electricity and telephone accounts which are usually due quarterly. Only 2 out of 13 such households are likely to have recorded the relevant payment in a 14-day diary. A large sample, spread continuously over a long period covering one or more complete quarter should still produce a valid estimate of mean expenditure. The drawback is that the occurrence of a large proportion of households with nil expenditure implies that these means will have relatively large variances. The solution adopted in the FES is to obtain data on certain infrequent expenditures at the preliminary interview, and to discard from the diaries any entries relating to such sectors. It can be argued following the model adopted in the third paragraph of the previous section that this substitution will improve the estimate of mean expenditure. The drawback is that the resulting hybrid data are not referable to any definite time period; however, this seems a fairly unimportant criticism.

Information from the preliminary interview is used extensively in the FES instead of material from the diaries, but mostly in those fields where there is a commitment to make regular payments at regular intervals. They cover payments in respect of goods and services such as housing costs covering rent, rates, insurance, consumption of gas and electricity through credit meters, use of a telephone in the accommodation occupied by the household; various licences including vehicle licences and insurance, payments by means of standing orders to banks, travel by means of season tickets and the acquisition of goods on hire purchase and other credit arrangements. Also on the household interview schedule are questions where the payments include some investment or savings component; in particular, mortgages and life assurance. In all the examples quoted the transactions occur at fairly regular intervals, thus keeping to a minimum reliance on memory. An interview technique seldom used in the FES is one where informants are expected to recall all transactions which have taken place in a period retrospective to the interview. The main exceptions are outright purchases of motor vehicles and payments to educational establishments. Here, the burden on memory is small although the memory period covers 12 months. In addition to the use of the interview technique to collect expenditure data in the restricted fields described above, it is also employed to obtain data over the whole income field. Here, the justification is that most income receipts occur with some regularity.

One means of trying to overcome memory bias is to ask informants to refer to any records or bills they may have kept. It is customary procedure for FES interviewers to ask informants to search for records either at the interview or during the 14 day period. (There are 'records consulted' boxes on the two schedules and periodically counts are made to make some assessment of reliability of answers. This is covered more fully in Chapter 14.)

11.11 Separate schedules for each household member

While there may be households where all the required data can be obtained from one person, it is always advisable to take each member individually so that information is obtained at first hand. This does not imply, of course, that each person should be dealt with separately and independently. Experience with the FES shows that in most households all members can be interviewed together; the important thing is to encourage each person to give his own account himself and not to allow the information to reach the diaries or the interviewer secondhand. To do so involves a risk of misunderstanding, of bias and of omissions. Material from some very early experiments showed that at that time a housewife was, on average, responsible for little more than half of total expenditure, although the exact proportion may have changed with the growth of teenage spending[6,7]. On the income side, reference to recent FES reports shows that between 10 and 15 per cent of household income is received by members other than the head of the household or his wife. There is therefore ample justification for the decision taken before the FES started and adhered to ever since, that each household member should be dealt with individually. The only exceptions are children below 16 years of age whose pocket money is included in their parents' diaries. Parents are supposed to note to whom gifts and presents have been made, eg pocket money to son. However, there are no details of how pocket money

has been spent. Furthermore where a child under 16 has any income from a spare-time job or from some other source, information is obtained about this at the end of the interview on income with the child's parent or guardian, together with an opinion as to whether the child disposes of this money himself or hands it to a parent. Thus, both household expenditure and income include an allowance for amounts attributable to children under 16. The loss of detail cannot be very serious. In the case of 16-year-olds barely one part in 200 of household expenditure is derived from diaries of 16-year-olds, the youngest age for which detailed information is available. However, it is true that the FES is thought to understate expenditure on sweets, chocolate and ice cream because of children's expenditure on these items.

Following this general principle, separate diaries are provided for each household member aged 16 or over in order to encourage each person to give his or her own account of spending. Besides reducing the risk that small items are forgotten, separate diaries also enable one member to avoid disclosure of spending habits to another, a matter of some importance possibly where teenage children are concerned, and sometimes as between husband and wife. With interviews it has been found that there is generally no need for completely separate documents. However, in order to avoid the risk of collecting data secondhand, the interviewer is reminded by instructions printed on the household schedule to take a particular question individually wherever the topic warrants it. Examples are questions dealing with hire purchase and other credit transactions. With income, interviewers have always taken each household member individually. Up to 1970 there were separate income schedules, but following some research carried out in 1967 (reported in Section 17.5) it was decided to use a schedule containing two columns to cover the data from two household members. This was found to be a more convenient arrangement both at the Field and Coding stages. The 1967 research confirmed that in the great majority of cases most members were willing to be interviewed together.

11.12 Data for sub-household units

The FES is planned as a household survey. Data for subdivisions, whether of individuals or of the main family unit forming part of a complex household structure will, generally speaking, be incomplete. This is true both of expenditure and of income. The main restriction arises from the fact that no information is obtained on intra-household transfers, except for money given to children under 16. This would require different methodology (see Section 17.6). It follows that it is not possible to build up a complete account of spending, nor of the income of any one individual forming part of a larger household. To take one example, the housewife who receives an allowance from the head of the household; this is not normally recorded since the information is unnecessary for compiling data on household expenditure and income. A similar situation arises with a boarder or with other adolescents or adults in the household. Furthermore, there is no need to seek out cases where one household members buys some item on behalf of another member. A second qualification arises from household expenditure which applies to the household unit as a whole, and which without some basis for allocation must be attributed to the head of the household or housewife. This applies to housing costs, fuel, heat and lighting. Similar problems arise with food expenditure, with telephone accounts, although here it is possible theoretically to allocate consumption on an individual basis, but only at the expense of considerable effort. Third, although the preliminary interviews cover each spender individually, the information thus collected when transferred to the computer tape is on a household basis and cannot therefore be retrieved on an individual basis. A consequence of the various limitations is that information on expenditure available for individuals is limited to items appearing in the diaries, excluding housing and related costs associated with the household accommodation, payments for hire purchase, telephone accounts and the purchase of motor vehicles. Information about income received by individuals is more comprehensive, excluding only transfers from one household member to another in the same household.

References

1. Eurostat. *Methodology of surveys on family budgets.* 1980.
2. Kemsley, WFF. Designing a budget survey. *Applied Statistics* Vol VIII No.2. 1959 p117.
3. Kemsley, WFF and Nicholson, JL. Some experiments in methods of conducting Family Expenditure Surveys. *Journal of the Royal Statistical Society, Series A (General)*, Vol 123 Part 3. 1960 p324—6.
4. Kemsley, WFF. The Household Expenditure Enquiry of the Ministry of Labour; variability in the 1953—54 Enquiry. *Applied Statistics* Vol X No.3. 1961 pp117—135.
5. Turner, R. Inter-week variations in expenditure recorded during a two-week survey of family expenditure. *Applied Statistics* Vol IV No.3. 1961 pp130—146.
6. Kemsley, WFF. Designing a budget survey. *Op cit.* p115.
7. Kemsley, WFF and Nicholson, JL. *Op cit.* p311.

12 Conceptual problems of definition

12.1 Household definition and absences

Definitions of head of household, housewife, income unit and employment are included in Appendices A2-A5. These and the household definition do not differ in concept from the definitions set out in Chapter 13 of the first handbook, as it is important to maintain continuity in fundamental classificatory attributes. The household is the basic unit both for samples and for almost all analyses of FES data. The concept is reasonably straightforward — a household comprises a person living alone or a group of people (not necessarily related) living at the same address, having meals prepared together, which implies common housekeeping. This is a standard OPCS definition; however, the FES definition adds the condition that a household must have exclusive use of at least one room. The full definition is given in Appendix A1. Problems can arise in two ways; first, in the distinction between a domestic household and an institution, and second through absences of individual members.

For reasons explained (Section 11.2), institutions are excluded from the FES. Even so, certain fringe cases are still encountered. If on checking at an address the interviewer discovers that in addition to the main institution there is also at the same address some completely separate accommodation where a household is responsible for all its own domestic expenses, the latter household is included in the survey. Boarding houses and households who sometimes take in a few boarders constitute a difficult problem. Commercial boarding houses would normally always be excluded, but the decision with private households depends on the number of resident boarders at the first call the interviewer makes; if there are four or more the household is excluded; so whether a particular household is included or not may depend on the season of the year. Another case which sometimes has to be excluded is a household living near or over a catering establishment where all or most of the household's meals are provided, so it is not possible to separate out the cost of food for the household from the main business of the establishment.

Since household expenditure and income are made up of the transactions of all household members, it is essential to have an unambiguous definition of what constitutes a household. Anyone who usually has at least one meal a day with that household is regarded as part of it. Persons who spend only part of their time in the household are members provided they usually spend four nights a week in the household. However, when a married person is a member the husband (or wife) is also counted as a member provided he usually goes home at least one night a week, or will be staying with the household for all, or most of the fourteen-day record keeping period.

Someone staying temporarily, or who has been living with the household for only a short time, is treated as a member provided he will be staying with the household for at least a month from the start of the records. Persons present at the initial interview but away for part of the seven days are usually asked to keep their diaries while away. However, there is a more fundamental question as to whether someone absent for all or some of the fourteen days should be regarded as a member at all. In the FES there are a number of rules which deal with this problem; they are set out in paragraphs (a) — (d) of Appendix A1.

a) *Persons absent at preliminary interview* — Some adjustment is necessary where someone, who would ordinarily be treated as a member if the interviewer had contacted the household on a different occasion, happened to be absent when the interviewer actually made contact with the rest of the household. If someone is temporarily absent the start of the diaries of all household members is usually delayed until his or her return provided the delay is less than seven days. If the delay is expected to be longer, the rest of the household is asked to start record-keeping without him. If he returns before the fourteen day period has ended the interviewer tries to interview him and, in particular, complete the income schedule. If he is absent for the whole of the fourteen days such details of income are recorded as the interviewer can ascertain, and subsequently a decision is made in the office as to whether he should be included in the household or not.

b) *Changes in household composition* — These involve cases where, although someone is definitely a member of a selected household at the preliminary contact, he will not be a member 14 days later, but instead will be living in another household or in an institution; and of course there are cases where the reverse situation applies. As far as possible, the rules adopted attempt to match income and expenditure with household composition. Anyone leaving a household for good before the fourteen days is completed is excluded from the household even if present at the initial interview. Other household members are asked to begin record keeping immediately or as soon as possible after the person in question has left. If someone is known to be joining the household within seven days of the interviewer's call, the start of the diaries is usually delayed until his arrival. If he is not expected until after seven days, he is ignored, and record keeping usually begins immediately.

Unexpected additions or departures from a household after the beginning of record-keeping are normally ignored, and the individuals excluded. However, anyone who suddenly becomes a hospital patient, or who dies within the fourteen days recording period, continues to be treated as a member. Whether the household is included in the final sample will depend on whether the remaining members have completed their records, and whether the individual in question has kept his own records until the time of going into hospital or death.

These rules apply to changes in household composition occurring within fourteen days of initial contact. There may have been changes prior to interview, of course, which although having no direct effect on diary expenditure, nevertheless, may have some bearing on expenditure reported in the interview. An example is where household size has changed a few weeks before interview so that the last gas, electricity or telephone account as reported on the A schedule relates to a household of a size and composition different from that at the time of interview. No information is obtained about such a situation, nor allowance made.

12.2 Accommodation and sharing

As used in the FES, the term 'accommodation' means the living area occupied by the selected household. Problems can occur in two ways; first where a dwelling is shared by two or more households, and secondly where a household has a second home.

By definition, each household must have exclusive use of at least one room, so that two or three friends living together but catering independently will not constitute separate households unless one, at least, has exclusive use of a room. The simplest case of sharing is where two or more households live in the same dwelling and where this constitutes a single rateable unit. In such a case part of the rateable value is allocated to each on the basis of the number of rooms occupied by each houshold, with an allowance for shared rooms. For this reason, if for no other, the household interview schedule contains a detailed question on the rooms occupied by each household at the selected address. The question distinguishes living rooms, bedrooms, kitchen, scullery, bathroom, garage and rooms used for business. Sometimes there is doubt as to what consitutes a room, but to standardize the definition as far as possible, all informants are asked to specify separately any other rooms. In making the calculations, spaces described by informants as cellars, utility rooms, rooms less than 6 feet square, and rooms and attics without windows, skylights or floorboards are disregarded. It will be seen that for purposes of calculation a garage is treated as a room unless it is rated separately and therefore comes within the scope of a separate set of questions (see Q.15 B Appendix C2).

It is convenient at this point to refer to another situation where rateable value is adjusted. This is where part of the rateable unit is used for business purposes. In the case of a self-employed person the proportion of rates allowed as a business expense is deducted from the rateable value. With an employee, a refund from the employer expressed as a proportion of rates is regarded as the proportion to be deducted. Where the remainder of a rateable unit is shared between two or more households, the business deduction is made first and the residential part then allocated between households in proportion to the number of rooms.

Besides its use in allocating rateable value between two or more households, the number of rooms is also put on to the computer tape, thus enabling users to make further adjustments. For instance, where one household at an address sub-lets to another, the gross rent received by the main household may be adjusted by a proportion of any joint expenses such as rent, rates or insurance paid by the main household. The second area where difficulty is sometimes found is in the treatment of second homes. Since a household is selected through the Electoral Register, it usually happens that the accommodation at a selected address is the one required. Any expenses on a second home are then classified separately according to the Item Code List (Appendix B8) if they happen to appear in a 14-day diary. In the unlikely event that a pre-selected address turns out to be that of a second home it is discarded as ineligible, even if at the time of an interviewer's call a family is staying there; to do otherwise would give residents at second homes a double chance of inclusion in the sample.

An oddity which occasionally occurs concerns someone, usually living on his own, who sleeps at a selected address but has no meals there. This falls outside the household definition; whether the case is treated as a household of one or as part of a larger household resident elsewhere depends on circumstances such as whether the individual has meals in another household, and any relationship between the individual and the main household.

12.3 Expenditure

The main information on expenditure is obtained from the 14-day diaries, and the notes printed at the beginning of each booklet are relevant when considering the definition and coverage of the expenditure data. It is clear from the first three notes that each household member is expected to give as complete an account as possible of all payments made during the period of record keeping; to quote:

1   This booklet should contain a complete record of everything which you yourself pay for ......
2   Please include everything that you pay for during the seven days ......
3   Write down the actual payments you make during the seven days.

Several comments relevant to the definition can be made. First, the FES requirement that each household member cooperates goes some way in ensuring complete information, and this is reinforced by asking for a complete account from each person. The emphasis is on payments rather than on acquisitions because this is a simpler instruction. It avoids ambiguity over the date as to when a transaction should be entered in the diary by concentrating on each payment separately. Otherwise an item where the transaction proceeds in stages could well lead to difficulty, and even result in double counting; for example, a consumer durable ordered on one day, a deposit paid on that or another day, delivery on a different day, and the balance paid on yet another day. Purchases on credit, however, do present certain problems and these are discussed in the next section.

Second, the emphasis on payments helps to stress that services are included, and this reinforces the impression intended to be given by the headings of the sub-sections on each of the seven pairs of recording pages, and also by the list of items at the end of the booklet. On the other hand, it is doubtful whether the diaries can be expected to give a complete account of all outgoings, especially of transactions which are not payments for specific goods and services.

Third, the notes stress that each diary should relate only to payments by the individual record-keeper and should not duplicate entries made by anyone else. In connection with this, intra-household money transfers are ignored in editing except pocket money to children under 16. Furthermore, no attempt is made to find out whether a recorded payment is on behalf of some other household member; this is in keeping with the fact that the FES is a household inquiry and not an individual one. This has the merit of simplicity; it avoids the need to discover who is the ultimate user of any item, or is intended as a gift to someone outside the household. Conversely, gifts in kind from someone outside are ignored. Only in the case of clothing is some information obtained about the wearer, and this is only to enable garments to be classified by age and sex. Since 1978 there has been an attempt to identify expenditure made on behalf of another household. (Question 3, page 18 of Appendix F2).

Fourth, the collection of some data by interview does not affect the general principle since most interview questions refer to payments. Duplication between the two sets of documents is eliminated by discarding diary entries in the sectors covered by the interview questions.

Fifth, although most entries are on a payments basis, a few listed below are on an acquisition basis:

Outright purchases of motor vehicles (Q35 Appendix C2)

Acquisitions through a budget account, mail order etc (Q43(d) Appendix C2)

Food and other goods from a household member's own shop or firm which would otherwise be sold commercially (Note 17, page 2 of Appendix F2)

Sixth, while secondhand goods are included at the price paid, in general no adjustment is made where a new item is purchased after selling a similar item secondhand. The exceptions are motor vehicles sold separately or traded in when buying another vehicle; also other goods part-exchanged when items are acquired on HP (Q's 35 and 42, Appendix C2 and Q69 in Appendix D2).

Seventh, the information collected relates to the personal sector. Whenever any business element finds its way into the FES, usually because the expenditure is of a mixed

character, the business component is estimated and excluded at the editing stage. Altogether four types can be distinguished:

i) refunds by employers of expenses incurred by employees;

ii) expenses resulting from employment claimed by employees as tax relief;

iii) refunds of expenses by charitable organizations, social clubs and similar bodies;

iv) expenditure incurred by self-employed persons, chargeable to a business.

These adjustments are made in the light of information at Questions 19, 20, 21, 26, 28 and 63 of Appendix D2 and Question 1 on page 18 of Appendix F2. Self-employed persons pose special problems, however, and these are discussed more generally in Section 12.10.

12.4 Purchases on credit

The emphasis noted in the previous section on recording payments rather than acquisitions to some extent takes care of items acquired on credit. For example, where a deposit is paid first and the balance paid off subsequently. The main drawback is that often not all the payments relevant to one transaction appear in one set of diaries. The mean expenditure is not affected by this feature, so that the main purpose of the FES is still fulfilled. However, it was recognised from the earliest days of the FES that it is sometimes useful to have a more complete picture of the whole series of transactions even when they take place over a substantial interval. Hence, for hire purchase and credit sale agreements the interview calls for more detailed information than it is convenient to collect in the diaries (Questions 40-42 of Appendix C2); these questions cover purchase price, down payment, regular instalments and their frequency.

Occasionally difficulties occur in classifying hire purchase transactions according to the FES Item Code because two or more items have been included in one agreement, but the items relate to different codes. The down payment and instalment are then proportioned at the editing stage according to the relevant cash prices and classified accordingly.

A similar situation occurs with some entries in the diaries, ie. where food, groceries or meat are paid for by monthly accounts during the 14 days. Here, the informant is asked to enter the payment of the bill in the diary on the day it was made. (The interviewer will have discovered whether the informant is obtaining credit on monthly account when the Regular Commitments sheet is asked at the initial interview — see Appendix G3). Informants are asked to describe each item on the bill. (If this cannot be done, they are asked to note all items and prices as *acquired*.) The payment is then broken down in proportion to the amounts of the separate acquisitions and these notional payments are classified by the appropriate item codes; the original acquisition entries are deleted. Similar treatment is given to other bills paid periodically, for example the milkman and newsagent.

An analogous situation arises with credit cards. Over the last few years these have assumed an increasing importance, and in 1979 it was found necessary to supplement the diary with an extra sheet on which informants record credit card account payments (see Appendix E2). Any payment of a credit card account made during the recording period is apportioned over the value of the items shown on the credit account. (Informants are additionally asked to record any goods or services acquired by credit card during the 14 days; however, the data is only required for research purposes ie to test the feasibility of moving to an acquisition basis.) Another group providing short-term credit covers mail order clubs, clubs run by shops, budget accounts and similar schemes based on revolving credit; they form the subject of interview questions associated with the hire purchase section of the household schedule. For these categories the FES uses data on the prices of goods and services acquired during the month retrospective to the date of interview (Q43(d) — Appendix C2); payments made into the relevant club etc are ignored.

While the FES collects a great deal of information bearing on the subject of credit, it does not cover the whole field. Although it covers personal loans, it does not deal with the wider subject of overdrafts and also loans which are not given for a specific purpose.

12.5 Postal orders and money set aside

The principle followed is that disbursement does not take place until the postal order, or money set aside, is used to pay for a specific item or service. For postal orders Note 2 on page 2 of Appendix F2 makes the situation plain. Any purchase of a postal order is to be recorded as and when it takes place and a separate note made whenever the postal order is used, stating the item or service involved. Where postal orders are used during the 14 days, poundage on the order is coded as a separate expenditure item; the face value of the postal order is attributed to any items or services paid for by the postal order and coded in the usual way. Where postal orders are not used during the 14 days, the poundage is still recorded as current expenditure; however the face value is deleted by coders.

Where money is set aside to pay future bills, it is ignored at the coding stage. Usually the money is for specific purposes such as payment of rent, gas or electric bills, and these are covered by specifc questions at the preliminary interview, while any such entries in the diaries are discarded. The interviewers' instructions remind interviewers about this possibility and ask that any entries of money set aside in the diaries should be annotated by the interviewer to facilitate coding action.

In certain cases where pre-payment slot meters are in use, rebates may be given. Details about rebates are collected at the preliminary interview for gas and electricity, and for television rental (see Q's 27A(a) and 32(a)(a1)(i) of Appendix C2).

12.6 Holiday expenditure

This subject is sufficiently important to merit a section to itself, especially as the subject of holiday expenditure is raised periodically as one in which the FES is deficient. Holiday expenditure as such is not separately distinguished; instead, expenditure while away from home, for whatever reason, is classified according to the standard coding frame for expenditure items. Payments to hotels, boarding houses, holiday camps, and the commission on the purchases of travellers' cheques and of foreign currency are separately identifiable in this frame; but other items are not. Any change to this situation would require additional questions about a wide range of items, together with an extension of the item coding frame. A decision would also be necessary on whether or not to cover all absences or only holidays of some minimum length.

However, there is a fundamental issue as to whether such an exercise would be worth doing at all since the results are likely to be misleading. A household away when the interviewer first calls cannot be contacted until later, so the diaries will not contain data on previous absences. The appearances of any holiday expenditure in diaries is therefore somewhat fortuitous. It consists of payments made in advance or on accounts settled on return from holiday, or entries made by people who happen to go away after starting record keeping. What is not included is expenditure of a household while away on holiday at the time when the interviewer first attempts to make contact. The FES is therefore unavoidably biased against holiday expenditure.

This situation could only be changed by drastically modifying the survey design. One modification would be to reorganize the fieldwork programme so that calls are made on each pre-selected household well in advance of the date when the diaries for that household are supposed to start; in fact, sufficiently far in advance to ensure that contact can be made with every household, even with those away for some time. Households might then be asked to begin their diaries on some definite future date irrespective of whether they will be at home or away on that date. Such an arrangement has never been adopted because it is likely to prove more costly and to produce a poorer response than the present procedure.

An alternative possibility is to extend the preliminary interview to cover holidays and other absences from home. However, only the sample for the last three months of a calendar year is likely to produce useful data about holidays in the same calendar year. If such questions are applied to samples interviewed earlier in the year the holiday information will be incomplete unless questions are extended retrospectively to cover some absences in the previous year. Probably the only consistent approach, applicable at whatever date a household happened to appear in the sample, is to go back a full twelve months from the date of interview, thus putting a heavy burden on the memory of people who may have found already that parts of the FES interview are difficult to answer. It is for these reasons that the FES does not attempt to deal with holiday expenditure as a separate topic.

12.7 Income

Almost all information about income is obtained at the preliminary interview and recorded on the Income Schedule. (See Appendix D2). This covers income received from sources outside the household, namely earnings whether as an employee or self-employed, some fringe benefits, occupational pensions, income from investments and property, interest on loans, social security benefits, analogous payments from other sources and other regular payments. Information on educational grants and scholarships is also available from the household questionnaire.

Transfers within a household are ignored, except for childrens' pocket money. This applies to all housekeeping allowances paid to a housewife, including payments by a boarder for board and lodging. The only exceptions, now of little importance, are wages paid by a member of a household to a domestic servant or other employees living in the household. (When this arises, the wages or salary appear in both the employee's income questionnaire and also in the employer's diaries.) Most windfall gains are ignored: these include legacies, money from the sale of a house or a consumer durable (trade-in value is usually treated as a reduction in the cost of the replacement item), sales of stocks and shares, Premium bond winnings and occasional money gifts. Nevertheless, information on certain windfalls has been obtained since 1976 (see Questions 69-71 in Appendix D2). Information on gambling winnings is limited to the kinds of gambling listed on page 18 of Appendix F2.

For employees and pensioners, who together account for a large portion of the sample, the information about earnings and/or pensions is on a current rate basis. The thinking behind this is that the current rate basis provides an estimate of income as close as possible to the diary recording period without requiring further interviewing after the preliminary interview. The simplest estimate on that basis is to obtain the last amount received, with a code indicating whether this is received weekly or at some other frequency. It has long been recognised that this is not entirely satisfactory for earnings since the last pay received may be subject to temporary variations ranging from short-time working to substantial, but unusual overtime, or accumulated back pay resulting from pay rises or even to more permanent changes. Holiday pay included in the last earnings received is dealt with by adjusting the period code (Question 7 of Appendix D2) to take in the holiday period as well as that covered by the earnings while at work. Adjustments for other variations are more difficult, and in an attempt to make some allowance, each employee is asked for an estimate of his usual pay. (Question 15 of Appendix D2). The concept is subjective, although there is an instruction on the income schedule that if the informant is 'unable to give usual pay because it varies considerably give average pay received (not basic)'. Some experimental data as to how informants define their usual pay is reported in Section 17.8.

Apart from short-term fluctuations in earnings there may also be editing problems whenever there has been a recent change in an individual's situation. Such a change would have been allowed for automatically if it had been possible to adopt a technique whereby earnings data are collected for a specific retrospective time period. Indeed, this is a convenient and logical technique to use for flow data such as income. However, for the reason explained above, a current-rate concept is used instead. An example of the problem occasionally presented by the use of the current-rate concept is an employee who has recently changed his job. To ask for last pay received would result in the earnings of the previous job being given. These would clearly relate to a past situation and the earnings reported are clearly out of date and are replaced, usually at the editing stage, by an estimate of what the employee expects to receive at the next pay day. Similar situations occur when an employee retires or becomes self-employed, or vice versa. The principle adopted is to change the income data to match the current position as recorded at Qs 1-4 of the Income Schedule.

This is not the end of the matter because with the current-rate concept precautions have to be exercised at the editing stage to guard against omissions or, on the other hand, against statistical double-counting of earnings. There is a possibility of double-counting if employment details are restricted to the main employment, and any other earnings are relegated to a catch-all question covering a retrospective period of twelve months. This may happen if during the twelve months two part-time jobs are replaced by one full-time one. The FES deals with this sort of situation by asking about all jobs, regardless of hours worked, on which the individual is employed at the time of interview. The question about miscellaneous earnings (see Q64 of Appendix D2) is limited only to those where the informant has carried out some particular piece of work or given advice on a single occasion, and this in circumstances which if carried out continuously would be regarded as self employment. Careful editing is necessary and, where appropriate, details are sometimes transferred to employee or self-employed sections of the income questionnaire. The entry is discarded altogether if the job appears to be one that would have appeared in Q4 of the Income Schedule if the interview had taken place at some time within the duration of the job, especially if it has been replaced by one providing current earnings.

12.8 Social security benefits

In itself, collecting information about social security benefits does not give rise to serious problems where payments are made regularly and are a basic amount. However, the multiplicity of benefits may lead to some confusion in the minds of recipients and sometimes to incorrect classification. For benefits not paid indefinitely, and Unemployment Benefit is a case in point, the informant is asked to give the number of weeks the benefit has been received in the last 12 months, as well as the last amount and whether it is being received at present.

The most difficult is Supplementary Benefit; when taking informants through the relevant questions interviewers ask that this benefit should be separated from other benefits and recorded at Q40 (see heading to pages 11 and 12 of

Appendix D2). However, some unpublished research confirms that where it is paid in supplementation of another benefit, many people cannot distinguish the two benefits. In practice, the material has to be taken at its face value, and it seems likely that some Supplementary Benefit is incorrectly classified, with a consequent under-statement both of total benefit and of the sample numbers receiving benefit.

12.9 Savings

The FES is not designed to produce data on savings either directly or indirectly. It has already been pointed out that although the survey produces valid estimates of mean expenditure, it does not cover all outgoings; nor is the FES income definition comprehensive of all sources of financing expenditure. Direct savings information is available for only a few specific fields, and mainly only from the preliminary interview; on re-payments of mortgages (see Q23 of Appendix C2) and premiums on Life Assurance policies (see Q37). As regards the diaries, the notes at the beginning of each diary do not mention savings specifically, the emphasis being on payments for goods and services, except for a brief reference to purchases of Savings Certificates, Premium Bonds etc in the list on page 19 of the diary. If any such entries occur they are regarded as short-term savings and classified to item code 803. (See Appendix B8). What is found in this code is probably fortuitous and dependant on the inter-pretation of the notes by the informant and on his or her opinion as to what the survey is about. Such information as actually gets into the FES probably represents only part of total savings; in particular, it seems likely that data on repayment of loans, purchases of stocks and shares and investment are deficient.

An alternative approach is to compare expenditure with income and attribute the difference to savings or dis-savings, but this is also unreliable. There is, first, the arithmetical objection that a relatively small residual derived by taking the difference between two large variables, each with a random element, is subject to large errors. Second, FES income and expenditure are not col-lected over a common time period, so that the two are not strictly comparable. Much of the expenditure data relates to the fourteen days following the preliminary interview, while all the income information is retrospective to that date. This in itself may make a substantial contribution to the residual difference when income and expenditure are compared for single households. The impact of this is reduced by using samples covering a long period, say of twelve months, although even then the absence of a completely identical time period will introduce time lags into some of the components. The effect may not be negligible in comparison with the relatively small residual savings. A third reason why comparison cannot be satis-factory is that expenditure does not cover all outgoings, nor income all incomings. Fourth, even if the FES were to produce valid data for separate households, it is doubtful whether a response rate of no more than 70% can yield reliable estimates of mean savings. The distribution of savings is highly skew and it is probable that the distribu-

tion is therefore sensitive to variations in response, although direct evidence is not available.

In summary, the definitions used for expenditure and income together with the time periods to which component items relate are such that the total expendi-ture and income available from any one budget will not balance except by chance. Moreover, any difference which is actually observed does not represent a meaning-ful estimate of household saving or dis-saving. Improve-ment is unlikely to be obtained without so elaborating and extending the survey as to change it into something rather different from the present FES and at the price of reduced cooperation from the public.

12.10 Self-employed persons

Being based on a nationally representative sample, the FES inevitably includes a proportion of households con-taining self-employed persons, and these often lead to difficulties both at the data collection and coding stages. The problem is important since somewhat over 6% of cooperating households have self-employed heads, and in addition there are almost as many other household members who are self-employed. First, the self-employed display a below-average response rate[1] although in some cases this may be caused partly by the difficulties for a self-employed person to provide the necessary informa-tion. Second, even with those who cooperate there are problems in establishing income, and sometimes in disen-tangling personal expenditure from that of the business, particularly where the accommodation is partly residen-tial and partly business. The difficulties are most acute with farmers and shop-keepers.

In theory, income should be straightforward since the relevant question asks:

'How much net profit (or loss) did you receive in the last 12 months from your business or profession? That is after deducting all expenses and wages . . . ' (Q27(a) of Appendix D2).

There are also supplementary questions where a partner-ship is involved. What is required is information that in the great majority of cases has already been calculated for taxation purposes.

In practice there are often difficulties, especially where someone leaves the financial side of the business to an accountant, including payment of income tax, so that the self-employed person can legitimately reply 'Don't know' to the questions about earnings. Slightly more helpful are those who produce business accounts, but as interviewers are not trained accountants, they may still not be able to disentangle the required information from the business accounts without assistance, especially where part of the profits have been retained in the busin-ess. This is possibly a factor leading to under-statement of self-employed income, (see section 14): a further circum-stance tending in the same direction is that a business year may end at any time in the 12 months prior to the date of interview, thus introducing a lag of twelve months.

The backward effect may be even more serious where the 'most recent twelve months for which figures are available' is an even earlier business year because of delay in making up the accounts.

In some respects the difficulties are so great that a self-employed person is quite unable to answer the direct question quoted above. The interviewer then makes use of a rough and ready alternative (Q27(b) of Appendix D2). Some light on the prevalence of these cases was thrown up by an ad hoc survey carried out in the second half of 1972 when self-employed earnings were obtained using similar questions to those in the FES. Of 243 self-employed, 68 per cent were able to answer the direct question, while of the others asked the alternative version fewer than 9 per cent were able to give all the alternative data, ie both the amount withdrawn regularly and the residual profit; another 9 per cent were able to give only turnover, while the remaining 14 per cent were unable to give even that. Little can be done about those who give no information, but for the 9 per cent giving turnover an estimate of income from profits is made from the profit margin believed to exist in that type of enterprise. Businesses making a loss, or which have not been in existence for a full year, are coded separately to enable adjustments to be made at the analysis stage. In many cases, especially among those who are not heads of households, the earnings must be small since the self-employed category includes mail order agents and baby-sitters.

The expenditure side can be almost as troublesome as earnings. Difficulties arise whenever a dwelling is used partly for business and partly for residential purposes. For this reason Q28 (Appendix D2) is inserted immediately following the main question on earnings; it asks about the proportion of accommodation and car expenses claimed as a business expense. The relevant items reported on the household schedule are then abated at the editing stage by these proportions; rateable value is reduced in the same proportion as rates. Where gas and electricity are paid by slot meter such payments in the diaries and rebates in the household schedule are also reduced. Where car expenses are involved the relevant payments, whether on the interview schedule or in the diaries, are abated. Should other expenses appear in the diaries and be claimed as chargeable to the business, abatement is made on the basis of information at Question 1 on page 18 of the diaries (Appendix F2). In a few cases a self-employed person will claim that the whole of an accommodation expense is chargeable to a business; it is then assumed that some at least of this amount should be treated as personal sector expenditure, and that, in effect, the business is providing a subsidy of unrecorded income. Various rules are applied to make a reasonable deduction for the business element. The balance of the claimed accommodation expense is treated (by the CSO) as imputed income (see codes 267 and 268 on page 21 of Appendix C2). Food items and goods which otherwise would have been sold commercially but are taken from a firm or shop owned by a household member have already been mentioned briefly in Section 12.3. They are also treated both as expenditure and income (see code 327 on page 9 of Appendix D2).

12.11 Direct personal taxation

The principle followed is that earnings and other income recorded in the income schedule should be in a form that provides gross income before tax. For income paid after deductions, that is employee earnings and occupational pensions, the PAYE deductions provide an estimate of tax (see Qs 9, 25 and 46 to 49 of Appendix D2). Payments direct to Inland Revenue and refunds of direct tax are dealt with by Qs 65 and 66; these cover tax liability arising from self-employed earnings and other income not taxed at source, and also additional tax from higher rate tax and investment surcharge. A reference to capital gains tax has been included with these questions (Q65(a3) of Appendix D2) to ensure that it is excluded when reporting tax paid direct to Inland Revenue. As regards investment income, Qs 51—57 ask for the amount of interest and dividends received net of tax; the corresponding standard rate tax is calculated at the computing stage, as also is the tax on Building Society interest at the prevailing special rate agreed between Building Societies and Inland Revenue.

This is straightforward as far as it goes. As with gross income, a sample of households should yield valid estimates of mean tax, although payments of direct tax will be lagged behind estimates derived from the questions on PAYE. Total tax will not necessarily be the correct amount corresponding to total income as estimated for the same sample of households. Furthermore, there is no guarantee that tax reported on a schedule for a single tax unit will correspond to the total income of that unit. This could only be achieved by calculating total income for the tax unit from the information reported at the interview, and then taking into account all the tax allowances to which the tax unit is entitled, a course which it has never been practicable to adopt. Sometimes the actual position is even more complex, especially where a change in situation has led to substantial editing of the income information as described in Section 12.7. In particular, if direct tax reported relates to a source no longer providing income at the time of interview, it is then deleted. This is done in order to maintain consistency although it leads inevitably to an under-statement of tax paid by the sample as a whole. Similar inconsistencies occur with data based on 'usual earnings' at Q15 since the only tax information is that relating to last pay.

Reference
[1]   Kemsley, WFF. FES: a study of differential response. *Op cit*. Appendix A5, p31.21.

13 Measures taken to ensure reliable results

13.1 General remarks

At each stage great care is taken to see that the detailed information is accurate and representative of the population in domestic households in Great Britain. The search after soundness and reliability begins with the sample design and is maintained throughout each stage of the inquiry until the documents containing the collected data are made ready for despatch to the Department of Employment for transfer on to computer tape. Many of the steps taken to achieve this have already been described in preceding chapters, and where this is so the following sections bring the main points together in a convenient summary.

One method of validation is not open, however, to the FES; for reasons explained in the preceding chapter, it is pointless to compare expenditure with income. What is needed instead is a comparison between all outgoings and all incomings. While this is not possible for the standard FES, feasibility studies have been made of this technique. A summary of the findings appears in Section 17.6. What this tends to show is that even if this technique could be applied to the FES, it is unlikely that the expenditure patterns would be altered greatly. Finally, it must be admitted that in spite of the care taken in design and execution, the results are subject to certain defects and limitations; these form the subject of Chapter 14.

13.2 Sample design

It will be clear that, apart from certain aspects mentioned in Sections 11.2 and 11.3, the sample design will produce a pre-selected sample representative of the whole population resident in domestic households . The selection at each of the three main stages plus the further stage of selecting a household at a multi-household address, is made at random with the appropriate probabilities, thus ensuring that the final pre-selected sample is representative in every sense. The design incorporates a measure of stratification the main benefit from which is to ensure regional representation and eliminate the regional component of variance from the results.

A complete sample drawn from all 168 strata into which the sampling frame is divided is secured every calendar quarter, and this is the minimum period over which the FES can claim to be representative. Since the survey is organized on a continuous basis and at an even rate, any interval containing a series of calendar quarters will also produce representative results.

13.3 Design of data-collecting documents

The procedure and documents used to collect the data from each household have been designed with the follow-ing objectives in mind; to collect complete and accurate data, with as little trouble as is reasonable to the co-operating household and with the highest possible response. From one point of view, the simplest and least expensive method of collection would be to obtain the data by interview. This might increase response, but, with a topic such as expenditure this would be an intolerable burden on memory, and this in itself would render the data suspect and unreliable. Accordingly, the FES is planned to keep demands on memory as low as possible. It does this by placing the main reliance on diaries, especially for information about those expenditure sectors which comprise numerous items. As regards the interview technique, the least satisfactory type of question is one where informants are asked to record transactions over a long period retrospective to interview. This technique is therefore employed sparingly, and only where there are likely to be few items to remember; Q 35 of Appendix C2 is an example, where informants are asked to remember outright purchases of vehicles over the past 12 months. Otherwise information collected by interview is restricted to topics where fairly regular payments are involved, and where it is possible to reduce the demand on an informant's memory as to the amount of the last payment and to the period covered by it. This 'current-rate' concept is also used extensively for income.

These main features of the design have been followed right from the start of the survey, as also has the requirement that each household member should be included individually and encouraged to take part. The necessity for this was established as long ago as 1950/51 during experimental work carried out by the Social Survey[1]. Reliance on only one or two members for information would, in many households, result in incomplete data. For this reason there are separate diary records for each person aged 16 or over, and the interview questions are arranged to ensure a separate recording of any expenditure made by individual members. Moreover, the incentive payment of £2 given to each household member for cooperation is only made providing that all co-operate.

The design of each document has been drawn up with need for accuracy and ease of entry very much in mind. In particular, the two interview questionnaires have been developed and improved as the survey has progressed. Many changes have been made to clarify definitions and to deal with the exceptional cases; one way in which they have been improved is by the addition of dependent and supplementary questions, sometimes to provide additional data in its own right, but often to make editing and coding easier and more accurate. Both schedules have the interview questions to the left, while on the right there is a columnar layout from which details for the computer are taken. For the Household Schedule this consists of two columns on the right; the first contains the amount of expenditure, or in some cases a number, and this followed in the second column by an identifying three-digit code which is usually pre-printed. Where the three-digit code is preceded by a capital A the entry on the left usually relates to an indicative code in the £ column. In all other cases the three-digit code identifies the amount in the £ column, while on the right of this code is a period code indicating the frequency of payment; this is usually inserted by the SSD Primary Analysis Branch unless pre-printed. Wherever possible, the answer is recorded by the interviewer in the £ column, thus reducing clerical work and transcription error. Where this form of direct entry is possible it is indicated by an arrow followed by a thin dotted line in the £ column. In cases where the recorded answer has to be converted to a numerical code or is subject to editing, the interviewer records the answer to the left of the columnar layout and the edited item is subsequently entered in the correct column.

The Income Schedule follows the same principle except that the columnar layout consists of two sets of colums on the right to enable data for two household members to be entered on the same form. This arrangement was introduced a few years ago partly to reduce the number of separate documents the interviewer had to handle at the preliminary interview, and partly because the entry of a household member and spouse on the same form facilitates editing of income data for a tax unit.

The layout of the diary, however, has remained virtually unchanged from the beginning of the FES, except for the expansion of the Meals Out Section. In order to encourage recording of entries as soon as possible after the actual spending and thus keep down memory errors, the main part of the diary takes the form of seven pairs of pages, one pair for each day covered by half of the fourteen-day period. Each pair of pages is identical, and is divided into sections corresponding to very broad expenditure categories. This sub-division is of some use in coding, but its main purpose is to emphasize the comprehensive nature of the FES, and to stress once more some of the points made in the notes on page 2 of the diary. As regards description of items, record keepers are left to use their own words except that the list on page 19 serves the dual purpose of a reminder that every kind of item should be entered, and also indicates the descriptive detail that is acceptable.

13.4 Fieldwork

Those selected as interviewers must have the ability, interest and personality to attract reasonable cooperation from the public. This is emphasized in training, as well as the need to understand and apply correctly field procedures and survey definitions. The field procedure is itself designed to give the best chances of cooperation. It avoids the risk of too rigid an application which would lead to a

loss in cooperation through an interviewer having insufficient time to contact every household on an address list, or persuade all members of a household to take part. The procedure described in Sections 6.1 and 6.5 is designed to be as flexible as possible consistent with good sampling practice and within constraints of the processing timetable.

The intermediate calls made after diary recording has started also have as their main purpose the accuracy of the final results. Besides encouraging households to continue once started, these calls enable interviewers to raise queries and check various aspects of the data in the light of the 'Regular Commitments' questions (Appendix G3) and the checking sheets (Appendices G4 and G5).

The Regular Commitments questions give the interviewer some warning that there may be diary entries relating to payments made by postal or money orders, by credit cards, by monthly accounts or by some other arrangement. Short-term credit arrangements such as these require the interviewer to take further action, as explained in Section 12.4.

Of the two checking sheets, the more important lists items which can be expected to re-appear once or twice in the diaries after taking into account the reported frequency. The form also contains a tabular layout to assist the interviewer to discover any discrepancies in reported earnings and deductions from earnings. The second checking sheet, used mainly by the less experienced interviewers, sets out several simple consistency checks which have to be made as a matter of course. Queries arising from these checks are taken up by interviewers at the intermediate and final calls, and notes are then made on the checking sheets for the guidance of Primary Analysis Branch.

In a few cases direct validation of the reported information is possible where the informant can produce relevant documents. This applies to employees, where 70—80 per cent are able to produce pay slips for last pay received; to gas and electricity accounts, and also to credit-card accounts. In the fourth quarter 1978 about 71 per cent of gas accounts were either seen by the interviewer or consulted specially by the informant at the time; for electrcity accounts the proportion was 74 per cent and for credit cards 68 per cent. In other cases, under half were able to produce any back-up evidence; 48 per cent for mortgage interest, 47 per cent for savings accounts interest, (Qs 51—55 combined of Appendix D2), 43 per cent for hire purchase (Q42 of Appendix C2), while only 18 per cent of households were able to produce their rates demands (Qs 18, 19 and 20 of Appendix C2).

13.5 Editing and coding

This stage of the work is described in Section 7.1, and its importance cannot be over-estimated. Accuracy is essential since, although manual transcription of data from one document to another has been eliminated wherever possible, some is inevitable; coding is also a function where great accuracy is vital, and it cannot be eliminated, at least from the diaries. However, much more than this is involved, especially in editing the collected information if the results are to be trustworthy. All consistency checks made by the interviewers are gone through again, and alterations made where necessary in the light of interviewer comments on the checking sheets. Other consistency checks are also carried out; for example between rateable value, poundage and rates paid. Besides discarding diary entries in sections covered by interview questions, adjustments are often necessary in editing to ensure that the final data conform to survey definitions; for example, where a rateable unit is occupied by several households, or is partly residential and partly business. Deductions have to be made where part of an item is chargeable to a business. The purpose of these operations is to improve the accuracy of the final results.

As mentioned in Section 7.2, sometimes editing throws up queries which can only be dealt with satisfactorily by seeking further information from the household.

Reference
[1]   Kemsley, WFF and Nicholson, JL. *Op cit.*

14 Reliability of the FES

14.1 General remarks

It will be apparent from the remarks made in the last section that a great deal of care is taken to ensure the reliability of FES results. Nevertheless, the FES data are, as with most budget surveys, subject to limitations and biases.

It is not a simple matter to assess the reliability of FES expenditure and income figures. In the United States, validation of survey answers through gaining indirect access to Social Security records insurance policies and consumer durable purchases has been attempted by Ferber and others[1]. This method is not adopted with FES informants because of the confidentiality pledge.

Follow-up surveys to the same respondents are impractical as they place an almost impossible demand on informants' memories. Nevertheless, there have been other attempts to assess reliability of FES results and this Chapter discusses the methods used and the findings. Broadly, the chapter is divided into two sections: first, an analysis of the relative reliability of FES interview questions, based on the quality of answers (an internal check on reliability); and second, an attempt to explain major discrepancies between FES grossed-up estimates of expenditure and income with the National Income and Expenditure figures (an external check on reliability).

14.2 Relative reliability of interview questions

Even though households cooperate in the FES, it is not always possible for informants to provide answers to all questions. Because of the interest in FES accuracy, an analysis was carried out on the relative reliability of interview questions. This was based on an analysis of various symbols or comments made on the interview schedules at the time of interview or during coding. The results described below are based on a special exercise carried out during the fourth quarter of 1978. For this purpose, each answer was classified into one of the following four categories:

(a) No symbol or note against an entry, indicating that the amount was given without estimation;

(b) E, indicating that the amount had been estimated by the informant;

(c) DK against an entry, indicating that the informants did not know the answer;

(d) Coding action (CA) where Coders in PAB had changed the original entry because the amount given was clearly wrong, eg a fixed fee like a TV licence was given wrongly.

The fourth category is kept to a minimum, as shown in Tables 14.2.1 and 14.2.2 and does not give the full measure of work carried out by Primary Analysis Branch, as imputation is carried out for all DK codes (Category (c)).

The proportion of entries in category (a), that is, those without a symbol, provides a crude measure of the relative reliability of different questions in the sense that a high proportion of No Symbol entries suggests, but does not guarantee, accurate data. The exercise was applied to all questions except to those with few answers. The sample in the fourth quarter 1978 consisted of 1,648 co-operating households. Altogether, they provided 64,811 entries for this exercise: 41,395 from Household schedules and 23,416 from Income schedules. The results of the count have been summarised in tables 14.2.1 and 14.2.2; however a more detailed breakdown of reliability by individual question is available on request.

Table 14.2.1 shows a distribution of 41,395 entries in the Household Schedule by the four categories. The overall reliability is 93 per cent. The problem areas, as indicated by a below-average percentage in the first column, are gas and electricity data and data from credit cards.

Table 14.2.1 Distribution of mentions by reliability code by topic area — household schedule
Percentage distribution based on 1,648 households—4th Quarter 1978

	No Symbol	Esti-mated	Did not know	Coding action	Total mentions = 100%
Housing					
i) Rent	96	2	1	*	1,098
ii) Rent free	90	3	Nil	7	29
iii) Owner-occupiers	91	4	4	1	2,589
iv) Insurance	95	4	2	*	2,130
Gas and Electricity	82	5	14	*	7,580
Other regular housing expenses	93	6	1	*	2,250
Transport	97	2	1	*	4,410
Life Insurance	96	3	1	*	3,719
Instalment credit					
i) Hire purchase	97	2	1	*	4,311
ii) Club	96	2	2	*	4,414
iii) Credit card	87	2	8	3	1,377
Rates	98	Nil	Nil	3	7,488
Total (Household schedule)	**93**	**3**	**4**	**1**	**41,395**

*Less than 0.5%

The relatively poor showing of gas and electricity is not inconsistent with the fact noted earlier (see section 13.4) that gas and electricity accounts are consulted by roughly 70 per cent of informants when replying to the questions. Three groups of questions have contributed to this: the quantity of gas or electricity consumed, (Q's 28(c2), (c,3) and (c,4) of Appendix C2) amounts paid under a Board Budgeting Scheme (Q27B(a)) and finally rebates arising from slot meter payments, (Q27A((a)(i)), items which in any case are not covered by account invoices. Even with accounts available, it is not easy to obtain this information. Although interviewers are specially briefed to read electricity and gas accounts, the presentation of accounts varies widely between boards and is exceedingly complex.

Another weak area is the credit card sheet (Appendix E2). This shows up badly because of difficulties with three detailed questions: the balance brought forward from a previous account, interest charged and the amount outstanding. Again this illustrates difficulties in reading complex accounts which vary in format and presentation.

The items just singled out all have proportions in the last three columns totalling 20% or more, although they are not shown separately in Table 14.2.1. The Household Schedule (Appendix C2) has a few other areas where the index reliability as measured by the first column is below 80 per cent namely, the frequency of receipt of lump sum rate rebates received over the last 12 months (Questions 18(b4)(ii), 19(b3)(4)(ii) and 20 (c4)(ii)); mortgage interest (Question 23(d)); central heating expenditure on oil over the past 12 months (Question 33(b)(i)) and bank charges (Question 38(b1)). The first two items may suffer from problems of memory; bank charges may be understated because of lack of knowledge.

Although at first glance, rates appear to come through the test without difficulty, they do present very special problems. The details are collected by interviewers from Local Authority offices, but, even so, the subject is sufficiently complex and liable to misunderstanding as to make it necessary to check at the coding stage all rate poundages and rateable values whenever a certain level of discrepancy is found. This explains the relatively high proportion of rates entries subject to coding action. The main difficulty lies with obtaining the various components of rates poundages (see Question 48 of Appendix C2).

Table 14.2.2 Distribution of mentions by reliability code by topic area — Income schedule
Percentage distribution based on 1,648 households — 4th Quarter 1978

	No Symbol	Esti- mated	Did not know	Coding action	Total mentions = 100%
Employee earnings	91	6	3	*	11,458
Subsidary job - employee	89	2	9	Nil	135
Self-employed	67	5	28	Nil	607
N.I. contribution	93	3	4	Nil	1,765
State & trade union benefits	92	5	2	1	3,258
Pensions and Trust	93	2	5	*	443
Investment income	80	7	13	*	4,946
Coal	100	Nil	Nil	Nil	18
Odd jobs	91	7	3	Nil	151
Income tax & N.I. paid direct	79	19	3	Nil	316
Windfalls	91	8	1	Nil	170
Children's income	83	13	4	Nil	149
Total (Income schedule)	**88**	**6**	**6**	*	**23,416**

*Less than 0.5%

The exercise was extended to all income schedules completed for the 1,648 households in the fourth quarter 1978, with the result shown in Table 14.2.2. Overall reliability for the Income Schedule (Appendix D2), as measured by the percentage in the first column is 88 per cent,

somewhat lower than for the Household Schedule. Quite clearly, the least reliable topic areas are self-employed income and investment income. As indicated in Section 14.3, these are two of the main areas of discrepancy with National Account figures. A detailed examination of the individual questions is illuminating, and indicates which are the more difficult items in the Income Schedule.

Many self-employed people have difficulty in producing net profit figures (Question 27a); 19 per cent said they did not know the amount of their profit and another 15 per cent had to estimate it, while just over 20% did not seem to know the date of their business year (Question 27a(i)). The alternative questions put to those who could not estimate their net profit (Questions 27(b3) and 27(c)) were not conspicuously successful; 55% of those asked the alternative questions were unable to give their residual profit, while turn-over figures were equally difficult to obtain. One problem facing interviewers is that they are often referred by informants to accountants for this information; however, some accountants, in turn, request a fee for any search and it is not possible to pay for this.

Investments are well-known as a subject which presents considerable difficulty and the fourth quarter count confirmed this. For only 60 per cent of accounts was a direct answer forthcoming about the amount of annual interest (Questions 51-55(a)); for 11 per cent, the amount of interest was estimated and for 29 per cent the amount of interest was not known.

The questions about income from stocks and shares (Question 57(c)) produced a less discouraging picture: 81% gave an answer, but as with other investment data, there could be no validation of the actual accuracy of the reply.

In addition to these two main problem areas, examination of the other Income Schedule questions shows up several more weak cases where the index of reliability is below 80%. Data on quantities of food supplied free (Question 17(c)) also produced a poor showing, but this was based on only 21 cases in the whole sample. Of the Social Security benefits, only Sickness Benefit (Q36A) was outstandingly poor, at 66 per cent. The other area which does not show up too well is children's income (Q 72) with 83 per cent, well below the overall level of reliability.

In conclusion, it is clear that certain questions prove to be difficult for informants. Over the years there have been continuous attempts to improve question wording, to brief interviewers to help informants, that is by asking them to produce documentary evidence and generally to make requirements as clear as possible. Still, it appears that certain areas seem incapable of improvement, either because informants do not know the answers or else are unwilling to provide answers. Although the FES obtains 100 per cent cooperation from all spenders, this is not to say that there is 100 per cent response to all questions.

14.3 Blue Book comparison

The external yardstick for assessing the validity of FES results has been the National Income Blue Book (NIBB) estimates, adjusted to the FES sample definition. For some years the Central Statistical Office has carried out a comparison between FES average household expenditure, grossed-up to give estimates of national expenditure, and the NIBB estimates, based on other sources[2]. This type of comparison is often carried out in other countries to validate their budget survey results[3].

In 1972 a fundamental review (The FES Review) was carried out into the functions and methods of the FES. Arising out of this Review, an experimental programme to improve FES methodology was recommended. One of the problem areas mentioned was the fact that FES grossed-up estimates appeared to understate the National Income and Expenditure figures derived from National Accounts (the Blue Book), particularly for certain types of expenditure, notably alcohol and tobacco expenditure. These discrepancies have persisted since then and Table 14.3.1 shows the results of the FES/Blue Book comparison in 1976.

Table 14.3.1 Consumer expenditure: FES/Blue Book comparison (1976)

Expenditure group	Grossed-up FES	Blue Book Consumers' Expenditure	$\frac{(i)}{(ii)} \times 100$
	£m (i)	£m (ii)	% (iii)
Strictly comparable*			
Food	13,560	14,085	96
Alcoholic drink	3,238	5,587	58
Tobacco	2,381	3,025	79
Housing (excluding imputed rent)	6,591	6,716	98
Fuel and light	3,683	3,528	104
Clothing and footwear	5,200	5,211	100
Sub-total (strictly comparable)	34,653	38,152	91
Less comparable*			
Durable	3,832	4,842	79
Other goods	4,805	4,450	108
Transport	7,782	8,832	88
Catering	2,820	2,103	134
Services	4,026	4,365	92
Sub-total (less comparable)	23,265	24,592	95
Grand total (consumers' expenditure)	57,918	62,744	92

These terms reflect the degree of comparability of the FES with other sources

NIBB consumers' expenditure estimates are derived from a wide variety of sources[4]. Also, in order to attempt a comparison with the FES, NIBB estimates have to be adjusted to the same domestic basis as the FES, which means that deductions need to be made from NIBB estimates for expenditure by businesses, by tourists and by the institutional population. In its paper on the FES/Blue Book comparison, the Central Statistical Office classifies major expenditure groups into those 'strictly comparable' with the FES and those 'less comparable', taking into account all these factors.

Of the major expenditure groups said to be 'strictly comparable' the FES comes within 91 per cent of NIBB estimates; 'less comparable' groups are within 95 per cent of NIBB estimates. The major discrepancies (of more than 10 per cent) where the FES understates NIBB, are Alcohol (—42 per cent, Catering (+34 per cent) Tobacco (—21 per cent) and Durable Goods (—21 per cent).[4,5]

The CSO have only recently commenced a similiar exercise (unpublished) which compares FES income sources with NIBB estimates. Preliminary figures (for 1976) showed that the greatest discrepancies occur for Self-employment income (—33 per cent), for Investment income (—67 per cent) and for Private occupational pensions (—51 per cent). For all three income sources, the FES understates the NIBB figures.

There are considerable problems in assuming that NIBB estimates can be compared with the FES. The grossing-up procedures are simplistic, depending as they do on simple ratios of total national expenditure (per expenditure group) or income (per source) divided by the number of households in the population. In addition, it is difficult to estimate reliably the proportions consumed by the business, tourist and institutional populations; the same estimates have been used for many years.

Finally, in the case of alcohol and tobacco expenditure estimates, the CSO has to convert consumption statistics into expenditure, using average cost per quantity factors; only rough estimates can be made of quantities, as quantities are not recorded in the FES.

Despite these difficulties, it is true that other budget surveys suffer from similar problems and report discrepancies in much the same problem areas: alcohol and tobacco expenditure, self employment and investment income. It is the extent of the discrepancy that is difficult to assess.

14.4 Possible causes of discrepancies

It is possible to group the main factors leading to the discrepancies between the FES and NIBB into four headings:

(i) problems in making the comparison (covered in the previous section);
(ii) limitations of survey design, eg. restricting the reference period for recording, use of retrospective questions, etc.
(iii) recording biases;
(iv) non response bias ie. the failure of certain sub-groups of the population to respond representatively.

Factors (ii)—(iv) are commonly called non-sampling errors.

With regard to (iii), recording biases can lead to over-statement, eg. where expenditure incurred outside the reference period is nevertheless recorded during the period 'telescoping' or 'end period effect'). However, for the major FES problem areas, the biases are in the direction of under-recording since the FES understates the NIBB figures.

The following are recording biases* that could lead to under-recording in the FES:

(a) *omission of an amount* where an informant entirely omits an amount due to:
— forgetfulness or memory lapse; or
—purposeful suppression;
(b) *understatement of an amount* where an informant provides an amount but either unknowingly, or deliberately, understates the actual amount;
(c) *concealment of an amount* where an informant either cannot separate out the amount from another already given, eg. the alcoholic drinks in Meals Out or deliberately conceals the amount in another item;
(d) *changes in behaviour prior to record-keeping* where an informant, because he is embarking on record-keeping, decides to reduce expenditure of a certain type, eg. on drinking, smoking, betting, before records are started;
(e) *changes in behaviour during record-keeping* where an informant becomes conscious of his or her spending because of record-keeping and decides to reduce spending during the period.

One of the aims of the experimental programme was to try to determine the causes of the large discrepancies between the FES and the Blue Book for Alcohol and Tobacco expenditure and also for Consumer Durables. The understatement of Self-employment income and Investment income were also to be investigated. The next sections examine in turn each problem area of the FES and suggest which non-sampling errors affect the discrepancy. The results of various experiments are given in order to substantiate conclusions, although it would be rash to claim that the conclusions are more than deductions.

14.5 Problem areas

(i) Alcohol and tobacco expenditure

There are a number of commonsense reasons for supposing that any understatement in alcohol and tobacco expenditure in the FES results would be due to some type of recording bias. First, this type of expenditure is 'stigmatised' and informants may be reluctant to reveal their behaviour. Second, there may be memory problems, particularly for alcohol expenditure. It therefore seemed advisable to commence the experimental programme with a test of the recordkeeping accuracy of the FES.

In order to test the accuracy of alcohol and tobacco recording on the FES, a new methodology was devised which required informants to balance all outgoings against all incomings over a 14 day period. The methodology is described in further detail in Section 17.6; however, effectively it made it possible to estimate the amount of unrecorded cash expenditure. Two experiments, the Family Budget Survey Experiment (FBSE) and the Family Budget Survey Pilot (FBSP), were carried out in February 1976 and February 1978 respectively.

* There are other typologies of recording bias.[5,6] See also Sudman, S and Ferber, R. *Consumer Panels*. American Marketing Association, Chicago, Ill. 1979. p67.

Both experiments served as controls against the FES during the same four week period.

The results of both experiments are shown in Table 14.5.1. There are very few statistically significant differences between the FES samples and the FBSP control,

Table 14.5.1 Comparison of Average weekly household (original) expenditure

Expenditure Group	Average weekly household expenditure					
	1978‡			1976†		
	FBSP	FES	FBSP-FES	FBSE	FES	FBSE-FES
	£	£	£	£	£	£
Housing	6.81	5.10	1.71	3.91	3.64	0.27
Fuel	6.56	4.89	1.67	4.67	3.27	1.67
Food	19.60	19.20	0.58	13.92	14.29	—0.37
Alcohol	3.62	3.74	—0.12	2.67	2.75	—0.45
Tobacco	2.55	2.63	—0.08	1.89	2.24	—0.35
Clothing	4.60	4.90	—0.30	2.23	3.00	—0.77
Durables	1.94	3.85	—1.91*	2.00	2.81	—0.81
Other Goods	5.16	5.24	—0.08	3.16	3.87	—0.71*
Transport	8.05	7.48	0.57	5.60	7.63	—2.03*
Services	8.82	6.89	1.93	6.34	4.41	1.93
Instalments	3.82	3.06	0.76	1.82	2.43	—0.61
Miscellaneous	.40	.20	0.20*	1.77	0.15	1.62
	71.93	67.00	4.93	49.98	50.49	—0.51
No. of hhlds =	123	567		113	586	
No. of spenders =	261	1,179		237	1,189	
Spenders per hhld =	2.12	2.08		2.10	2.02	

‡*Family Budget Survey Pilot (Feb-Mar 1978) and FES (Feb-Mar 1978)*
†*Family Budget Survey Experiment (Feb 1976) and FES (Feb 1976)*
**Significant at greater than 2 standard errors*

due to the small FBS samples. Nevertheless, with respect to a number of expenditure groups, notably alcohol and tobacco, the direction of the differences is the same. Average weekly household expenditure figures for alcohol and tobacco in both FBS experiments were less than the averages obtained in the FES samples. The conclusion drawn was that, even with the intricate balancing methodology of the FBS experiments which helped account for every penny spent, missing alcohol and tobacco expenditure was not revealed; and concomittantly, this implied that recording of these items by FES informants was probably reliable. In fact, if all unrecorded out-goings in the FBSP (46p per week) were arbitrarily assumed to be unrecorded alcohol expenditure, this would improve the estimate by only 13 per cent. This still would leave considerable shortfalls with NIBB figures. Therefore the discrepancy with National Accounts figures does not seem to be due mainly to under-recording.

Recalling the various possible recording biases, it is true that the FBS methodology only controlled for omitting an amount, (bias (a)) and understating an amount (bias (b)). Further research was therefore carried out to see if biases (c), (d) and (e) could account for understatement of Alcohol and Tobacco expenditure.

An experiment was carried out to investigate whether there was concealed alcoholic drink (bias (c)) in meals taken out at restaurants. Informants who entered a

'Meals Out' amount in their diaries were written to asking if they had taken alcoholic drink with their meal and had forgotten to separate it from the Meals Out total. Response was 87 per cent. The results showed that alcoholic drink expenditure concealed in Meals Out amounted to only 5 per cent of total Meals Out expenditure. (It should also be pointed out that if an informant deliberately wishes to misdescribe an item, for example a pint of beer is described as a 'packet of fish fingers', there is no way of overcoming this problem.) However, on balance it was judged that bias (c) was small and did not contribute greatly to the overall discrepancy.

Bias (d) (changes in behaviour prior to record keeping) poses almost insuperable problems of detection. There is no way of discovering 'normal' behaviour if contact with a survey causes that behaviour to change. One method attempted has been to ask informants to remember their alcoholic consumption over a past period. However, this assumes that informants are prepared to be more honest about their past behaviour than they are about keeping records. This may not be the case. Also, the retrospective questions can lead to understatement due to memory bias. In fact, the retrospective method was used in several OPCS drinking surveys and showed no improvement over the FES when their results were compared with NIBB figures.

Bias (e) (when spending is reduced during recordkeeping) is not a major source of recording bias on the FES, as shown in a study of 1978 FES data. Total expenditure declined only 2—3 per cent between the first and second weeks. (This represents an improvement over the inter-week bias figure of − 7 per cent referred to in the first edition of the Handbook*.) With respect to alcohol and tobacco expenditure, a study carried out on data collected over four weeks in February—March 1978 revealed an increase in expenditure of 2.7 per cent between the weeks for alcohol and no change in expenditure for tobacco. This study was based on the original recordkeeping of informants; normally items recorded which also are on the Household Schedule are edited out of the diaries.

The possibly surprising conclusion drawn from this series of experiments was that none of the recording biases could account for the understatement of FES Alcohol and Tobacco expenditure against NIBB figures. It is possible that the size of the discrepancy is to some extent due to the methods the CSO uses to adjust NIBB figures to make them comparable to the FES definitions. However, there is also evidence that suggests that non-response bias is the main factor explaining the discrepancy for alcohol expenditure. This is covered in the next section.

It is clear from the OPCS drinking consumption surveys that alcoholic consumption is very skew: 3 per cent of the Scottish sample consumed 30 per cent of all sample consumption[7]; similar results were obtained in England and Wales[8]. Response was very high, yet estimates still understated NIBB figures by − 47 per cent. This suggests that a minority of non-respondents account for a very high proportion of all alcoholic consumption. It can therefore be assumed that both the specialised drinking surveys and the FES fail to pick up the very heavy drinkers who are either not easily contacted or do not want to take part in surveys or are, in fact, excluded from the FES sample*.

There is support for the argument that heavy drinkers are either missing from the FES sample entirely or are likely not to be contacted because they would be away from home when their household is visited. An OPCS study[9] of the occupations of those who died from cirrhosis of the liver in England and Wales in 1970—72 showed the following highest rankings of death risk from cirrhosis: publicans and innkeepers (1); ships' deck hands, engineering officers and pilots (2); bar staff (3); deck and engine room ratings, bargees and boatmen (4); fisherman (5); proprietors and managers of boarding houses and hotels (6) and restauranteurs (7). These highest death risk occupations are all excluded from the FES sample or else are likely to be absent when their household is sampled and therefore may not keep records even if their household cooperates.

Finally, as shown in Table 5.2.1 there is usually a higher non-response rate in December due to non-contacts than during the rest of the year. This could mean that there may be understated alcoholic expenditure in the sample at the time when expenditure on alcohol is at its peak.

The evidence that the understatement of FES Tobacco expenditure is due to non-response bias is not so easy to obtain, although results from the 1978 General Household Survey indicate an association between heavy drinking and heavy smoking[10]. It is possible that heavy smokers are also often heavy drinkers and are underrepresented in the sample for the reasons just given. The shortfall of − 21 per cent is not as great as with alcohol expenditure.

(ii) *Consumer durables*
FES Consumer Durable figures understate NIBB figures by 21 per cent. Memory bias could lead to understatement as details about purchase of consumer durables by hire purchase and credit sale are obtained retrospectively. (see Question 42 in Appendix C2) Only 43 per cent of informants with hire purchase agreements have records to consult and, as data is sought for arrangements incurred during the three months prior to interview, this could lead to a downwards bias. Sudman and Ferber[11] have shown that understatement increases over time with retrospective questions about consumer durables (see also Kemsley[6]).

---

* Kemsley, WFF. *FES Handbook. Op cit.* p 92. For a more detailed analysis of the current inter-week bias in the FES the reader is referred to an unpublished paper entitled *Inter-week variation in the FES (February-March 1978)* obtainable from the authors.

* This conclusion has been confirmed with reference to the results of the specialised drinking survey in England and Wales and was reported in a paper given by P Wilson of OPCS read at the Annual Conference of the Institute of Statisticians at Kings College Cambridge in July 1980.

There is considerable inter-week bias in expenditure on consumer durables: expenditure declines in the second week by 25 per cent. The bias probably is due to demonstration effect because there are only 14 days in which to record consumer durables. This could lead to overstatement; however it is conceivable that the record-keeping period is too short to accurately measure consumer durables. A number of European budget surveys ask informants to keep forward diaries over a year in order to obtain a more normal picture of consumer durable acquisitions, albeit with consequent risk of panel conditioning and lower response.

The conclusion is that the understatement with NIBB for Consumer Durables is due to a limitation in the survey design, where consumer durables purchased outright are only recorded over a period of 14 days.

(iii) Self-employment income
The 1971 Census/FES comparison study[14] showed higher non-response for the self-employed than for other employment statuses. Therefore non-response bias could account for some of the understatement with NIBB figures, particularly at the top 1 per cent of the tax unit distribution, where the CSO has shown some bias exists. Another factor could be the marked lack of reliability to the answers to the questions about self employment income shown in Table 14.2.2. (It may be more than a coincidence that the least reliable answers to questions on the FES are also two of the three areas with the greatest income discrepancies, self-employment income and investment income.) Genuine lack of knowledge seems to be part of the explanation: self-employment informants often rely on accountants to prepare their tax figures. On the other hand, it is also possible that suspicions may exist about whether the information may be passed on to the Inland Revenue, despite assurances to the contrary by OPCS interviewers. In fact, the NIBB figures may also suffer from understatement.

Very little can be done either about improving knowledge of up-to-date figures or about easing suspicion. Accountants normally request fees to provide figures. There is also evidence that the Self-employed feel increasingly besieged by requests from 'the Government' to provide statistics, particularly since the introduction of VAT.

(iv) Investment income
Understatement of dividends and interest on the FES is not surprising as most other budget surveys experience the same shortfall. Questions about this type of income (as well as about private occupational pensions) may be considered by many people to be an intrusion of privacy. In fact, in recent years, there have been about 20 cases a year where FES informants cooperate on all questions except for the investment income questions, where they flatly refused on the grounds of intrusion of privacy.

The answers to the questions asking for 12 months income from interest and dividends are not relatively reliable. Table 14.2.2. showed that 60 per cent of answers were reliable. This could be due to genuine lack of knowledge because passbooks are not up to date or not available. It could also be due to concealed refusal to give the information.

It is unlikely that changing the wording of questions will improve results for investment income. In 1978, the 29 per cent of informants with investment accounts who could not give 12 months interest were asked to provide current balances in their savings accounts so that interest could be estimated. Seventy-nine per cent could give an answer. The interest estimated from the current balances only provided marginal improvements to the discrepancy with National Accounts; however, the results seemed to indicate that there were genuine knowledge problems, as opposed to concealment problems, in giving 12 months' interest. Informants were willing to provide current balances as an alternative.

There is also evidence that informants tend to forget children's accounts. The FES has a question which asks about income received by children in the household (Q 72 of Appendix D2).

In addition to the factors given above, the FES is said to be biased (only) at the upper 1 per cent of the income tax unit distribution and this non-response bias could be one of the main causes of the FES understatement of dividends and interest.

In conclusion, the discrepancies with National Accounts are probably mainly explained by non-response bias and less due to under-recording. However, there may well be concealment of certain sources of income. To overcome the problem of deliberate concealment is neither easy nor assured of success. There is a suggestion that sensitive information, such as savings information, is more forthcoming on long-term panels where it is possible to ask check questions at quarterly recalls by interview. The informant is thought to be more forthcoming with information as he or she gains trust in the interviewer. Naturally, there is the problem of panel mortality as well as the problem of obtaining a sufficiently high initial response rate; however, there is a suggestion that any adverse effects on sample averages due to panel mortality are more than offset by improvements in reporting of sensitive information.[15] The FES is well-established in its commitment to its traditional design and because of processing deadlines for the RPI and for the annual report, might not be flexible enough to convert to a panel design. Nevertheless, there is a trend in most European budget surveys and in the United States toward this approach.

References
1   Ferber, R. The reliability of consumer reports of assets and debts. Studies in Consumer Savings No.6. University of Illinois, Urbana Ill. 1966. See also Studies in Consumer Savings Nos.2 and 3.
2   FES/Blue Book. Op cit.
3   For example see US Bureau of the Census. 1972-1973 US Consumer Expenditure Survey: a preliminary evaluation. Technical Paper No. 45. US Department of Commerce, Washington DC 1978.

4   Maurice, R. *Op cit*. pp 190-201.
5   Prais and Houthakker. *The analysis of family budgets with an application to two British surveys conducted in 1937—39 and their detailed results.* University of Cambridge, Department of Applied Economics Monograph 4. Cambridge University Press. Cambridge, 1955. pp39—42.
6   Kemsley, WFF. Collecting data on economic flow variables using interviews and record-keeping, in Moss, L and Goldstein, H (Eds). *The recall method in social surveys*. Studies in Education (New Series) 9. University of London, Insitute of Education 1979. p127.
7   Dight, S. *Scottish drinking habits*. HMSO 1976.
8   Wilson, P. *Drinking in England and Wales*. HMSO 1980.
9   Donnan, S and Haskey, J. Alcoholism and cirrhosis of the liver. *Population Trends 7*. HMSO 1977 pp 18-24.
10 OPCS. *General Household Survey 1978*. HMSO 1980, pp 145-149.
11 Sudman, S and Ferber, R. *Experiments in obtaining consumer expenditures of durable goods by recall procedures: a preliminary report*. Survey Research Laboratory, University of Illinois. Urbana I11. 1970.
12 Pearl, R. *Op cit*. p 45.
13 Eurostat. *Op cit*.
14 Kemsley, WFF. FES: a study of differential response. *Op cit*. Appendix A5, p31.21.
15 Ferber, R and Frankel, M. *The collection, measurement and evaluation of savings account records*. Report 1 under contract HEW-100-77-0112. HEW Office of Survey Development, Washington DC. Survey Research Laboratory, University of Illinois, Urbana, Ill. 1978. p64.

15 Major changes to the FES

15.1 Sample design

Modifications to the sample design or sampling procedure have been made in 1967, 1970, 1975, 1977, 1978, 1979 and 1980. For the first ten years from 1957 to 1966, the sample produced between 3,000 and 3,500 co-operating households in a year, derived from 128 primary sampling units; a description will be found in the first Handbook, pages 6 and 7. These 128 units were selected with probabilities proportional to the mid-1955 electorate, and were divided into 8 sets of 16 and a set was allocated to each of the 8 half quarters of the year. With the small number of areas available at the first stage, regional representation was necessarily imperfect, and, in practice, a representative sample could only be secured by taking data for a whole year. Moreover, seasonal variations might become confounded with regional biases so that in a regional analysis seasonal variations might give rise to spurious effects.

In 1967 a new design was introduced. The sample was doubled in size and re-designed so as to overcome these objections. The main difference was that the number of PSUs was increased to 168 each quarter and arranged so that each calendar quarter was representative in itself. The stratifying factors were also improved, and a rotating system of selection incorporated at the first stage. A complete description of the design will be found in the first Handbook on pages 8 to 13. It is similar to the one now in use and described in Chapter 4. In 1967 the 168 PSUs were selected with probability proportional to the mid-1965 population estimates. In 1970 the sampling frame was updated and based on mid-1968 population estimates; this up-dating led to a few small changes in the distribution of PSUs between regions.

The next change, that in 1975, was brought about by the re-organization of local government, which in England and Wales took place in 1974 and in Scotland in 1975. The newer local authorities are, on average, considerably larger than the pre-1974 areas. Whereas in the earlier design the 168 PSUs were drawn from 1,782 administrative areas, the corresponding strata for the 1975 design contained only 455 separate areas. Another modification made at the same time was the updating of the sample frame based on the mid-1973 population estimates, as well as minor alterations to all the stratifying factors. In late 1974, when the new sampling frame was being drawn up, the details of the Clydeside conurbation were not available, so that, for 1975 and 1976, Glasgow was included with the other three cities of Scotland in the sample stratification. However, for purposes of analysis, Glasgow was re-classified and grouped with the rest of the Clydeside conurbation. Local government reorganisa-

tion in Scotland was not completed until 1977. In 1978 the measure of size for PPS selection of districts was changed from total population of the district to total electorate in the district to be more consistent with the selection of wards at the second stage, as wards are selected PPS according to their total number of electors.

Prior to 1977 interviewers were asked to interview all households at a selected address (up to a maximum of three); they then discarded, from the list of pre-selected addresses the next available address, following the one giving rise to the additional household. This was subject to the restriction that it must not have already been visited by the interviewer. (This restriction was necessary in order to avoid introducing selection bias). This procedure was felt to lead to clustering of households at multi-household addresses.

In 1977 a change was made to the procedure at multi-household addresses as it was assumed that households at this type of address were under-sampled, particularly single-person households. Also, as mentioned above, the previous procedure led to clustering. The new procedure attempts to pre-select multi-household addresses, using the number of surname changes as an indicator. Where the Electoral Register shows four or more surnames at an address, Sampling Implementation Unit gives a greater chance of selection to the address. Four surname changes were set as the indicator of the presence of a multi-household address, as research showed that the majority of addresses with three or less surnames were, in fact, single-household addresses. At the same time (1977) the instruction to delete the next address(es) was dropped.

The number of surnames is not a precise indicator of the number of households at the address and occasionally the interviewer finds concealed multi-households where there was no prior indication from the Electoral Register. New procedures for dealing with 'concealed multi-households' were initiated in 1979 so that interviewers took a random sub-sample of three households from each address containing four or more households which had not been identified from the number of surnames on the Electoral Register.

15.2 Schedule design

In discussing changes, the matter of schedule layout must not be overlooked. Modifications to schedule design, while not affecting content, have usually been made to assist interviewers in collecting and recording data, or to assist handling and processing the information. Changes and alterations in design can be expected to contribute towards improving the quality and accuracy of the final results. Throughout the history of the survey there have always been at least two interview schedules; a Household Schedule containing, as a minimum, information on household composition, on accommodation and on housing expenses, while the other questionnaire has dealt with income. Sometimes some of the individual and personal expenditure items have appeared on yet another schedule, while in some years these topics have been included on the income schedule. But since 1968 all expenditure data other than that collected through the diaries, has been recorded on the Household Schedule.

The first major change in layout occurred in 1961 when the introduction of an electronic computer led to the widespread use of pre-coded questions to facilitate processing. From this time all the interview schedules have usually had the questions printed on the left of a page with the codes pre-printed in a corresponding position of a column on the right. The next major change was in 1968 when the schedules were completely and thoroughly re-designed after discussions with the Technical Branches, particularly the Field Branch. While the content remained almost unchanged, the interview questions were expanded to facilitate fieldwork and editing, as mentioned in the following section. In 1970, following a small scale study, the Income Schedule was further modified to provide recording columns for two individuals; previously a separate form had been used for each person. A year later in February 1971 there was decimalisation of the currency, and for most of that year the diaries contained two columns side by side catering for both new and old currency. Informants were told to enter details in whichever form they wished, but preferably in the form in which the price was expressed. For reasons of space it was not possible to re-design the two interview schedules to cover both forms, and provision could only be made for the new currency. Amounts in old currency, whether in diaries or interview schedules, were converted before the documents left SSD for DE. Interviewers were encouraged to make these conversions, and they were then checked in Primary Analysis Branch.

Finally, the diaries—since informants are allowed to use their own words in describing each entry, and this has usually proved adequate in applying the coding frame, there has never been much incentive to vary the form of the recording pages. In 1975, however, the recording space allocated to food was substantially increased by moving other sub-headings to the right-hand page of each pair of pages for that day. In 1977 the 'Meals out' section was also expanded and divided into:

(a) Meals bought and eaten at workplace
(b) Meals eaten in other catering establishments
(c) Take-away meals.

15.3 Content

Broadly speaking, the content of the survey has remained more or less unchanged since it began in 1957. Theoretically, expenditure and income have always been defined as described in Sections 12.3 and 12.7 respectively. On the other hand, comparison of interview schedules in any two consecutive years shows that there have been few years without change. Some changes have been small, others almost trivial, but all have been made in a continuous endeavour to improve the quality of the data. Many have been made to meet the increasing sophistication of editing procedures, while others have been made to meet the increasing complexity of everyday economic life, such as the introduction of new state benefits, business expenses and credit cards. Editing problems became more acute with the doubling of the sample in 1967, and the employment of many more interviewers unfamiliar with the survey. Also, there was a high rate of refusals for further information. In its turn, this led to a major revision of the interview schedules in 1968.

An important innovation made in 1968 was the introduction of special checking sheets, up-to-date versions of which appear in Appendices G3 and G4. These replaced some limited information collected since 1961 and recorded on one or other of the interview schedules.

An improvement in content, also made in 1968, was the addition of questions relating to supplementary or secondary employment. Also 1968 saw the introduction of an interview question on the outright purchases of motor vehicles over 12 months retrospective to the time of interview. Strictly speaking, this was not a change in content since data on such purchases had always been obtained, but up to 1968 the information had come from the diaries. The change was made to increase the number of mentions and thus the accuracy of the final results, particularly when used in the calculations on re-distribution of income.

However, it is in certain topics peripheral to the collection of expenditure data, where substantial additions have been made. These reflect the increasing use of the FES. In 1961 the demographic detail for the household composition box was expanded to include marital status, together with a finer classification of full-time education. In 1978, a question about terminal school-leaving age was added. Questions about hours worked by employees were added in 1964, and a corresponding item for self-employed in 1977. Ownership of durables — possession of a motor vehicle and ownership of a garage, television and telephone — have been covered for most of the time in conjunction with questions about related expenditure. Ownership of a refrigerator and washing machine was covered in 1959, 1960 and 1964-66, and then have been continuously included in every year since 1969. Central heating was added in 1969 and deep freezes were added in 1977.

Over the years questions have been added to improve calculations of redistribution of income. In 1968 questions were introduced about outright purchases of motor vehicles over 12 months prior to interview; about education grants received and payment of tuition fees over the previous 12 months; about tax paid direct to Inland Revenue and about lump sum tax rebates, again over a 12 month period. Questions were also added about Redundancy Pay and Death and Maternity Grants received. In

1976, questions were added about National Insurance contributions paid direct as well as luncheon vouchers received in the last 7 days. Finally in 1978 and 1979 informants were asked to quote their PAYE code as shown on their pay slips to enable consistency checks to be made on tax estimates derived from the FES. Only 50 per cent of employees were able to provide the PAYE code based on pay slips. As this is a lower proportion than those who have pay slips (70—80 per cent) this indicates that PAYE code was not provided in all cases.

The FES has always included questions which ask employees whether or not their last pay received was their 'usual pay'. Questions were asked both about usual net and usual gross pay. Until 1970 questions were asked of those informants whose last pay was not said to be usual as to whether their pay varied a good deal or not. If their pay varied a great deal they were asked how much they received 'on average'. In 1970 the questions were revised. The new wording was 'Do you usually receive the wage/salary you mentioned before?' A prompt note was added: 'If unable to give usual pay because it varies considerably, give average pay received (not basic).' The definition of 'usual' has always been left to informants, rather than trying to impose a strict statistical definition. However, informants' answers often lead to further queries at coding stage.

Another topic added in 1976 was that of windfall income. Except for certain gambling winnings recorded in diaries, the FES had always excluded windfall receipts from the Income Schedule. In 1976 questions were added to cover sales of secondhand cars, amounts received from endowment and life assurance policies and also from insurance policies relating to property and cars, even though this list by no means exhausted all potential sources of windfall income. The main reason for adding these questions was to try to balance FES expenditure against income. Gradually these questions have been dropped as it was realised that their addition made little difference to balancing, and it was recognised that the FES, with its existing methodology, could not be expected to balance on a household basis anyway.

A further area of change has been concerned with obtaining fuller details about gas and electricity accounts. From 1970 to 1976 informants with gas supplied were asked whether their gas supply was Town gas or North Sea gas. This question was dropped in 1977 when there was universal conversion to North Sea Gas. In 1977 questions were added to discover whether electricity units were charged at off-peak or full-rate; also the month and year of the last gas and electricity accounts were added. Finally, informants with oil central heating were asked for 12 month expenditure. As indicated in Section 14.2 informants have great difficulty in obtaining details about the off-peak and full-rates charged, as well as with units of gas and electricity consumed.

There have been considerable changes to the wording of questions about rates rebates over the years. There has been a question for a number of years to cover the case

where rates rebates are deducted from the last rates payment; however, it was not until 1975 that a question was added to cover the case where a rates rebate is received by lump sum refund.

Editing of business expenses has become more complex in recent years. Prior to 1976, business expenses reclaimed were obtained by a single question in the Household Schedule and at the end of each diary. In 1976 the Household Schedule question on business expenses was transferred to the Income Schedule and there was a major expansion of questions to cover motoring expenses, refunds of expenses from subsidiary employment, special questions on expenditure claimed as a business expense by self-employed informants, and finally, expenses refunded by organisations for which informants did unpaid work. Business expenses are always deleted from expenditure; since 1978 the deleted business expenses have been coded for certain categories of expenditure (meals out, alcohol, etc).

Finally the area of instalment credit expenditure has undergone considerable changes. Until 1968, there was a separate C Schedule which asked for instalments paid on hire purchase and mail order for items acquired in the three months prior to interview. Instalment transactions through clubs, by credit account, budget account and bank loan were excluded. Commencing in 1968, the C Schedule was dropped and the instalment questions were added to the Household Schedule. Furthermore, the informal instalment credit transactions (clubs, budget accounts, etc) were now included. For club transactions, informants were asked to remember goods or services obtained over the calendar month previous to interview. In 1972, an instruction was added to the diary records to cover the situation where a monthly credit card account was paid: informants were asked to write down the amount paid if payment occurred within the record-keeping period; they were also asked to itemise the separate goods and services covered by the account. In 1977 fuller instructions were given in the diary to itemise all details on the account, including interest charged, balance brought forward as well as the value of goods and services acquired. Informants were asked to record goods and services acquired during the 14 days as well. In 1978 procedure for obtaining credit card information changed: informants were asked if they had paid part or all of a credit card account during the calendar month prior to interview. If they had, they were asked to provide full details of the account paid. In 1979 the procedure changed yet again. At the beginning of recordkeeping, informants were given a special credit card account sheet (Appendix E2) which gave preprinted entries of the information required. There are still problems with the procedures for dealing with credit card transactions, notably informants' lack of knowledge of details and the high proportion of expenditure which is coded as miscellaneous because of the apportionment procedures. The possibility of converting credit card transactions from a payment basis to acquisitions is currently being investigated.

15.4 Field procedures — quota sizes and payment

There have been no substantial changes in field procedure, in spite of the modifications and improvements to the schedule layout. Over the period, however, the importance of intermediate calls has become increasingly recognised, so that whereas in the early days it was left to the interviewer to decide whether to pay more than one such call, it is now considered essential that at least two intermediate calls should be made. This tendency was reinforced by the introduction of the various checking sheets in 1968.

A major change made in 1967, when the sample design was improved, was a reduction in quota size. Up to 1966 each quota was intended to cover 6 or 7 placing weeks, and consisted of 36 or 42 addresses respectively, a rate of 6 per week. In 1967 this was reduced to 16 per placing month. This was done in order to increase the number of PSUs for a given sample size and thus help to improve regional representation.

In July 1971 the token payment given to each household member for cooperation was increased from £1 to £2 to offset the falling value of the £1. Commencing in the latter half of 1979, an experiment has been underway to examine the effect of raising payments on response in the Greater London Area.

In 1973, the youngest age at which individual household members were asked to keep diaries, or answer individually the interview questions, was raised from 15 to 16 in line with the raising of the school leaving age at the beginning of the 1972-73 school year.

16 Follow-up surveys using FES as a sampling frame

16.1 Summary

On a few occasions, households cooperating in the FES have provided a sample for a further survey. One important advantage of such an arrangement is that the FES can then be linked with the results of the follow-up survey. It can also be used to provide samples stratified by variables not generally available, or restricted to certain groups such as those with high or low incomes. The follow-up technique makes a particularly efficient use of field resources since any hard core of refusals has already been eliminated. Furthermore, the good will and rapport established during the various visits of the FES interviewer can be expected to smooth the course of interviewing in the follow-up exercise, especially by making for an easier introduction, even when the same interviewer cannot be employed. On the other hand, there will be a small number who refuse to take part in a further survey simply because they have already cooperated in the earlier FES.

Response rates on follow-up surveys so far carried out are summarized in Table 16.1.1. They are described in more detail in the remaining sections of this chapter. Some general comments may be of interest although it is not easy to make inferences from so few cases. Were it not for the National Food Survey and Wealth Study exercises the general conclusion might be that re-interviewing was fairly successful, especially as in both these cases special circumstances may explain the poor showing of the re-interviews. In the case of the NFS (1969) a low re-interview response rate may have been obtained because housewives were, in effect, being asked to continue record-keeping for a further week and on a subject not regarded as important as the whole of expenditure. The feasibility studies for a Wealth Study in 1976 and 1977 produced the kind of response generally associated with inquiries into investment, assets and savings. Not even linking the topics to the FES has overcome the reluctance to take part in such inquiries.

On the other hand, when a suitable topic has been under study quite a good re-interview response rate has been achieved. However, the response rate when calculated on the sample originally selected for the FES can never be exceptionally good because 30 per cent is always lost at the FES stage. All the rates shown in Table 16.1.1 have therefore to be reduced in the ratio of about 0.7 if the true overall response rate is to be ascertained; it may even be lower if further losses due to removals and deaths are incurred before the FES sample can be re-interviewed.

16.2 National Food Survey experiment (1969)

This follow-up study was undertaken to see whether housewives who had already cooperated in the FES could

Table 16.1.1 Follow-up surveys to FES

Survey	Re-interview response rates (per cent)	Cooperating FES households (= 100 per cent)	Date of FES sample
National Food Survey 1969			
Introduced by:			
a) SSD interviewer	69	113	1969
b) Letter from SSD	33	129	1969
Family Income Supplement 1971			
a) 1969 sample	98	101	1969
b) 1970 sample	96	123	1970
Layfield Committee 1975	91	1,609	1974
Feasibility Studies for a Wealth Survey			
a) 1976	68	182	1974
b) 1977	79	123	1977

be persuaded to take part in a further inquiry similar to the NFS by keeping diaries of food purchases for seven days. Such an arrangement would have certain advantages over the present one where the NFS has always been conducted as a separate survey. Organized as a follow-up survey, the NFS sample would then be the same as the FES, and this would be an improvement on the simpler and less sophisticated design used for the NFS. Secondly, such an arrangement would enable data from the FES to be linked to the NFS. In the event, the feasibility study indicated that overall response was poor and the idea was abandoned.

The NFS is carried out by interviewers employed by the British Market Research Bureau Ltd and it was considered essential to use interviewers who were already experienced on the NFS for this experiment in order to maintain comparability. This had two consequences for the design of the follow-up survey. First, the sample areas had to be restricted to those common to both surveys; the second half of 1969 was chosen as a convenient time for the experiment, and during this period 11 such areas were available. Some were in use more than once, and altogether 25 FES quotas were selected as suitable for the experiment, providing in all a sample of 395 housewives from cooperating FES households. The second consequence of the decision to retain BMRB interviewers for the follow-up survey was more serious in that special steps had to be taken to avoid infringing the FES confidentiality pledge. This, among other things, guarantees that names and addresses included in the FES sample will not be passed to anyone outside OPCS. This undertaking would be broken if any BMRB interviewer had been given sufficient details from the FES sample to identify an FES informant. The difficulty was overcome by asking the selected housewives if they were willing to co-operate in a further survey into food. At the same time it was explained that the interviewer for the follow-up survey would not be an FES interviewer, but one employed by a market research firm working on the NFS under the supervision of SSD. It was also explained that this would involve disclosing the housewife's name and address to that firm but neither the latter nor the BMRB interviewer would have access to the information provided by the housewife in the course of the FES.

This preliminary request for assistance in an NFS type of inquiry was made in two different ways. In one, sub-sample A, the request was made by the FES interviewer at the end of the 14-day recording period. This group comprised 113 housewives drawn from 11 quotas which were in the field during September and October 1969. In the other, sub-sample B, the request for further diary recording was not made until after all the documents completed for the FES had been returned to London, when a letter was sent by Social Survey Division to each of the 129 housewives selected for this part of the experiment. They were drawn from 14 quotas which were in the field during August and September 1969. Interviewing for the Food Survey followed shortly afterwards in November and December 1969. No payment was made to any housewife who took part in the follow-up survey; this was consistent with standard practice in the NFS. Each housewife had, however, received the usual payment for cooperating in the FES, which at that time was £1.

The two methods attracted widely different response rates, as can be seen from Table 16.2.1.

Table 16.2.1 Response to NFS as a follow-up to FES

| | Initial request by: | | | |
| | Interviewer - A | | Letter - B | |
	House-wives	per cent	House-wives	per cent
Effective sample (1)	176	100.0	219	100.0
Cooperating in FES (2)	113	64.2	129	58.9
Cooperating in NFS (3)	78	44.3	42	19.2
Re-interview response rate (3) as per cent of (2)		69.0		32.6

In this table no allowance could be made for deaths or removals, but they are unlikely to be many in view of the short time between the FES and the follow-up survey. Of the 129 in sub-sample B, 63 replied to the letter refusing to have anything more to do with a diary type survey, while there were only 18 direct refusals out of the 113 in sub-sample A. Relatively, therefore, there were about three times as many refusals when the request was made by letter as when it was put personally by an interviewer. The response in sub-sample B was so very poor as to rule out any approach by letter. However, not even the better response in sub-sample A was good enough to justify using this method to recruit samples for the NFS. The overall response of 44 per cent is low compared with that usually attained by the NFS — 50 to 55 per cent.

16.3 Family Income Supplement (1971)
As part of a larger exercise involving the General Household Survey, a sample of low earners was interviewed at the request of the Department of Health and Social Security following the introduction of a new Social Security benefit in the summer of 1971. The purpose of the survey was to discover what was known by the public about the new benefit, and how many of those who appeared to be qualified as beneficiaries had, in fact, applied.

The FES was used as a sampling frame since from the information supplied by cooperating households it was possible to select a sample fulfilling the qualifications for the benefit. The sample was in fact extended to include those just above the FIS earnings level to allow for changes in employment since the time when the person had taken part in the FES. It consisted of those family units where the head was an employee working full time, that is 30 hours or more, and earning less than £2 above the then limit for FIS eligibility, which at that time was £20 for families with one dependent child, and rising by £2 for each further dependent child. Dependants were defined as children up to 16, plus those from 16 to 19 years who were receiving full-time education. The FIS sub-sample was selected from the 1969 and 1970 samples of cooperating households. In complex households containing more than one family unit, only that conforming to the conditions described above was selected. Earnings as recorded in the FES were up-dated to 1 June 1971.

The selection of individual cases was made by DHSS from their copies of the FES base tapes. In order to meet the requirements of confidentiality these tapes contain no details which enable any individual to be identified, neither the name nor address. Instead, DHSS provided a list of selected serial numbers and from these Social Survey Division produced address lists for interviewers working on the follow-up survey. After eliminating a few cases where comments made at the time of the original FES interview suggested that further visits would be unwelcome, the total sample consisted of 244 out of 13,253 households who had cooperated in the FES over the two years 1969 and 1970.

The response was very good, averaging almost 90 per cent. Most non-response was attributable to those who had moved; even so, the proportion lost through removals appears to be lower than for a sample representative of the whole population. This can possibly be explained by all the families having low earnings and dependent children. Eliminating removals leads to the remarkably high re-interview response rate of 98 per cent in 1969 and 96 per cent in 1970, as shown in Table 16.3.1.

Table 16.3.1 Response to FIS Survey as a follow-up to FES

| | 1969 FES sample | | 1970 FES sample | |
	No.	%	No.	%
Family Units from FES cooperating households	112		132	
Moved away since FES	11		9	
Available for re-interview	101	100.0	123	100.0
Interviewed about FIS	99	98.0	118	95.9
Refused or no reply	2	2.0	5	4.1

Table 16.3.1 does not give the overall response rate because the response rate for the original FES sample is not known for those with low earnings. While there is ample evidence as to the existence of differential response in the FES, there is no dependable information as to whether the response of those with low earnings is above or below the average level. In the absence of such information the best estimate of the overall response is to use the average rate for 1969 and 1970, that is 67.5 per cent. Applied to the average yield of 89 per cent (that is 217 as per cent of 244) this gives an estimate of 60 per cent as the overall response rate.

Two further observations may be pertinent. Of those successfully interviewed, only a small proportion actually had entitlement to FIS — 47 out of 217 interviewed — so that the yield from this fieldwork was low. Where the relevant proportion of the population is extremely small as in these examples, 47 out of 13,253 or 0.35 per cent, any direct approach would be costly and an efficient use of resources. The FES provides a most convenient sampling frame, especially where one of the sample stratifiers is income. On the other hand, as the FES is limited in size, the total number available in such a follow-up is spread so thinly over the whole country as to make re-interview fieldwork disproportionately expensive.

16.4 The Layfield Committee Inquiry (1975)

During April and May 1975 the FES sample which had co-operated in the second quarter of 1974 was re-interviewed for the Layfield Committee on Local Government Finance. This is the only occasion when a complete sample of FES cooperating households has been re-interviewed. The main purpose of this exercise was to provide the Layfield Committee with data on changes in the rates paid by a household in relation to changes in income over twelve months. (Some results will be found in the *Report of the Committee into Local Government Finance.* Cmnd 6453. HMSO 1976 Annex 19.)

Each household member in the 1974 sample aged 17 or over at the time of the 1975 visit was re-interviewed using a standard 1975 income schedule. There was also a simplified household schedule covering the standard questions on household composition, accommodation and housing costs. No diaries were kept.

The response to the re-interview is given in Table 16.4.1.

Table 16.4.1 Re-interviewing an FES sample about income

	House-holds	Response rates	
		Overall	Re-Interview
Original FES sample Q II 1974	**2,504**	**100.0**	
Cooperating in 1974	**1,770**	**70.7**	
Not available for 1975 interview:			
Moved from 1974 address	138		
Died or in hospital	10		
Other reasons	13		
Total not available	**161**		
Available for 1975 interviews	**1,609**	**64.2**	**100.0**
Re-interviewed:			
Whole 1975 household (17 +)	1,425	56.9	88.6
Not complete, but HOH at least	36	1.4	2.2
No 1975 interview	148	5.9	9.2

Response is high, particularly if the 161 not available to be interviewed are excluded. Most of the reasons for non-availability were because of removals or deaths; they account for about 6.5 per cent of the original sample, a relatively small proportion bearing in mind that a year had elapsed since the original FES interview. Excluding these 161, the re-interview response rate is 91 per cent. In all cases except 36, all members of a household, that is all aged 17 or over, were re-interviewed. In the remaining 36, or 2.2 per cent, interviews were obtained with the HOH, but one other member at least could not be interviewed. It will be seen that complete household income for the two years 1973—74 and 1974—75 was available for about 57 per cent of the original sample.

These re-interviews also provide information on changes in household composition over twelve months, but this is limited of course to those aged 16 or over in 1974. Of the 1,609 available for the second set of interviews, changes in composition had occurred in 147, or 9.1 per cent. Most households (101) had lost one or more members through removal or death; 39 households had gained someone aged 17 or over without losing any of their 1974 members, while the remaining 7 had both lost and gained members. Some of the losses can be explained by a young person leaving his or her original household and setting up a new household elsewhere.

16.5 Feasibility studies for a Wealth Survey

Surveys into savings, investments, finances and other assets present many difficulties, not least that of securing cooperation from an adequate proportion of the sample. At best, such a survey may appear to the public as no better than a statistical exercise without practical justification except to gratify some academic curiosity. In this respect, a Wealth Survey stands in marked contrast to the FES, for which good reasons can be advanced and which are acceptable to the majority of the population. At worst, it can arouse suspicions as to the future intentions of government policy on taxation. Even where an interviewer does not initially share these feelings, exposure to those who do in the course of fieldwork may lead to a loss in interviewer morale and ultimately to a decision to give up working on the survey.

With this background in mind, plans for any survey into the topic are bound to be cautious. It is in this situation that former FES cooperators may be expected to provide a useful sampling frame. Previous cooperation on the FES should provide a useful introduction, and also remove the main core of refusals. It also permits of stratification by various variables and, in particular, the over-sampling of those groups who find serious difficulties in providing the required information.

In the first of two studies the data collected in the course of the FES was used to over-sample for self-employed and those with investment income. A sample of 200 was selected from those who cooperated in the third and fourth quarters of 1974. However, it was restricted to a few areas, 20 in all, so that fieldwork could be concentrated on the more experienced interviewers. The questionnaire put to each person in the sample, and to the spouse if married, was a long one, running to some 80 pages covering the possession of land and other items, financial affairs generally and the business interests of the self-employed. Fieldwork took place in February and March 1976, with the response shown in Table 16.5.1.

Table 16.5.1 Feasibility studies for a Wealth Survey

	1976 Individuals		1977 Households	
	No.	%	No.	%
Re-interview sample from cooperating FES households	200		125	
Moved, or died, before re-inteview	18		2	
Available for re-interview	182	100.0	123	100.0
Interviewed	123	67.6	97*	78.9
Refusals	48	26.4	25	20.3
Non-contacts	11	6.0	1	0.8

Including 6 where only part of household could be interviewed

After excluding 18 removals, 182 were available for this study, of whom 123 were interviewed; a re-interview rate of 68 per cent with 26 per cent refusals and the rest non-contacts. Re-weighting to correct for the over-sampling had little effect. The re-interview response rate was reduced slightly to 67 per cent and the refusal rate increased to 27 per cent. Expressing this in terms of the original sample by applying the FES general response rate to that data gives an overall response rate of only 43 per cent.

Since it was not clear from the first study how the outcome from re-interviewing compared with the response to a completely fresh sample, a second study was made in June 1977. This consisted of 125 households selected from those who had taken part in 25 of the areas worked in February and March 1977 for the FES. The results are shown in the second column of Table 16.5.1.

Although the re-interview rate of 79 per cent is marginally better than that for the first study, the overall response rate was really quite poor being in the range of 50 to 55 per cent, in line with the 56 per cent achieved by a small control sample. This suggests that the re-interview technique had little advantage over a separate and independent sample. Both studies confirm that these topics attract a poor response; indeed, interviewers may encounter active hostility in the field, a possibility that does not appear to have been avoided completely by re-interviewing a sample known to be favourable to cooperation on the FES.

17 Experiments by Social Survey Division into FES techniques

17.1 Work in 1950 and 1951 prior to the FES

The Social Survey began research work on budget surveys several years before the beginning of the FES by conducting six experimental surveys during the period 1950 and 1951. These surveys and their results are described in a Social Survey Report[1] and in a paper to the Royal Statistical Society[2]. To quote the foreword to the latter paper:

'The Ministry of Labour's Household Expenditure Enquiry in 1937/38 provided valuable information about the pattern of expenditure at that time of working-class households in the United Kingdom. As the war was accompanied by severe changes in real incomes and consumption, it was recognized that another inquiry of this kind would be needed after we had emerged from the aftermath of the war and the economic outlook had begun to seem fairly settled. In view of the lack of recent experience in conducting sample surveys on this subject, it seemed advisable before embarking on a new inquiry to investigate the relative efficiency of different methods of collecting the required information.'[3]

This section summarises the main results of these early experiments, many of which influenced the way in which the FES developed. The results confirm that a substantial proportion of consumers' expenditure could not be obtained from the housewife alone, nor could a survey safely be conducted through the post. In an experiment using the mail barely 20 per cent response was obtained when all contact was through the post, while as regards the records thus obtained, about one quarter of the entries could not be assigned to detailed item headings. A substantial proportion of the records were returned late, thus, first arousing doubt as to whether the data related to the correct time period, and secondly delaying processing operations. The data showed considerable discrepancies when compared with interview information; in particular, total expenditure was higher than that from a follow-up interview. In another experiment two types of recording diaries were used; one was an open booklet without headings, while the other was divided into sections corresponding to the main expenditure categories. There was no significant difference between the data in the two booklets. As regards interviews, the experiments did not set out to make a general comparison between information obtained from records and that from interviews. The question did not really arise because even at that early date the two methods were regarded as complimentary rather than competitive. However, some rather fragmentary information was obtained in the course of one experiment. It appeared that interview information about expenditure in the week preceding an interview was somewhat above that recorded in the diaries.

It also appeared that making a payment to record-keepers made a substantial improvement in response rate. In one experiment, each interviewer's quota was divided into three parts; in one part no payment was offered to anyone and 33 per cent of households cooperated; in the second part the equivalent of 25p was given to each household member who cooperated and nearly 45 per cent cooperated; while in the third part 50p was given which led to a response of nearly 50 per cent. It was also found that extending the record keeping period from one week to four weeks led to only a small reduction in response. Checks were also made on the representativeness of cooperating households. There was some under-representation of higher-rated property, of owner-occupiers and the self-employed. The experiments also included two attempts to reconcile expenditure and income. These were so unsuccessful that no further attempts were made until after many years had elapsed. (See Section 17.6).

In an experiment using a four-week record book differences were found between the level of expenditure in the first week and that in subsequent weeks. This feature was subsequently explored in much greater detail in later surveys, especially in the 1953—54 Household Expenditure Enquiry of the Ministry of Labour[4].

Finally, one of the experiments attempted to collect expenditure data by interview asking retrospectively about the previous day's expenditure. The response from complete households was little more than 70 per cent[5].

17.2 Experiment into interviewer variability (1958—1961)

Interviewer variability tends to occur where different interviewers can deal with the same topic in slightly different ways. Where a survey topic is factual and objective there should be little room for interviewer variability, in contrast to the situation when opinions and other subjective topics are under investigation. Spending is an activity where one would not expect to find any room for subjective interpretation or variation. Nevertheless, there are two points in the collection process where some such subjective variation may conceivably occur. First, in the way in which each interviewer deals with individual addresses in the quota. Secondly, there may be some residual element of memory in the collection process even although the main reliance is placed on the 14-day diary.

To test whether these were serious problems various experiments were made in the early days of the FES. For this purpose certain address lists in the standard FES were split into two; instead of the whole list being given to one interviewer, the two half quotas were assigned at random to two interviewers. Fieldwork by both members of the same pair was carried on over the same period and at the same rate. Effectively the two interviewers had equivalent and inter-penetrating samples, but otherwise the standard procedure was undisturbed. This arrangement was applied to a number of areas, and it provided data for making a test into the existence of interviewer variability in a number of variables. For this purpose mean variance within interviewers was compared with mean variance between interviewers, using the F-ratio test as a measure of interviewer variability.

The main work on this problem was carried out in 1958 and the early part of 1959[6]. Quotas were split in 24 of the FES areas. The main finding was that there was no evidence of interviewer variability when a reasonable response rate was achieved by each interviewer separately. On the other hand, variability appeared when an interview with poor response was compared with an interviewer displaying a high response. It would seem that the sample achieved by someone with a poor response was not a representative selection from the pre-selected list of addresses on which the interviewer was working, but was biassed in various directions.

The same technique was later applied to a wide variety of interview questions in surveys carried out from 1958 to 1961[7]. Various methods of estimating expenditure were examined by this technique to see whether any were liable to a significant degree of interviewer variability. Those which required the informant to recall past transactions over a retrospective time period were found to be suspect as displaying the presence of interviewer variability. This, in itself, would seem to be a justification for putting the main reliance on diaries in the FES as a means of collecting expenditure information. The exceptions to this general finding were cases where the expenditure sector consisted only of occasional and infrequent items. In such cases there was no evidence of interviewer variability. The examples given in the paper quoted above included purchases of motor vehicles, and thus helped to justify the treatment of this topic by interview on the main FES schedule.

The other interview technique, which is also used extensively by the FES, estimates expenditure as the product of the last payment and its frequency, and this also came in for some comment in the paper. The most satisfactory results were obtained when the payments occurred regularly, but even then there was some doubt over the data on frequencies. In line with these results the FES questions using the technique are restricted as far as possible to cases where payments occur regularly, even if the actual payments differ from time to time. The method is applied to both expenditure and income estimates, but the question on frequencies has been replaced by one asking about the period covered by the last payment.

17.3 Diary records restricted to food (1960)

In the first quarter of 1960 a small experiment was carried out using the FES interview schedules standard at the time, but with diaries restricted to purchases of food. This was part of an investigation then taking place into differences between the NFS and the FES. The immediate purpose of the experiment was to provide data similar to that from the NFS but under FES conditions. Each household member aged over 15 was interviewed about income, was asked to keep a diary of any food expenditure, and was paid £1 for cooperation.

A total sample of 468 households was selected from 12 out of the 32 areas sampled in the standard FES in the first quarter of 1960; six in each half quarter. The food recorded in the diaries of the standard FES in the same 12 areas was used as a control. The main results are shown in Table 17.3.1.

Table 17.3.1 FES restricted to food — 1960

	Food experiment	Control from FES
Original sample	468	470
Cooperating households	319	292
Response (per cent*)	72.0	65.2
Mean expenditure on food per household per week	£4.63	£4.07

*After excluding ineligible addresses from original sample

The experiment produced a somewhat higher response than the standard FES, but little importance should be attached to this bearing in mind the small samples and the once-off character of the experiment. More to the point is that restricting the diaries to food appears to have led to a higher recorded expenditure. While the samples were too small to say whether the higher expenditure of 14 per cent was restricted to any individual food categories, it was noted that a consistently higher proportion of experimental households recorded expenditure under any given food heading compared with the position in the control group. There was also definite evidence of inter-week bias. Recorded expenditure in the first seven days was higher than in the second seven; by 5 per cent in the experiment and 4 per cent in the control.

The general conclusion from this small scale experiment would seem to be that limiting the coverage of diaries to a single topic (food) has resulted in a higher recording. Why this is so is more difficult to explain. Several factors may be involved; behavioural change, differential response and memory. It has been argued earlier that memory probably plays only a small part, but differential response may well be involved. Although whole households were included in the interview, most of the recording burden will have fallen on the housewife, so that the kind of households which cooperate or refuse may differ slightly from the standard FES. Behavioural change may well differ also from that in the FES since temporary changes in spending behaviour need only apply to a small sector of expenditure.

17.4 Acquisitions of durable goods over past 3 months (1966)

Very little information on the outright purchases of durable goods is collected by interview in the standard FES. Most data on these topics are obtained from diary entries. The exceptions are acquisitions on hire purchase and similar credit schemes, and since 1968 outright purchases of motor vehicles. In 1966 an attempt was made to find out whether the preliminary interview could be extended to collect information about the acquisition of consumer durables over a retrospective period of three months. At that time the old sample design of 128 areas a year was still in use, and for the 1966 experiment all 32 areas drawn in the fourth quarter were used. Each was divided into two equal, random, inter-penetrating sub-samples. In one sub-sample, the control, the standard FES procedure was used; while in the other sub-sample the additional questions on durable goods were put to each household member in addition to the standard interview. All co-operating households also completed diary records. Furthermore, in 16 of the 32 areas extra samples were drawn additional to the main samples and equal to them in size. These extra samples were drawn with the main purpose of trying out an extended income interview schedule. But each was also split into two equal, inter-penetrating sub samples. The durable goods experiment was extended to the extra samples by treating one sub-sample in each area as the experimental group, putting the questions on durable goods to households in that sub-sample and taking the other sub-sample as the control group. In both main and extra samples the experimental and control groups were balanced as regards area and interviewer. The response rates achieved in the experimental and control groups are shown in Table 17.4.1.

Table 17.4.1 1966 Experiment with durable goods schedule

	No durable goods schedule (Control group)	Additional schedule (Experimental group)	Whole sample
FES main sample Q IV 1966			
Effective sample	603	590	1,193
Cooperating households	434	430	864
Response rate(%)	72.0	72.9	72.4
Extra sample			
Effective sample	304	297	601
Cooperating households	209	223	432
Response rate(%)	68.8	75.1	71.9
Main and Extra samples			
Effective sample	907	887	1,794
Cooperating households	643	653	1,296
Response rate(%)	70.9	73.6	72.2

While it is evident that the extra schedule of questions did not result in a loss of public cooperation, it should not be concluded that the reverse was true. In both the main and extra samples the additional schedule produced a slightly higher response rate than the corresponding control group, but this probably came about because the interviewers would have made an extra effort to deal with something new and unusual. The remainder of this section deals with the data on durable goods reported by the 653 co-operating households in the combined main and extra samples. The results from the income part of the experiment form the subject of the next section. The durable goods schedule asked about expenditure in the three months retrospective to the date of interview. For this period each person was asked which, if any, of a list of 23 electrical appliances had been purchased outright, whether any motor vehicles had been bought outright, or payments made to a builder or contractor for heating in-

stallations, additions, alterations, repairs or decorations to the household accommodation.

Only about 1 in 3 of the 653 households answering the additional schedule had items to report, and then usually only one or two. Consequently, little extra field time was involved in handling the extra questions. The median time of interview per household was about five minutes, compared with a total of one hour to one and a half hours spent in interviewing household members prior to the commencement of diary records in the FES. For the experiment a separate questionnaire was provided for each adult, but in view of the short time required to get the extra information and because most household members are interviewed together, it would have been more convenient to deal with these topics on a household basis.

Since the information was obtained by interview for a retrospective period, the validity of the results depends on the accuracy of recall. It is not possible to devise a direct test as to whether items were forgotten, but some check was made by examining whether informants appeared to know exactly when items were acquired on the assumption that confusion over dates is likely to lead to incorrect reporting. With this in mind the additional schedule called for the exact date of acquisition, both month and date of the day. Altogether 391 items were reported as acquired within three months preceding the date of interview. For 64 of these the informant was unable to specify the exact date of acquisition. When analysed according to the interval between month of acquisition and the month of interview, a distinct and progressive failure of memory was found, increasing with the length of reference period. It was concluded that information on all categories of durable goods was liable to a margin of uncertainty which was likely to be more serious for small items such as radios and electric fires[8].

An attempt was also made to compare expenditure data from the additional durable goods schedule with the corresponding entries in the diaries of the control group. This was not made without some difficulty because whereas the diaries produced an even flow of data, the interview information came from a three-month period prior to the date of interview which itself was spread over three months; thus the number of weeks covered by the recall tailed in and out. After correcting the experimental data by reweighting to improve comparability with the control data, it appeared that the average expenditure per household in the experimental group was higher than that in the control group by nearly half as much again. Further examination showed that the experimental group recorded fewer purchases per household-week than the control group, but that purchases which were recorded were larger than the average purchases in the control group.

17.5 Income questionnaire experiments (1966—1967)

Information on income has often been regarded as being more difficult to collect than expenditure. Many early budget surveys ignored income or confined their interest to the earnings of the chief wage earner. Even when some information was collected, it was often only for classificatory purposes and the details were brief and simple.

In keeping with this attitude, the income schedules used in the early years of the FES, although covering all major income sources, were deliberately restricted in length. With increasing experience over the years it became clear that improvements could be made to the clarity of the data by using more elaborate questions; particularly by adding supplementary questions to deal with complex and unusual circumstances. However, the Social Survey were inhibited from making any progress along these lines by the need to keep the income schedule to its then current size of 4 pages, because at that time it was thought that heavy and long documents would discourage interviewers and lead to a loss of public cooperation.

In 1966 all the interview schedules were subjected to a thorough review, and the opportunity was taken of testing a greatly expanded questionnaire. This was 12 pages in length and spelled out in greater detail certain kinds of situations not clearly defined in the current schedule, often by the use of additional dependent questions. The main difference was in the treatment of multiple jobs. In the standard income schedule of that time only the most remunerative job was dealt with in full; any others were supposed to be picked up by a question about miscellaneous income; some of the dangers inherent in this procedure are explained in Section 12.7. In the experimental schedule each job, subsidiary as well as main, was treated separately and in full. The opportunity was also taken of employing a wider definition of 'working'; hitherto, the standard Social Survey practice had been to ignore jobs of 10 hours or less a week. Among other changes were a more detailed treatment of absences from work, occasional bonuses and other additions to pay, information on earnings for periods prior to the last pay, a more detailed treatment of income tax and the inclusion of questions on certain forms of windfall income.

This extended schedule was tried out in the last half quarter of 1966, that is in the second half of the period covered by the durable goods experiment described in the previous section. It was restricted to the same 8 areas from which the extra sample for the second half quarter of the durable goods experiment was drawn. A 2×2 factorial, experimental design was used; one factor was the extended income schedule versus the standard version; the other factor contrasted the presence or absence of the durable goods schedule. The sample in each of the 8 areas consisted of four equal, interpenetrating sub-sambles, one for each of the four treatments in the 2 x 2 factorial design. Since the two sub-samples using the standard income schedule formed part of the standard FES, the time allocated to the experiment had to conform to the FES programme. However, the total quota in each of the areas was too large for a single interviewer to handle in the time available, so 2 or 3 interviewers were employed in each area. The quotas given to each interviewer consisted as far as possible of equal numbers of each treatment so that the design was balanced by area and interviewer. The total numbers assigned to

the 4 treatments are shown in Table 17.5.1. (Incidentally, they also form part of the cases included in Table 17.4.1, and as in that table the two upper cells were part of the standard FES.)

Table 17.5.1 1966 Income Experiment

	No durable goods schedule	Additional durable goods schedule	All
Standard income schedule B			
Effective sample	152	152	304
Cooperating households	103	104	207
Response rate(%)	67.8	68.4	68.1
Extended income schedule			
Effective sample	149	149	298
Cooperating households	103	110	213
Response rate(%)	69.1	73.8	71.5
All households in experiment			
Effective sample	301	301	602
Cooperating households	206	214	420
Response rate(%)	68.4	71.1	69.8

It will be seen that the sub-samples using the extended income schedule produced a higher response rate, 71.5 per cent, compared with the simpler schedule, 68.1 per cent. Moreover, the response for the whole FES sample for the fourth quarter 1976 was 72.4 per cent. A possible interpretation is that interviewers found it necessary to exert more effort with the longer income schedule and the extended durable goods schedule in order to maintain their normal performance, but that this was at the expense of the simpler cases; hence the relatively low response of 67.8 per cent in the upper left-hand cell. However, an analysis of variance on the four cells showed that the treatment differences were not significant, nor was the difference between the 67.8 per cent achieved by the standard cases in the experiment and the overall 72.4 per cent of the standard FES.

The most reassuring part of the experiment was that it showed that the extended income schedule had in no way led to diminished public cooperation. At the time this was a most important conclusion since it implied that a longer schedule could be incorporated in the standard FES without serious adverse reactions from the public. In fact, the new 1968 schedule consisted of 8 pages, double the size of its predecessor, thus enabling many of the improvements piloted in the experiment to be included.

Perhaps the most important change was the treatment of subsidiary jobs which from that time have always been the subject of a separate set of questions. Another innovation tried out in the experiment was not adopted; this was an attempt to collect data on earnings for periods preceding the last pay; for the weekly-paid, questions had been asked in the experiment about earnings for the three pay weeks prior to interview and for monthly-paid the previous two months' earnings. The attempt was not an unqualified success because so many of the answers were estimates by informants unsubstantiated by pay slips. Accordingly, the 1968 schedules continued the previous practice of limiting the main earnings questions to pay received last time.

Another idea given a trial run in the experiment was the collection of data on windfalls, such as payments received from insurance policies, sales of household goods, legacies and winnings from Premium Bonds. The questions appeared to produce the required information but the incidence was so low that the whole proposal was dropped not to be revived until 1976 when several questions on windfalls were added to the income schedule.

One other consequence of this experiment deserves mention. Records were kept of the interviewing situation in each household, and it was found that, excluding one-spender households, joint interviews were held in about two-thirds of households. This was something of a suprise to many of those concerned with the FES, and was contrary to well-established opinion. From the earliest days it had been considered advisable to interview each person separately, particularly about income, and if possible in isolation from the rest of the household. While it was accepted that some joint interviews were inevitable, it was believed to be essential to keep the number to a minimum otherwise there would be a risk of losing public support. However, over the years the Social Survey had succeeded in getting much more income data than had ever been thought possible before the days of the FES. The interviewing procedure gradually developed could not therefore be faulted on this score.

With this background in mind a special exercise was carried out at the end of 1967 to discover what actually happened in different interviewing situations. The months November and December 1967 were chosen for this second experiment in order to give interviewers as much time as possible to become accustomed to the new sample design introduced at the beginning of that year but before re-designed schedules were brought in for 1968. For this study special records were kept by interviewers in 89 out of the 112 areas used in these two months. For each household, interviewers recorded the times the interviews began and ended on each schedule, and the reasons for taking separate or joint interviews. In all, records were kept for 904 cooperating households. This showed that, excluding time spent introducing the survey, explaining its purpose and the use of the diaires, just over 50 minutes on average was taken up with interviewing each household, of which the income schedules accounted for 20 minutes.

However, the information more immediately relevant to the present purpose is that derived from the times of start and finish of the interview on each income schedule. This information is reproduced in Table 17.5.2.

Table 17.5.2 **Number of different times given for B schedules in the same household**

Number of spenders (16 +)	1	2	3	4	5	6	All
1	157						157
2	355	175					530
3	59	44	54				157
4	13	14	9	10			46
5	2	1	6	1			10
6	1					1	2
7					1	1	2
	587	234	69	11	1	2	904

This table was compiled by comparing the times of interviews for each spender; for example, if in a two-person household the starting and finishing times were identical the household was classified into the first column as a joint interview; if not, it was put into the second column. From this table it can be seen immediately that a substantial proportion of households with two or more spenders were interviewed jointly. Out of 747 households with two or more spenders, 430 or 58 per cent, were joint in the sense just described. Furthermore, in many of the more complex households two or more spenders were interviewed together and only one or two separately. For instance in a three-spender household, besides the 59 completely joint interviews there were 44 where a pair were taken together and only one separately.

This, however, was not the full measure of joint interviewing when account was taken of interviewer comments and of those present during each interview. From interviewers' comments about two-spender households it was clear that in most of the 175 households in the second column of Table 17.5.2 both spenders had been present throughout both interviews. In only 42 out of the 175 did it appear that each spender was interviewed separately without the other being present, usually on separate days, but if on the same day, at different times. Even more relevant to the main purpose of the experiment was the finding that in only two out of 42 cases of separate interviews had one or other of the two spenders actually asked for a completely separate interview. Apart from these two cases, the reasons given for separate interviews were either that it was more convenient to take them separately or that both spenders were not at home together at the time when the interviewer called.

Similar circumstances applied to the larger and more complex households. When members were not interviewed together it was usually because one member was not available at the same time as the others or because one member, such as a young person, wished to go out for the evening before interviewing had been completed for the whole family. There were extremely few cases where an informant asked for an interview entirely separate from the rest of the household. Because of the importance of confidentiality it has long been FES interviewing practice that if anyone is dubious about revealing income details in the presence of other spenders or child household members, then the interviewer asks the informant to write the details directly on to the interview schedule instead of giving the details orally. The 355 joint two-spender households were examined for this possibility, but in fewer than 10 cases did it appear that any income details had had to be collected in such a way as to ensure that they were not overheard by others present at the interview. Similar results were found with larger households.

The general conclusion from this study, was that the provision of separate schedules for each household member was unnecessary, and moreover, especially inconvenient where the interviewer had to complete two or three income schedules at one and the same time. It would be better to have recording spaces for two or more persons on the same form, and this would have the further advantage that when details for a husband and wife are entered on the same schedule it might sometimes be easier to edit the data on a tax unit basis. As experience had shown that the main interviewing could not proceed until all or most household members were present together, and this study confirmed that it was rarely essential for any member to be interviewed entirely separately, it was decided to change the basic schedule design.

Following this experiment a small scale pilot was carried out in mid 1969 with a three-person schedule. The general reaction from the Field was favourable, partly because it was easier to handle and partly because it presented a less formidable appearance to informants. The only serious criticism was that three sets of columns side by side led to a cramped design, and one that was difficult to scan across to find the correct recording box. As a compromise, a two-person design with two columns of recording spaces on the right was adopted in 1970, and this has remained a feature of the basic design ever since.

17.6 Family Budget Survey experiments (1976 and 1978)

Arising out of the need to assess the accuracy of record-keeping by FES respondents a new record keeping methodology was devised which would act as a control against the FES (see Section 14.5). This methodology, called the Family Budget Survey (FBS), required radically new tasks of interviewers and informants alike as it involved arithmetically balancing all outgoings against all incomings over a 14 day period. Two FBS experiments were carried out to test this methodology — one, the Family Budget Survey Experiment (FBSE), held in February 1976 and the other, the Family Budget Survey Pilot (FBSP) held during four weeks covering February—March 1978.

Informants were given diaries which provided for daily entries of cash outgoings on the left hand page, faced by a page where they could record daily cash incomings. Prior to recording cash outgoings and incomings during the day, they were asked to count separately all cash in pocket and cash set aside in the house. At the end of the recording day, they were asked to count all cash in pocket and cash set aside. Counting cash acted as a control on accuracy of record keeping. Accounts were balanced each day by adding incomings received during the day to cash in hand at the beginning and then subtracting outgoings. The resulting difference should have equalled the cash in hand they had counted at the end of the day. Any discrepancy could be attributed either to missing outgoings or incomings, depending on the sign of the difference. Interviewers were asked to follow up any discrepancy when they made mid-week calls and to probe for missing items.

Both experiments were designed to try to help informants record all transactions, and a number of consistency checks were designed to test the adequacy and comprehensiveness of the records. Not only were there daily cash balancing checks on accuracy, but because changes in balances were recorded for bank and savings accounts as well, it was possible to check the accuracy of withdrawals and deposits. Furthermore, it was possible to check accuracy of record keeping by comparing amounts passing between accounts, eg the amount of cash received from cashing a cheque (recorded as an incoming to cash) should equal the amount of the cheque drawn in the bank account. Also intra-household transfers could be checked by comparing the separate diaries of spenders.

In addition, a further step was adopted to try to maximise record keeping accuracy. It was assumed that balancing daily entries of incomings and outgoings would be most effective in discovering missing entries if the arithmetic balancing was carried out by either informants or interviewers. In order to assist in this, interviewers were provided with pocket calculators and daily cash reconciliation sheets. This was an innovation, as normally all arithmetic calculations on the FES are carried out by either Primary Analysis Branch or by the FES Research Unit; however, it was felt that if discrepancies were calculated in head office, there would be too great a lapse in time for informants to remember missing amounts.

In the first experiment, the FBSE, interviewers were given the option of offering special diaries enabling the informant to balance arithmetically his or her own cash transactions each day during the second 7 days of record keeping. It was thought that if informants themselves balanced cash transactions and found amounts to be missing, their memories would be fresher about these missing amounts. If successful, balancing by informants would be preferred to balancing by interviewers who were only able to balance accounts twice during the 14 days. The results of the attempt to get informants to remember missing amounts were disappointing. First, only 12.5 per cent of missing amounts were fully accounted for by informants; 8.5 per cent were partly accounted for. Second, there were several biases in the characteristics of the sample who were willing to balance their own records. Examination of the characteristics of those who successfully balanced their records showed that they tend to be male, under 60 years of age and non-manual employees. The amounts that were remembered were not alcohol or tobacco expenditure. (See Section 14.5(i).)

Finally, there was a marked difference in arithmetic accuracy between informants and interviewers. Interviewers balanced informants' diaries during the first week; therefore a comparison could be made at coding stage between the arithmetic accuracy of informants and interviewers. Interviewers, (provided with pocket calculators and a special balance sheet) had arithmetic accuracy ranging from 95 to 98 per cent, when measured as a ratio of all calculations. Informants' accuracy rate was only 51 per cent. (Admittedly, informants were not issued with pocket calculators.)

In consequence, it was decided not to ask informants to balance their own diaries in the second experiment, the FBSP, which was undertaken to give further evidence of the findings of the FBSE. The record-keeping standard of informants in both experiments was very high and consistent between both experiments. Cash incomings were perfectly balanced against cash outgoings for 3088 out of 3696 recording days (83.5 per cent) in the FBSE sample. FBSP informants achieved an equivalent proportion (83 per cent). However, the proportions of informants who kept perfect records throughout the entire fortnight was far lower: 32.7 per cent (FBSE) and 31 per cent (FBSP). Nevertheless, the amount of unrecorded cash over the fortnight was small. On the FBSP, the amount of unrecorded expenditure per household per week was £0.46, only 1 per cent of total outgoings. Unrecorded incomings were slightly higher (£0.52 per household per week).

The main purpose of the experiments had been to provide a control of accurate record keeping against which record keeping on the FES could be measured (See Chapter 14). Alcohol and tobacco expenditure recording was of particular interest. As shown in Table 14.5.1, the balancing methodology did not appear to improve record-keeping of alcohol and tobacco expenditure. This implied that record-keeping on the FES was as accurate as on the FBSE and FBSP, where great pains had been taken to ensure accurate record-keeping. Furthermore, even if the entire unrecorded outgoings of £0.46 are assigned *arbitrarily* to the alcohol or tobacco expenditure average in Table 14.5.1, this would by no means account for the discrepancies with National Accounts shown in Table 14.3.1. The conclusion was that under-recording of alcohol and tobacco expenditure was not a substantive cause of the discrepancies with National Accounts estimates.

These conclusions need to be tempered by the fact that sample sizes for the FBSE and FBSP were small: 113 and 126 households respectively, and hence differences thrown up by comparisons with the FES are not statistically significant. Also response for both experiments was low: 57 per cent and 59 per cent, respectively; this amounted to 10—14 per cent below the FES in the same period. However, comparison of the income distributions of the FES and FBSP showed them to be virtually identical.

Several points can be made about the FBS methodology. First, the balancing of all outgoings against all incomings yields intra-household transfers, something that the FES does not. Results from both experiments were identical: 83 per cent of all money transferred within a sample household was given to the wife/mother. Second, the methodology appears to have provided a better measure of savings (during the 14 days) than the FES; this could be attributed to asking informants interview questions about outgoing and incoming transactions in separate bank and savings accounts and asking them to note changes in balances over the 14 days. (The FES, on the other hand, relies on savings entries made in diaries and does not emphasise consulting savings accounts). Third, the balancing methodology also seemed successful in overcoming 'end-period' effect, probably because informants counted cash before starting records; how-

ever, there was greater inter-week bias for alcohol and tobacco expenditure than in the FES. The major drawbacks to the methodology are low response and response bias by age, which appeared to be greater than on the FES. One conclusion was that this methodology was not suitable for the elderly. One reason given was that the methodology revealed too much and did not allow informants to 'keep any secrets' about their financial affairs. Despite this, a higher proportion of those aged 60 and over kept perfect records for the fortnight than any other age group.

An additional drawback of the FBSE and FBSP design was that balancing was only carried out over 14 days; this meant that only the accuracy of incomings received weekly, fortnightly and (some) monthly, could be tested with certainty. The time reference period would have to be extended for income sources like dividends and interest, occupational pensions and probably also for self-employment income. However response would almost certainly be lower still if informants were asked to balance accounts over a quarter, a half-year or a year.

Finally, certain diagnostic questions were asked of FBSE informants at the end of the 14 days. Of particular methodological interest were the answers to two questions. First, informants were asked:

'For how long would (each of) you be prepared to keep records?'

193 out of 264 spenders (73 per cent) said that they would be prepared to keep records for four weeks or longer. However, when replies were analysed by the condition of 100 per cent co-operation for all spenders in the same household, only 45 per cent of all households would have cooperated*.

FBSE informants were also asked if they thought that keeping records had affected their normal spending in any way. Only 12.7 per cent of all spenders felt that their spending had been affected, these mentioned cutting spending because they became more aware of prices or because they realised how much they were spending on smoking, drinking and luxuries. (In an earlier study, 20 per cent of women and 5 per cent of men co-operating in the FES thought that record keeping had affected their spending[11]). However, it is worth noting that 69 per cent of those who felt that their spending behaviour had not changed, in fact, had increases or decreases of 10 per cent or more in expenditure between the weeks. The conclusion drawn is that relatively few people are consciously aware of changes in levels of expenditure during record keeping. It is also true that there was not a systematic change in expenditure between the weeks throughout the sample: 109 spenders increased spending in the second week, 116 spenders decreased spending in the second week. This suggests that behavioural change due to record-keeping is not uniform nor systematic in one direction, even though there is an overall net decrease in spending between the first and second weeks.

---

*The figure of 45 per cent is very similar to Kemsley's estimate of 47 per cent of the original samples[9]. It is also remarkably close to the figure of 44 per cent found by Sudman and Ferber[10].

17.7 Feasibility study into Annual Income (November 1976)

One of the recommendations of the FES Task Force was that OPCS examine the feasibility of providing income information over a consistent 12 months' period, retrospectively from the time of interview. This would be particularly useful for the Central Statistical Office use of the FES in its income distribution studies. Data from the FES is used to estimate non-taxable incomes and is merged with income data from the Inland Revenue Survey of Personal Incomes, which itself is given on a 12 months financial year basis.[1][2]

Preliminary work based on the OPCS Census Interview Follow-up to the 1 per cent Postal Income Survey held in June 1972 had shown that the Inland Revenue P60 form could provide a reliable source of employee earnings for the tax year. However, it was realised that tax year figures could become quickly out-of-date, particularly in periods of rising wage inflation. Furthermore, there had been no attempt to validate the 12 month estimates of those who did not possess P60 forms. Therefore, it was decided that a further feasibility study should be carried out which depended on wage slips as a source of 12 months' earnings estimates. If employees could produce 12 month pay slips records, then it might be feasible to obtain accurate 12 month figures. The study also would investigate the feasibility of obtaining 12 months estimates for certain sources of income besides wages and salaries.

During November 1976, interviewers were given the option of asking informants to participate in a short supplementary interview following the completion of the main interview and before the introduction of record keeping. Out of an effective sample of 1188 informants, 1014 (85.4 per cent) cooperated in the Feasibility Study. Only 0.3 per cent refused; the remaining 14.3 per cent were not offered the supplementary questionnaire by interviewers, who were concerned that cooperation in record keeping might be jeopardised.

There were 541 informants whose main source of income was from wages and salaries. The charcteristics of the November sample compared closely with those of the 1976 FES; however, the November sample had a higher proportion of inactive or unemployed and manual workers. Also, when comparing the distribution of pay period with that of the 1976 New Earnings Survey, the November study had a higher proportion of weekly-paid workers (73 per cent) than the New Earnings Survey (62 per cent).

Co-operating informants were asked what records they kept of their main source of income. Those giving wages/salary as their main source were asked to estimate their earnings from employment over the previous 12 months. They were then given a self-completion form to complete during the fortnight onto which they copied details taken from their pay slips for the past 12 months.

The main purpose of the study was to ascertain the proportions of informants who could produce pay slips or other records (depending on the income source) for 12 months. (Normally, interviewers ask FES informants to try to obtain the pay slips of the last pay received, and this is done by 70—80 per cent of all employees).

Two hundred and seventy-nine (52 per cent) of the 541 co-operating employees whose main income was wages/salary said that they kept pay slips as a record of their pay (43 per cent of the weekly paid and 77 per cent of the monthly paid said that they kept them).

Tables 17.7.1 and 17.7.2 relate to the 190 employees (68 per cent of 279) who had only one job, whose pay periods were weekly or monthly and who recorded pay slips. The results show that the coverage provided by the pay slips they recorded deteriorated rapidly as the record went back in time — especially in the case of weekly-paid workers.

Table 17.7.1 Pay slips recorded by those weekly-paid informants who said that they kept them - percentage of informants with pay slips covering at least . . . weeks by different measures of coverage*

Percentage	Number of weeks/pay slips												
	1	5	10	15	20	25	30	35	40	45	50	52	Base (=100%)
recording at least . . . pay slips	97	78	67	56	54	47	38	33	29	18	10	3	116
with an uninterrupted record of at least . . . pay slips	81	49	32	24	20	18	15	11	10	9	7	2	116
whose earliest pay slip for the reference year is at least . . . weeks before interview	96	88	77	75	68	65	60	50	45	41	33	31	116

This table is restricted to individuals who had only one job during the preceding 12 months.

Table 17.7.2 Pay slips recorded by those monthly-paid informants who said that they kept them - percentage of informants with pay slips covering at least . . . months by different measures of coverage*

Percentage	Number of months/pay slips												
	1	2	3	4	5	6	7	8	9	10	11	12	Base (=100%)
recording at least . . . pay slips	100	96	91	89	86	84	81	77	76	72	62	49	74
with an uninterrupted record of at least . . . pay slips	93	84	78	77	76	74	73	65	64	61	58	49	74
whose earliest pay slip for the reference year is at least . . . months before interview	100	96	92	92	91	91	88	81	80	78	74	66	74

This table is restricted to individuals who had only one job during the preceding 12 months.

There is room for disagreement about how complete a record would be necessary to obtain reasonably accurate 12 months' earnings data. However in broad terms the picture that emerges is that about half the monthly paid workers, but only about 10 per cent of weekly paid workers, have a complete or nearly complete set of pay slips for the previous 12 months. This casts serious doubt on the feasibility of collecting accurate 12 months earnings figures from pay slips.

There was evidence that other records (P60's and bank statements) were kept by weekly-paid workers. However, it would be necessary to obtain deductions from wages; this ruled out bank statements which only give net income. The reason for ruling out P60's has already been given.

Additional work was carried out to test the validity of informants' initial 12 months estimates against the figures recorded from their pay slips. Unfortunately there were only 55 cases which provided sufficiently full 12 month records and out of these, there were only 12 weekly paid employees. Comparisons were nevertheless made between informants' estimates and their pay slips for the 12 months. Over 70 per cent were able to give estimates which were within ± 10 per cent of their actual earnings. Mainly there appeared to be a tendency to under-estimate actual earnings. However, it was difficult to assume that results of this validation could be applied to the remaining 486 employees whose estimates could not be validated, as keeping records was likely to improve estimates.

Unemployment Benefit, Sickness Benefit, Invalidity Pension and Allowance, and Industrial Injury Benefit were major sources for which 12 months' receipts from State Benefits would be sought. The November experiment also included questions on the General Household Survey which simply asked if records were kept of these benefits; however it was not noted whether records were complete for the full 12 months, as was done on the FES. Table 17.7.3 shows the results of the record keeping question on the GHS.

Table 17.7.3 Whether or not beneficiaries of Unemployment, Sickness and Invalidity benefit during the past 12 months had any record of income received

	Unemployment benefit		Sickness benefit		Invalidity benefit	
	No. of benefici-aries	%	No. of benefici-aries	%	No. of benefici-aries	%
Record kept	11	17	15	11	10	59
No record kept	53	83	115	89	7	41
	64	100	130	100	17	100

Source: General Household Survey, November 1976.

The picture here too is discouraging. Although 59 per cent of GHS informants receiving invalidity benefit kept some record of the income received, the proportions keeping Unemployment benefit records and Sickness benefit records were far lower: 17 per cent and 11 per cent respectively.

Overall, the conclusion was that moving to a 12 months income period would not be feasible if consultation of records was an important assurance of accuracy. Weekly-paid employees form the majority of employees and they are least likely to keep payslips. Nothing definite could be concluded about the accuracy of earnings estimates made without consulting records. Twelve month reference periods are used in the United States but only where income is a classificatory variable; on FES it is used to estimate individual income sources.

Further work has been carried out by the CSO on the November 1976 data.

17.8 Informants' definitions of annual earnings and usual earnings (1979)

Background

In June 1979 a further experiment was carried out to test the feasibility of obtaining accurate annual gross income data. Unlike the Annual Income Feasibility Study (Section 17.7) the June experiment concentrated only on earnings from employment, as wages and salaries comprise over 75% of all household income sources.

The Annual Income Feasibility Study had validated estimates by informants of 12 months' earnings, using 12 months' actual earnings obtained from their pay slip records; however, it had not attempted to ask informants how they arrived at their estimates. Therefore one of the purposes of the June experiment was to try to discover how informants arrived at their 12 months' earnings estimates, eg by consulting documents or by some form of arithmetic reasoning or by vague reckoning. This would help determine whether there was a logical basis for the estimates. However, in the June experiment, 12 months' estimates were validated by P60 forms, which gave 12 months' earnings over the tax year (5 April 1978 to 5 April 1979).

The other purpose of the experiment was to discover how informants define their 'usual earnings'. The FES Income questionnaire has for many years included a question which asks employees whether their last pay received is their 'usual pay' (Section 12.7). If the last pay is not the usual pay, employees, are then asked to give their usual gross and net pay. There has never been an attempt by SSD interviewers to define the period over which informants should calculate 'usual pay'. This has been left up to informants. However, there is interest in the period over which informants estimate their 'usual wages or salary', as usual pay forms the basis of the normal gross income from wages and salaries which is used by DE in the FES income definition (see Appendix 7 of the *1978 FES Annual Report*).

Finally, as shown in Section 17.7, there was evidence in the Annual Income Feasibility Study that some weekly-paid workers did not keep records of pay to the same extent as monthly-paid workers.

As in the Annual Income Feasibility study, SSD interviewers asked informants to participate (on a voluntary basis) in a short interview following the completion of the main FES interview and prior to record-keeping. One main difference between the two studies was that in the November 1976 experiment informants were allowed 14 days to search out pay slip records, whereas the June 1979 experiment did not stress this.

There were 520 employees in the June sample: 321 weekly-paid workers; 6 fortnightly-paid, 12 four-weekly paid and 177 calendar-monthly paid employees as well as 4 others with longer pay periods. (The proportion of weekly-paid workers (62 per cent) coincided exactly with that found in the New Earnings Survey in 1976.)

Annual earnings estimates
Informants were first asked to give their gross earnings over the 12 months (ending last Saturday) for all jobs. Then they were asked:

'Would you explain how you arrived at this figure for your annual wages/salary?'

In the event 466 employees provided answers to the questions. In 83—85 per cent of all cases it appears that a considered approach was taken to the problem of estimating earnings over 12 months, either by searching for documents or by carrying out arithmetic calculations. Roughly the same proportion of weekly-paid and monthly-paid workers consulted some document (pay slip, P60 etc) before giving an answer, 34 per cent and 36 per cent respectively. Also, exactly the same proportion (49 per cent) used some form of arithmetic reasoning to give an estimate. Above all, the proportion of weekly-paid employees who based annual estimates on only one pay slip was virtually the same as for monthly-paid workers (5 per cent and 4 per cent respectively). This indicates that there were no differences between weekly-and monthly-paid workers in their arithmetic or documentary approach to the problem of estimating 12 months' earnings. The problem still remains of how accurate these estimates of annual earnings are compared to the current approach in the FES, which is based on the last pay slip, and where records are produced in over 70 per cent of cases.

Usual pay experiment
Question 15 of the Income Schedule asks (of employees):

'Your last wages/salary was £........ Is this the amount you usually receive?'

Those who say 'No' are then asked what their usual gross and net pay are. Having once established the usual pay, employees in the June experiment were then asked questions about the length of period over which they had been receiving their 'usual' pay.

As pointed out in Sections 12.7 and 15.3, FES informants are left to define what they mean by 'usual pay'; it is a subjective concept. The purpose of the experiment was to find out how usual pay was defined by informants.

Ten per cent of the sample did not answer the question. Of the 466 employees who did answer the question, roughly 70 per cent said their pay was usual, and the remaining 30 per cent said their pay was not usual. Thirty-four per cent of weekly-paid workers (99 out of 292) said their last pay was not usual; this was 10 per cent higher than the proportion of monthly-paid workers whose last pay was said not to be usual (43 out of 174). Therefore weekly-paid workers' pay seemed less stable than monthly-paid workers' pay.

The answers to the questions which asked informants how long a period they took into account when defining usual pay are illuminating. The results are shown in Table 17.8.1.

Seventy-two per cent of responding employees took into consideration periods of longer than 2 months; however, only 38 per cent considered periods from six months onwards. The overall modal group lies in the two to six month period (34 per cent of all employees).

The four-weekly and calendar monthly-paid employees show a higher cumulative proportion of periods for longer than six months (48 per cent) than weekly and fortnightly-paid workers (31 per cent).

Table 17.8.2. again shows the length of period taken into account when estimating usual pay, cross-analysed by pay period. However, there is a further cross-analysis according to whether or not the last pay received was said to be the usual pay.

It is apparent that where the last pay is not the usual pay, the usual pay estimate is less stable. Table 17.8.2 shows that 41 per cent of those whose last pay was usual had the impression that they had received that pay for longer than six months; This can be compared with those whose last pay was not usual where only 29 per cent thought they had received their usual pay for longer than six months.

Table 17.8.1 Length of period taken into account in estimating usual earnings by period of payment

Length of period	Period of payment								
	Weekly and fortnightly			Four weekly and monthly			Total		
	No.	%	Cum %	No.	%	Cum %	No.	%	Cum %
One month	56	19	19	24	14	14	80	17	17
From one month up to and including 2 months	39	13	32	15	9	23	54	11	28
From 2 months up to and including 6 months	108	37	69	51	29	52	159	34	62
From 6 months up to and including one year	29	10	79	38	22	74	67	14	76
One year	26	9	88	33	19	93	59	13	89
More than one year	34	12	100	13	7	100	47	11	100
Total	292	100		174	100		466	100	

Table 17.8.2 Length of period taken into account in estimating usual earnings by period of payment by whether (i) last pay was not usual pay or (ii) last pay was usual pay

Length of period	Period of payment								
	Weekly and fortnightly			Four weekly and monthly			Total		
	No.	%	Cum %	No.	%	Cum %	No.	%	Cum %
	(i) last pay was not usual pay								
One month	37	37	37	12	28	28	49	35	35
From one month up to and including 2 months	13	13	50	2	5	33	15	10	45
From 2 months up to and including 6 months	23	23	73	14	32	65	37	26	71
From 6 months up to and including one year	8	8	81	3	7	72	11	8	79
One year	7	7	88	9	21	93	16	11	90
More than one year	11	11	99	3	7	100	14	10	100
Total	99	99		43	100		142	100	
	(ii) last pay was usual pay								
One month	19	10	10	12	9	9	31	9	9
From one month up to and including 2 months	26	13	23	13	10	19	39	12	21
From 2 months up to and including 6 months	85	44	67	37	28	47	122	38	59
From 6 months up to and including one year	21	11	78	35	27	74	56	17	76
One year	19	10	88	24	18	92	43	13	89
More than one year	23	12	100	10	8	100	33	10	99
Total	193	100		131	100		324	100	

In fact, it is possible to be more specific about the length of period for the 70 per cent of responding employees who said their last pay was usual. This is because respondents were more precise about the number of months they had received their usual pay. The overall median length of period for the weekly and fortnightly-paid was 5.3 months; the median for the four-weekly and monthly-paid employees was 8.3 months. Again, this shows that pay of weekly- and fortnightly-paid employees is less stable than the pay of calendar-monthly- and four-weekly-paid employees. However, the lengths of periods considered for all employees whose last pay was usual is somewhat surprising as it is tempting to assume that informants take the course of least resistance. It is easy to say that one's last pay slip shows one's usual pay, and no further thought is required. In fact, the results in Table 17.8.2 indicate that some thought is given to normal pay by those who say that their last pay was usual. This is encouraging in that, as mentioned above, 70 per cent of FES employees said that their last pay was usual; this means that for the majority of employees, the concept of usual pay is relatively stable.

It is not possible to be as explicit for the remaining 30 per cent whose last pay was not usual because their answers were not as precise; nevertheless, Table 17.8.2 shows that 50 per cent of the weekly and fortnightly-paid workers whose last pay was not usual, were thinking of periods up to and including two months; only 33 per cent of the four-weekly and calendar-monthly paid employees thought that their usual pay extended over two months.

A final aspect of the June experiment was that those informants who said their last pay was not usual were asked how they arrived at their estimates of usual earnings. The results were analysed by pay period as it was thought that weekly-paid workers would not rely to the same extent on documents as monthly-paid workers. It was also thought that they might not use arithmetic reasoning as much as monthly-paid workers.

The results showed that proportionally more (34 per cent) of the calender monthly-paid workers consulted documents than weekly-paid workers (19 per cent). However,

this was partially offset by a higher proportion of weekly-paid workers (40 per cent) carrying out arithmetic calculations to arrive at an estimate of usual pay than was the case with monthly-paid workers (23 per cent).

If one takes consulting documents and arithmetic reasoning together, a slightly higher proportion (59 per cent) of the weekly-paid workers carried out what might be termed a 'considered and statistical approach' to the calculation of usual pay than did the monthly-paid workers (57 per cent).

The conclusions drawn from the study are:

(i) Answers to the question about usual pay are not given casually — considerable thought and some arithmetic reckoning is carried out. There appears to be no difference between weekly-paid employees and monthly-paid employees in this respect. Nevertheless, the problem remains of how accurate these answers are;

(ii) Where last pay was said to be usual, the time periods considered were longer than might be expected; this implies that the 'usual pay' question does provide a reasonably stable estimate of normal earnings, although, again, this estimate is based on the informant's opinion.

It is important to add that the stress in this experiment was on the gross pay, and it has been found that net pay varies more than gross pay. Furthermore, the use of 'usual' pay in the FES normal income definition is mainly as a classificatory variable, intended to relate roughly to household expenditure.

References

1. Kemsley, WFF. *Some technical problems in planning budget surveys.* Central Office of Information M 78. HMSO 1952.
2. Kemsley, WFF and Nicholson, JL. *Op cit.*
3. *Ibid.* p307.
4. Kemsley, WFF. The Household Expenditure Enquiry of the Ministry of Labour. *Op cit.* pp117—135.
5. Kemsley, WFF. Collecting data on economic flow variables. *Op cit.* pp119—120.

6 Kemsley, WFF. Interviewer variability and a budget survey. *Applied Statistics* Vol IX No.2 1960, pp122—8.

7 Kemsley, WFF. Interviewer variability in expenditure surveys. Journal of the Royal Statistical Society, Series A (General), Vol 128 Part 1 1965. pp118—139.

8 Kemsley, WFF. Collecting data on economic flow variables. Op cit. p121.

9 Kemsley, WFF. Designing a budget survey. *Op cit.* p117.

10 Sudman, S and Ferber, R. Experiments in obtaining consumer expenditure by diary methods. *Journal of the American Statistical Association* Vol 66 No. 336 1971. p728.

11 Kemsley, WFF. Designing a budget survey. *Op cit.* p118.

12 Estimates of the distribution of income in the United Kingdom. Economic Trends. *Op cit.*

Appendix A Definitions used at the fieldwork and coding stages

A1 Household

(a) *General definition.* A household comprises a person living alone or a group of people living at the same address and having meals prepared together, and with common housekeeping. A person (or persons) living at the same address, but not boarding with the same household, and having separate catering arrangements constitutes a separate household.

A household must have exclusive use of at least one room. If two or more share a room and do not have exclusive use of at least one other room, they constitute a single household.

(b) *Persons resident only part of the time.* A person living with a household who usually has one meal a day with that household is normally regarded as part of it. Anyone who is absent from time to time constitutes a special problem in an inquiry where the household is under observation over a period of time. Household members who are present at the initial interview and are then away for part of the 14 days, are usually asked to keep their records during the period they are away. However, there is a more fundamental question as to whether a person who is absent for all, or part of, this time should be regarded as a member of the household at all. In the FES there are a number of rules dealing with this problem, and on these depend the final decision as to whether a particular individual should be included or not.

Persons who spend only part of their time in the household are members provided they usually spend at least four nights a week in the household. However, when a married person is a member, the husband (or wife) is also counted as a member provided that either he usually goes home at least one night a week or he will be staying with the household for all or most of the record-keeping period. A child under 16 at boarding school is also regarded as a member provided he spends his holidays with the household. A person staying temporarily with the household, or who has been living with the household for only a short time, is a member provided he will be staying with the household for at least one month from the start of the records.

Someone who used to live with the household but has been away for more than one month from the main interview is not a member unless he will be returning within seven days. This rule applies to someone in hospital.

(c) *Persons absent at time of interview.* Some adjustment is necessary for members who are absent when the interviewer makes contact with the remainder of the household. If a member is temporarily absent, the start of the records is usually delayed until his return provided the delay is less than seven days. In other cases the rest of the household starts record-keeping without him. If he is absent throughout the whole 14 days of record-keeping, such details of his income are recorded as the interviewer is able to ascertain, and a decision is then made subsequently in the office as to whether that person is included in the household or not.

(d) *Change in household composition during the record-keeping period.* Anyone leaving the household for good within a few days after the main interview is not asked to keep records and is excluded from the household. The other members are asked to begin record-keeping immediately, or as soon as possible after the person in question has left.

If someone is known to be joining the household within seven days of the interviewer's call the records are usually delayed until his arrival. If he is not expected until after seven days he is ignored, and record-keeping usually begins immediately.

Unexpected additions to, and departures from, a household are normally ignored and the individuals excluded. However, someone who becomes a patient in a hospital or who dies within the 14 days of record-keeping is regarded as a member. In such cases the household may or may not be included in the final sample of cooperating households, depending upon whether the remaining persons have completed their records and whether the individual in question has completed his record until the time of going into hospital or of death.

A2 Head of household (Schedule A, line 1)
This is the member of the household who:
(a) owns the household accommodation; or
(b) is legally responsible for the rent of the accommodation; or
(c) has the household accommodation as one of the benefits of his employment; or
(d) has the household accommodation by virtue of some relationship to the owner, lessee etc who is not himself a member of the household.

If the individual thus defined is the wife of a member, the latter is taken as the HOH.

If the HOH is absent and not in the household, then the housewife becomes HOH, but not head of the Income Unit.

If two members of different sex have equal claim to be the HOH, the male is taken; while if two members of the same sex have equal claim, the elder is taken.

A3 Housewife (Schedule A, item 3)

The housewife is the person, regardless of sex, other than a domestic servant, who is responsible for most of the domestic duties. If two members share these duties the one responsible for most of the duties is regarded as the housewife; if two members of different sex share equally, the woman is taken as the housewife, while if two members of the same sex share equally, the elder is taken. If a servant is employed to carry out most of the domestic duties, the housewife is the person to whom the servant is responsible.

A4 Income Unit (Schedule A, item 8)

This is similar in concept to the tax unit used by Inland Revenue. A married couple is treated as a unit and given a separate reference number. Other individuals are treated as separate units with separate reference numbers unless they are children under 25, who have never been married. Each child is regarded as part of his parents' unit, coded as a dependant, and given the same reference number as his parents' unit unless he falls into one of the following categories:

(a) Child under 16 with an income equal to or more than the single persons tax allowance;

(b) Child aged 16 or over but under 25 with an income equal to or more than the single persons tax allowance (excluding educational grants);

(c) Child aged 16 but under 25 and not receiving full-time instruction at a university, college, school or other educational establishment nor undergoing whole-time training for a trade, profession or vocation for a period of not less than two years.

These cases are treated as separate units; they are based on information received in the normal course of the FES, and will not in every case be identical with the corresponding classification of Inland Revenue. Note that the foregoing definitions relate to 1979 and are liable to vary with changes arising from Finance Acts. Foster children in the care of the local authority are not coded as to income unit, although an identifying code 7 is entered in the reference number column of item 8.

A5 Employment Status (Schedule B, Q.1)

Before coding Q.1 the interviewer has to find out whether the informant has more than one job, and if so, to choose the most remunerative. The relevant definitions of the various categories are:

(a) *Employee*. (Code 1) This applies to anyone who at the time of interview has an arrangement with an employer to work for the latter for a wage or salary. It also applies to someone on an employer's books who has not yet started work, but it does not apply to a person whose employment has terminated before the time of interview and who has not yet entered into a new arrangement with an employer. The classification applies to anyone temporarily away from work because of illness, accident, holiday, strike, temporarily laid off, short-time working, as long as the individual has a job to which he will be returning. It also includes sandwich students who have an arrangement to work for an employer, casual or seasonal workers who are working at the time of interview or have an arrangement to work for an employer in the future, or are on an employer's books. It excludes anyone whose only remuneration is income in kind, eg free accommodation but no wage or salary. It also excludes someone who normally works abroad and is paid in foreign currency.

(b) *Self-employed*. (Code 2) This includes all who are responsible in their work to themselves. The category includes partners, but not directors, managers who are classified as employees. The classification applies irrespective of the level of earnings or the number of hours worked provided it is of a fairly regular nature and not a 'once only' job.

(c) *Out of employment but seeking work*. (Codes 3 and 4) This includes a person who at the time of interview does not have an arrangement with an employer, but is seeking work. It also includes someone who is sick but would be seeking work with an employer if not sick. In this context seeking work means having registered at an Unemployment Benefit Office or at another employment agency, or answering advertisements or advertising for a job.

(d) Sick or injured but not intending to seek work (code 5). This includes all persons who are permanently unfit to work because of sickness or injury.

(e) *Retired* (Code 6) This covers those not now working or seeking work as defined above, but who have retired from their full-time occupation at about the normal retiring age for that occupation.

(f) *None of these* (Code 7) This includes:

(i) All persons never in employment and not seeking employment.

(ii) Persons of independent means.

(iii) Women engaged in unpaid domestic duties even if they have previously had paid work.

(iv) Women who have left paid employment before retirement age, and are not self-employed.

(v) Students aged 16 and over who are attending full-time education, other than sandwich students who have an arrangement with an employer.

(vi) Persons whose only remuneration is income in kind.

Appendix B   Coding Frames Applied in Primary Analysis Branch

The frames described below relate to 1979

B1. Period code
The coding frame is:

Code	Period
1	Weekly
2	Two weekly
3	Three weekly
4	Four weekly
5	Monthly (calendar)
6	Quarterly
7	Half-yearly
8	Yearly
9	Ten times a year

This code applies to all amounts reported on schedules A and B, and is entered to the right of the three-digit identifying code. In cases where the question relates to a time period of fixed length the appropriate code has been preprinted on the schedule, e.g. Q.23(d) on schedule A.

B2 Starting date
This code is entered in the OFFICE USE box on the upper right corner of schedule A to indicate the starting date of the records, and is as follows:

(a) Year is indicated by two digits, being the final digit of the year in question.

(b) 'Week' is indicated by a two-digit number regardless of the year; for this purpose each calendar month is divided into the four starting weeks defined in Section 5.2, and the four 'weeks' are numbered consecutively from 1 to 48. January is given numbers 1 to 4 and December 45 to 48.

B3 Relationship of each individual member to head of household
Code
0	HOH
1	Wife or husband
2	Son or daughter (including stepson/daughter)
3	Son-in-law or daughter-in-law
4	Father or mother
5	Father-in-law or mother-in-law
6	Brother or sister
7	Grandson or grand-daughter
8	Other relative (e.g. neice, nephew, brother-in-law

This code is applied to each household member and placed in the OFFICE USE boxes on Schedule A page 1, item 2.

B4 Type of tenure
Code
1	Rented from a Council, or New Town Corporation unfurnished
2	Rented from someone else, unfurnished
3	Rented from someone else, furnished
4	Owned with mortgage
5	Owned outright
6	Neither owned nor rented

This is applied to each household and entered in A120 against Q.16A of schedule A. Code 6 'neither owned nor rented' is restricted as far as possible to genuine rent free cases. For example, where a widow has her rent paid by a son outside the household, the accommodation is treated as rented whether he pays the rent direct to the landlord or to his mother. (The amount will also be shown as a receipt in Q.60B or 60C of Schedule B).

In the case of a caravan the tenure code will be entered in A120 against Q.16B. The code is then interpreted as relating to the caravan, irrespective of whether the occupier owns or rents the site. A caravan being bought on hire purchase is coded 5.

B5 Employment status
The codes are as in Q.1 of the B schedule, namely:
1	Employee
2	Self employed or employer
3 + 4	Out of employment, but seeking work
5	Out of employment, but not seeking work due to sickness or injury
6	Retired
7	None of these

The definition of each category will be found in Section A5. The code in Q.1 is transferred to A201 after the various questions on earnings have been edited.

Sometimes changes are necessary either because an entry in Q.64 is transferred to the main questions, or because there are difficulties over which is the more remunerative occupation.

B6 Occupational code

This applies to Q.4 of schedule B, and the code is entered in A210, A212 or A214. The coding frame is based on the Occupation Unit Groups in the *Classification of Occupations* 1970.

FES Code	Description	Occupation Unit group[1]
1	Professional and technical workers	115 181-191 117 195-220 150
2	Administrative and managerial workers	002 154 173-180 142-143 156 147 159 149 171
3	Teachers	192-194
4	Clerical workers, e.g. clerks, commercial travellers, agents	127-128 148 138-141
5	Shop assistants	144
6	Manual workers, skilled	007 040-046 083-089 151-152 009 048-052 091 162 013-016 055-063 093-096 167 018-021 067-072 100-101 169 024-028 074-075 103-105 030-038 077-080 118-126
7	Manual workers, semi-skilled	001 047 097-099 153 003-006 053-054 102 155 008 064-066 106 157-158 010-012 073 116 160-161 017 076 129 164-165 022-023 081-082 131 168 029 090 135-137 170 039 092 145-146 172
8	Manual workers, unskilled	107-114 163 130 166 132-134
9	Members of H.M. Forces	221-222

[1] *Classification of Occupations 1970, General Register Office, H.M. Stationery Office (pp.xxiii-xxxv)*

B7 Industry code

This applies to Q.4 of schedule B and is entered A211, the code is based on the two-digit order number of the Standard Industrial Classification. (H.M. Stationery Office 1968) The 1979 frame is given below.

1979 FES Code	Industry	Order No.	Minimum list heading*
1	Agriculture, forestry, fishing	I	
2	Mining and quarrying	II	
3	Food, drink and tobacco	III	
4	Coal and petroleum products	IV	
5	Chemicals and allied industries	V	
6	Metal manufacture	VI	
7	Mechanical engineering	VII	
8	Instrument engineering	VIII	
9	Electrical engineering	IX	
10	Shipbuilding and marine engineering	X	
11	Vehicles	XI	
12	Metal goods not elsewhere specified	XII	
13	Textiles	XIII	
14	Leather, leather goods and fur	XIV	
15	Clothing and footwear	XV	
16	Bricks, pottery, glass, cement, etc.	XVI	
17	Timber, furniture, etc.	XVII	
18	Paper, printing and publishing	XVIII	
19	Other manufacturing industries	XIX	
20	Construction	XX	
21	Gas, electricity and water	XXI	
22	Rail transport	XXII	701
23	Other transport and communication, Post Office	XXII	702-709
24	Distributive trades, wholesale and retail	XXIII	
25	Insurance, banking, finance and business services	XXIV	
26	Professional and scientific services	XXV	
27	Miscellaneous services (laundries, cleaning and dyeing, motor repairs, distributors, garage and filling stations, repair of boots and shoes)	XXVI	892-895
28	Miscellaneous services (other than code 27 above)	XXVI	881-891, 899
29	Armed Forces (not Police or Fire Service)	XXVII	901·1-901·4
30	National Government Service	XXVII	901·5, 901·6
31	Local Government Service (Police and Fire Service only)	XXVII	906·1, 906·2
32	Local Government Service (other than Police and Fire Service)	XXVII	906·3

Where only part of order included in FES code

B8 Item code for entries in record books

This three-digit code is applied to every entry in the D records except those deleted as duplicating expenditure sectors covered in the interview. The code is entered in the right-hand column against the amount. For operational purposes the SSD Primary Analysis Branch compile and maintain an alphabetical index of items, with the corresponding code number. The code list in the following pages, however, is in number order with a short description on the right, followed by a third column headed 'Additional Examples'. As the latter heading implies, the information in the third column is not intended as an exhaustive list of all the descriptions that have been found in record books. It contains additional information which either shows how certain unusual cases are classified or helps to define further the particular category. Changes are made from time to time; the list which follows relates to the position as at December 1979.

Item Codes 1979	Description of items	Additional Examples
	Food for home consumption	
101	Bread, milk loaves, rolls	Balmcakes, breadcakes, batch, baps, Take and bake, Butteries, dough cake, Fadge, Flat cake.
102	Flour, plain and self-raising	Saffron flour
103	Biscuits shortbread, wafers etc. (including chocholate covered)	Ryvita, Macvita. rusks, oatcakes, marshmallows, crunchies, cookies, macaroons, gingerbread men, cheese nuts, waffles, Toasties, Wigwams, slimming biscuits, Penguins, Kitkat, Choc-teacakes, Jaffa cakes, Yo-Yo, Breakaway, Squiggles, Twix.
104	Cakes, currant bread, fruit pies, pastries, scones, etc.	Crumpets, malt loaf, pikelets, cheese cake, teabread, bannocks, bracks (Irish), Parkin, Bread pudding, Chorley cakes, Petit Fours, Apple dumpling (pastry). Torta fruit, buns, frozen (cooked) cake (eg gateaux, eclairs, sponge)
105	Composite purchases of bread, flour, biscuits and cakes which cannot be allocated reasonably to particular codes	Including payment to baker
108	Dry cereals (including prepared breakfast cereals)	Ready Brek, Nuggets, Muesli, Puffed Rice, Familia, Special K, Flying Start, Alpen, Country Store, Coco crispies, Quaker Oats, Oatmeal, semolina, spaghetti, blancmange powder, cornflour, soya flour, farola, farinoca, sago, arrowroot, broth cereals, baby cereal, Farex, pearl barley, wheatgerm
111	Beef and veal, including minced meat	Beefburgers (unless meal out) and steaklets, minceburgers, beef loaf, sirloin, inlift, hough, sheet-ribs, beef-ham (raw), hamburgers
112	Mutton and lamb	Lap (breast), gigot.
113	Pork	Spare ribs, pork slices and cuttings
114	Bacon and ham, uncooked	Hock, knuckle, ulster fry, ham shank, Belfast Gammon
115	Offal (uncooked)	Liver, sweetbreads, tripe, pigs' trotters, sheep/pigs' head, chawl, cheek, elder, chitterlings, heart, oxtail, tongue, kidneys
121	Cooked including canned ham	Forespur
122	Sausages (uncooked), sausage meat	
123	Cooked meat and meat products (provided not sandwiches and meals out), canned and bottled meat	Pork pies, puddings, patties, pigs pudding, mealy pudding, bath chaps, pork fingers, bridies, hot dogs, haslet, meat squares, meat and potato pies, brawn, cooked sausages, scotch eggs, sausage rolls, pork pestle, pork cheese, hodge. Chicken rissoles, hot pot, shepherds pie, polony, saveloy, luncheon meat, corned beef, spam, beef in a bag, frozen roast beef (sliced).

Item Codes 1979	Description of items	Additional Examples
123 (continued)		Sliced braised beef, meat croquettes, sausages in batter, haggis, black/white pudding, Brunchie chopped pork, steak & kidney pancakes, Cooked tongue, veal and ham pies, ham and egg pies, chicken pies, game pies, frankfurters, liver sausage, escargots (snails), delicatessen meats — cooked pork and beef, garlic sausage. Canned meat, bottled meat, canned meat puddings, corned beef, spam, (exclude meat and fish pastes), canned braised beef, canned sliced beef, canned beefburgers, canned sausages, canned sausage rolls, canned tongue, canned escargots, canned frankfurters, canned cocktail sausages.
127	Poultry, rabbit, game and venison — cooked, uncooked, canned, bottled and frozen	Chickens, ducks, turkeys, chicken in aspic, capon, turkey loaf (raw), hares, partridges, pigeons
129	Meat not otherwise defined	Bones, goat meat, steak and kidney (uncooked)
130	Meat protein substitute	Mince savour
131	Fish-fresh	Smoked, buttered and Undefined
132	Fish-canned and bottled	Roll mops
133	Fish-frozen	Frozen fish fingers, frozen fish in a bag, frozen fish croquettes, frozen fish and chips
138	Fish and chips with or without peas. (cooked items only)	Fish cakes (cooked), fried fish, fish croquettes cooked with or without chips and/or peas. If fish and chips *separately* entered, code chips 856. Fish (fried), fish and chips, fish chips and peas, fish cakes with/without peas. Fish supper, fish tea. Where any of these appear in the 'Meals Out' section of the diary, code 138 *unless* there is evidence that a drink has been taken with the item *or* there is evidence that the item formed part of larger meal when code 877/8/9 as applicable.
140	Eggs, fresh and dried	
141	Butter	
142	Margarine	
143	Fresh Milk	
144	Fresh cream, canned cream skimmed milk, dried milk, canned milk, yogurt, milk babyfoods and other milk products (excluding cheese and butter.)	Coffee mate. Top of the milk. Frozen youghurt and other frozen milk products, mousse, sour cream.
146	Cheese, including processed	Cream cheese
149	Lard, cooking and other oils and fats	Vegetarian fats, olive oil, suet, Trex, peanut butter, shortex, pork scratchings, dripping

Note If specific vegetables are not distinguished as between fresh, canned, bottled, etc., treat as fresh vegetables

Item Codes 1979	Description of items	Additional Examples
150	Canned and bottled baby, junior and geriatric foods (other than milk)	
151	Fresh vegetables	Cabbage, cauliflower, broccoli, runner beans, brussel sprouts, mushrooms, onions, peas, carrots, spring greens, spring onions (syboes), leeks, shallots, broad-beans.
154	Canned, bottled and dried vegetables	Canned vegetable juice, baked beans.
155	Frozen vegetables	
156	Potato products and processed potatoes	Potato sticks, Puffs, Hula Hoops, 'Wotsits', Toggles, Ravers, chips, potato cakes/scones/pies/

Item Codes 1979	Description of items	Additional Examples

156 (continued)

farls, potato croquettes (includings croquettes unspecified), tinned potatoes.

158   Potatoes (raw)

Note If specific fruit is not distinguished as between fresh, canned, bottled etc., treat as fresh fruit.

160   Fresh fruit

Apples, pears, oranges, tangerines, satsumas, bananas, rhubarb and other undefined.

163   Fruit, canned, bottled, frozen or dried, fruit juices (excluding squashes), tomato juice, nuts.

Fruit salad, pears, peaches, pineapple, frozen apples, prunes, sultanas, currants, raisins, Appletree dessert, Britvic, rose-hip syrup, Optrose, Delrosa, Ribena

165   Tomatoes, fresh, canned, bottled and frozen

Tomato puree

171   Tea

Nestea, Herbal tea

172   Coffee, coffee essence

Nescafe

173   Proprietary and non-proprietary food drinks (excluding milk baby foods)

Cocoa essence, Nesquik, chocolate squeezy, Ovaltine, Horlicks, Milo, Bournvita, Instant Postum, Bengers Food, Malted milk, Slender (slimming milk drink)

181   Sugar

182   Syrup, Lemon curd, honey, jam, marmalade

Treacle, molasses, choc spread, sunny spread

183   Ice cream

Iced lollies, arctic roll, Dark Secrets

184   Soft drinks (squashes, cordials, crystals)

Lucozade, citrozade, essences for making soft drinks, sparklets, milk shake syrups, Triple 'C'

185   Sweets and chocolates

Drained and glace fruit, (except drained cherries, glace cherries, and candied peel (192)). Crystallised fruits, Picnic bars, Marathon, Curly Wurly, Chinese figs, Stem ginger.

191   Packaged and canned foods, prepared and semi-prepared.

Cake and pudding mixtures, canned puddings (eg rice, treacle), Xmas pudding, doughnuts and cakes uncooked and frozen, frozen pastry, packet icing, almond paste (incl. Ground almonds), ready made trifles and custard, instant whip, jellies (incl. jellies set with fruit), ice poles, ice pops, Peach melba/ Sundaes (unless ice cream, code 183), cream dessert (fool), cream topping, ice-cream and yoghurt powders, made up stuffing (eg Paxo), mincemeat, savourmix, hors d'oeuvres, coleslaw, chicken salad, mixed salad, vegetable salad, canned pease pudding, canned macaroni cheese, canned cheese and spaghetti, canned ravioli, canned risotto, canned spaghetti sauce (eg tomato), bolognaise sauce, curry sauce, white sauce, cheese and onion pies, pea fritters, pineapple fritters, packet dumpling, cheese or fish pancakes, cheeseburger, all cheese spreads, pizza pie, Toasty grills, toast toppers, meat, fish and 'fowl' pastes (ie spreads), paté, potted meat, 'ready-to-heat' meals, 'Make a meal', skillet meal, Duo cans (eg chicken/rice), canned chicken & mushroom casserole, canned creamed mushrooms, rum butter, canned sausage and beans, ravioli, instant dessert powders.

192   Flavourings, colourings, additives

Salt, pepper, mustard, vinegar, gravy salt, Oxo, Marmite, Bovril, King Beef (extract), herbs (eg mint, parsley), spices (eg ground ginger, root ginger,

Item Codes 1979	Description of items	Additional Examples
192 (continued)		cinnamon, all-spice), curry powder and paste, breadcrumbs, fish dressing, candied peel, angelica, glace cherries, drained cherries, candied fruit and flowers, dessicated coconut, nibbed nuts, flaked/ blanched almonds etc., sweet cake decorations, sweet and savoury flavourings and essences, baking powder, baking soda, cream of tartar, isinglass, pectin, gelatine, rennet, soup cubes/ squares, yeast, chicken essence, hops and malt for making home brewed beer, cocktail cherries, artificial sweetners (eg slimcea, sweetex, sugaree), cooking chocolate, powdered garlic, rice paper, Jif Lemon.
195	Pickles, sauces, chutneys	Pickled eggs, onions, walnuts, etc., mayonnaise, tomato ketchup, pickled cabbage, cranberry sauce, apple sauce, salad cream, jar of beetroot.
196	Sandwiches, rolls with filling	
199	Food undefined	Grocery bills which cannot be separately allocated, Xmas club hamper, money paid to someone else for a meal out.

Alcoholic drink

NB Drinks include tips and where separable alcoholic drinks bought with meals out.)

201	Beer, stout, ale, shandy, cider.	Perry, Barley wine.
202	Wines, other than those bought by the bottle	Sherry, vermouth, ginger wine.
203	Spirits, liqueurs, other than those bought by the bottle	
205	Wines bought by the bottle	Wine from the cask (ie bought in bulk), tonic wine, Clan Dew.
206	Spirits, liqueurs bought by the bottle	
209	Alcoholic drink incompletely described or itemised	Month's supply of wines and spirits, round of drinks.

Tobacco

211	Cigarettes, cigarette tobacco and papers	
212	Pipe tobacco	Chewing tobacco, twist
213	Cigars, snuff	Whiffs, Manikins

Housing

216	Structural, Space heating	Gas-fired central heating, water and hot air, including materials for do-it-yourself installations and labour charges.
		Storage Heaters: under floor heating (by electricity) including materials for do-it-yourself installations and labour charges.
		Radiator and hot air systems, including materials for do-it-yourself installations and labour charges.
		Open fires, closed fires, fireplaces, including materials for do-it-yourself installations and labour charges. Raeburn solid fuel cooker.
		Oil fired central heating, including materials for do-it-yourself installations and labour charges.
		Gas/Electricity Bills for previous address — delete.

Item Codes 1979	Description of items	Additional Examples
221	House purchase including deposits for new main dwelling for household other than the one in which they are now residing, or for members of household moving away from home (but exc. for rented property — see 799) incl. deposit, mortgage instalment.	Mortgage, Payments to 'Self-build Association' Purchase of garden plot. Road construction charges. (Including electricity/insurance etc. for new homes prior to moving in).
222	Caravan purchase including deposits.	
223	Structural additions and enlargements, ie payments to contractors and for do-it-yourself items not coded at 231—239 for household's main dwelling, dwelling into which a household is planning to move as its main dwelling, dwelling into which household member is planning to move (eg after marriage).	Bathroom added, Garden shed, new garage, Double glazing, Car port, Cement base for garage, Built-in furniture, Materials and labour costs. Unspecified house improvements (over £300). Alterations for solar heating.
224	Repairs, decorations and replacements, payments to contractors. (Do-it-yourself expenditure should be coded 231—239) for households as above.	Materials and labour costs, rewiring, private road repair charges, unspecified house improvements (under £300).
225	Electricity account payments for a permanent second dwelling.	
226	Gas account payments for a permanent second dwelling.	
227	Telephone account for a permanent second dwelling.	
228	Expenditure on provision of a *permanent* second dwelling eg country cottage, town flat incl. maintenance on a permanent second dwelling.	Rent, rates, water rates, mortgage and insurance on structure. Structural additions and enlargements (as code 223), repair, decorations and replacements (as code 224). (Excluding expenditure on temporary holiday homes and new homes prior to moving in). Include installation charges for gas/electric cooker if made by someone else other than vendor eg builder where purchase price is not entered. (If purchase price included with installation charge, code to 413 or 411, etc as appropriate).
229	TV licence for a permanent second dwelling.	

Purchase of materials and tools for house maintenance

Item Codes 1979	Description of items	Additional Examples
231	Paint and distemper	
232	Wallpaper	Dadoline
233	Timber and hardboard	Hardboard to make a pelmet, wooden floor tiles.
234	Other materials	Formica, roofing felt, sand, aggregates for cement, glazed tiles, wire netting, linseed oil, putty, Polyfilla/cell, heavy glues. Fablon, spare-parts for the structural space-heaters (ie, code 216). Paving slabs for path. Creosote, pipe lagging, polythene sheets, Rentokil, glass, paint stripper.
235	Fittings	Kitchen units, power points, door handles, ready-made hardboard pelmets, all electric door bells. Trellis, sash cord, wooden fence, window catch, bathroom cabinet.
236	Tools	Paint brushes, scrapers, rollers. Paint kettle. Extension ladder, scaffolding tubes.
239	Composite or undefined of items in codes 231—236. Hire of equipment for house repair or maintenance.	

Item Codes 1979	Description of items	Additional Examples

Fuel, light and power

240	House coal, slack, coal bricks, anthracite and boiler fuel (excluding coke and premium smokeless fuels).	Phurnacite, multiheat, dry steam coal, Welsh nuts, beans, peas and grains, stovesse and stove nuts. Trebles, ovoids, ordinary household coal used in open fires, etc.
242	Coke and premium smokeless fuels	Gloco, Sebrite, No2 Gas Coke, Hard cokes (including Sunbrite), gas cokes other than for open fires, Coalite, Rexco, Cleanglow, Phimax, Burnbrite, Homefire, Roomheat, Wonderco.
253	Paraffin	
254	Gas, slot meter payments.	
255	Electricity, slot meter payments.	Include payments at a permanent second dwelling.
		Exclude slot payments to account meters where residents have their own key.
259	Other fuel and light and fuel *undefined*.	Nightlights, firelighters, candles, calor gas, firewood. underfloor heating charges where source of heating unknown.
261	Fuel oil, *other than for central heating*.	

Clothing and footwear

Note Adults' clothing is defined as clothing for persons age 16 or over; for children 5—15 and for infants aged under 5. The various types of children's wear are defined as for adults.

301	Men's outerwear.	Overcoats, raincoats, mackintoshes, duffle coats, capes, spats, suits, jackets, blazers, trousers, waistcoats, cardigans, shorts, dressing-gowns, kilts, bathing costumes, knee pads, overalls, all sports clothes, riding and ski-ing clothes.
303	Men's underwear.	Vests, pants, combinations, pyjamas, shirts, collars, including paper collars.
304	Men's hosiery.	Socks, stockings.
311	Women's outerwear.	Raincoats, mackintoshes, capes, duffle coats, overcoats, frocks, dresses, suits, costumes, jackets, skirts, blazers, blouses, twin-sets, jumpers, cardigans, slacks, shorts, gym tunics, dressing-gowns, aprons, overalls, bathing costumes, beach suits, leotard.
313	Women's underwear.	Vests, knickers, panties, combinations, slips, petticoats, underskirts, corsets, roll-ons, suspender belts, brassieres, bodices, pyjamas, night-dresses, negligees, bed jacket, briefs.
314	Women's hosiery.	Stockings, ankle socks, tights.
321	Boys' outerwear.	
323	Boys' underwear.	
324	Boys' hosiery.	
325	Girls' outerwear.	
327	Girls' underwear.	
328	Girls' hosiery.	
329	Infants' clothing.	Pram sets, socks, hats, babies' napkins — terry and muslin, mittens, including other items of clothing bought for a child under 5. Exclude bedding.
330	Clothing materials.	Leather to make clothes, materials for school sewing.

Item Codes 1979	Description of items	Additional Examples
331	Men's and boys' headgear.	
332	Haberdashery, women's and girls' headgear and headgear not fully described.	Hats, caps, berets, gloves, scarves, handkerchiefs, ties, braces, belts, garters, laces, sewing-cotton, knitting wool and needles, ribbon, buttons, suspenders, pins, patterns, zips, embroidery silks, school badges, tape measure, darners, insoles, nightdress case, webbing, needles and threads etc for school sewing.
334	Other clothing charges, clothing undefined.	Hire of clothing, dressmaking charges (excluding repairs and alterations), dressmaking dummy.
341	Men's footwear	Boots, shoes, slippers, wellingtons.
342	Women's footwear	Shoes, slippers, fur bootees, leggings (mock boots)
343	Children's including infants' footwear	Daps
349	Footwear undefined	

Durable household goods

Item Codes 1979	Description of items	Additional Examples
401	New and second-hand furniture.	Tables, chairs, beds, bedroom/dining room suites. Table sewing box. TV fitment, fireplace wood surround.
404	Floor coverings including laying and making up charges.	Rubber-backed carpets, tufted carpets, rugs, mats and matting; jute carpets, needle-loom, sheepskin rugs, coir matting, underlay, Rug wool, carpet tiles, flooring tiles (vinyl, plastic and rubber): sheet plastic flooring. Lino sticky tape.
405	New and second-hand house textiles, including making up charges.	Blankets, sheets, (include rubber) duvets/continental quilts and covers, bedspreads, eiderdowns, curtain materials, rufflette tape, teacosy, adhesive binding, tea towels, Rydura dusters, cushion covers, table cloths (including plastic).
407	New and second hand mattresses.	Cot/pram mattresses, pillows, bolsters, cushions, Kapok, a baby's changing pad.
409	New and second-hand radios, televisions, record-players, tape recorders.	TV aerial and cost of fitting. Amplifiers including fitting, Music Centre — Radio, Record players, cassette, speakers, Radio clock, video cassettes.
411	New and second-hand gas cookers.	Include installation charges where installation known to be by vendor, or where not known who did the installation; if by someone else (eg builder) code installation charges to 224 or 228.
412	Gas and electrical non-structural space heating appliances, new and second-hand gas and electric durables not codable elsewhere.	Ordinary gas-fire or convector fire, conventional plug-in electric fires and convector fires, gas washing machines, gas refrigerators, gas drying cabinets, gas hand agitated washing machine, water heaters and boilers, pokers, electronic TV game, electronic calculators, type-writers and paint sprayers, dishwashers.
413	New and second-hand electrical cookers.	Include installation charges where installation is by vendor. If by someone else (eg builder) code installation charges to 224 or 228.
417	New and second-hand electrical washing/drying machines.	Washing machines, spin dryers, drying cabinets.
419	New and second-hand Electric Refrigerators, freezers.	
422	Spare parts for radios, television, gramophones, tape recorders.	Valves, blank cassettes (under £2.00).
423	Spare parts for gas and electrical durables.	Electric sewing machine needles.

Item Codes 1979	Description of items	Additional Examples	
431	China glassware and pottery (*not* mirrors).	Pyrex ware.	
434	Major household appliances not powered by gas/electricity excluding parts other than fittings. Major durables undefined.	Non-electric sewing machines, paraffin and other non-structural space heaters, oil-fired cookers and water heating systems, non-electric calculators and typewriters, knitting machines and ribbers, garden furniture, wheel barrows, lawn mowers, garden rollers, carpet sweepers, fire extinguishers, rotovators, water softeners, garden and beach umbrellas, emergency power unit.	
436	Household items not codable elsewhere, including spares for items at 434.	Doorstop, chamois leather, metal clothes post, wick for oil lamp or stove, sink plug, solder rawl-plugs, emery cloth, mouse-traps, fire-guard, lino knife, flex, electric plug or adapter if not defined for specific purpose or appliance, nails, screws, hooks, tools (eg pliers, screw-drivers, hammer, files, saws, chisels). Garden-tools (eg shears, hedge clipper, hoe, handbill scythe), garden hose, household oil, rope, tilley lamp, sawbench. Wine-making apparatus, padlocks, hinges, draught excluder, gardening gloves, industrial gloves, sand-paper, fuses, step ladder, French polish, varnish, teak oil.	

Asbestos mat, basin, bin, bowl, bread board, brass log box, clothes horse/line, coal scuttle, curtain rail, coat hangers, colander, dustpan, fire-irons, fish slice, frying pans, kettles, kilner jars, ironing board, laundry basket, milk cooler, metal bath, mashers, napkin ring, pail, potato peeler, pressure cookers, all plastic household goods, plastic foam for kneeler, odd pieces of hose, scourer, shoe horn, stair grips, strainers, sandwich box, saucepans, tub, trays, teapot spout, tray sets, tin openers, vacuum flask, wooden salad bowl and servers, waste-paper basket, pegs, clothes prop, bathroom scales, soap holder, foam filling for cushions, venetian blinds. Chopsticks, bake stone, keys, cash box, pastry brush, tub, peg bag, Carpet bar/strip, table top for washing machine, picnic table, teapot stand, watering can, oven gloves.

Light pendants and chandeliers, lampshades, and materials for making, light bulbs, infra red bulbs, torches, batteries (unless specific use implies coding elsewhere) gas mantles, lighters and flints.

Scissors, penknife.

Brooms, mops, shoeshine sets, bath brush to clean bath, clothes brushes.

Vehicles

Code	Description	Additional Examples	
501	New cars	Motor vans used for private purposes.	H.P. cases only
502	Second-hand cars.		
503	New motor cycles.	Motor assisted cycles.	
504	Second-hand motor cycles.	Motor assisted cycles.	

Item Codes 1979	Description of items	Additional Examples
505	Other new and second-hand vehicles.	Bicycles, perambulators, carrycots, motor cruisers, yachts, dinghies, trailers, canoes, gokarts, fairy cycles, tricycles.
508	Repairs and other service charges to vehicles other than cars and motor cycles.	Boat house hire, cycle garage fee, push chair/cycle hire.
509	Car accessories, parts and replacements new and second-hand.	Car seat for baby, car paint, brake fluid.
510	Motor-cycle accessories, parts and replacements new and second-hand.	Crash-helmet, motor-cycle paint.
511	Other vehicle accessories, parts and replacements, new and second-hand.	Cycle clips, Pram straps, pram harness, outboard motors, paddles.
546	A.A. and R.A.C. subscriptions.	Other non-profit making motoring associations (eg Civil Service Motoring Association).
547	Petrol and oil	
548	Car and motor-cycle repairs and servicing.	Labour and material costs should not be split. Car battery charging.
549	Other car and motor-cycle costs.	Tolls, parking fees, garaging, car polishes, shampoos, anti-freeze, safety test for older cars, underseal.

Travel

551	Rail or tube fares other than season tickets.	Train/boat ticket. Reservation of railway seat, S/Citizens Rail Fare Card, OAP Passes.
552	Bus, coach fares (regular services only) other than season tickets.	Tram, trolleybus, OAP Passes.
553	Air travel.	
554	Water travel other than season tickets.	Ferries, River 'bus, Hovercraft
555	Taxis, including hired cars with driver.	
556	Hire or self-drive cars.	Mileage charges for use of firm's car for private purposes. Expenditure on the motability scheme.
557	Monetary contribution towards cost of travel in friends' etc vehicle.	
559	Other travel and transport, and transport undefined.	Removals, transport of baggage and animals, coach trips/outings (may include meals and drinks where they cannot be coded separately). Transport of car by air, Charge for delivery of furniture, Cliff lift.

Other Goods

601	New and second-hand musical instruments and parts.	
603	New and second-hand records, etc.	Pre-recorded Cassettes (over £2.00) record tokens, Record rack, record cases, Baton, cassette cases, 'dustbugs'
611	Non N.H.S. spectacles, but not sunglasses.	If combined private/N.H.S., code ⅔rds at 611 ⅓rd at 612.
612	N.H.S. spectacles.	
621	Medicines and medical aids (other than NHS) including items undefined as to N.H.S. or other.	Slippery elm food, surgical goods and dressings, sanitary towels, babies bottles, bottle teats, Dettol, T.C.P., Glucose, cough sweets, Bemax, Froment, Milton, Virol, hearing aid/battery, cod liver oil and vitamin tablets, Metercal, Elastic stockings if not N.H.S., Lipsil, contraceptive pills, contact lenses

Item Codes 1979	Description of items	Additional Examples

621 (continued)

soaking fluid, insect repellent, Calamine lotion, Complan, hearing aid rental, teething ring, baby wipes, Ayds (slimming tablets), Disposable nappies. Nappy liners.

622   Cosmetics.

After shave lotion, 'Aqua-marine' lotion, astringent lotion, barrier creams, bath essences/salts, brilliantine and hair creams, bubble bath preparations, cleansing cream, cold cream, colour rinses, deodorants, depilatory creams, waxes and gloves, eye shadow, eyebrow pencil, face packs, face powder, powder in compact, foundation creams and lotions, hand creams and lotions, hair glitter, hair setting lotions, hair sprays, home perms, lipstick, lipstick brushes, lipstick towels, liquid make-up, mascara, 'Nailoids', nail polish/varnish, nail varnish remover, night cream, orange sticks, patches, perfumery, including cologne and toilet water, powder brush, powder puffs, preparation for tanning the human skin, eg, 'He-tan' (not soothing lotion such as calamine), proprietary hair bleaches and dyes, rouge, skin food, talcum powder and treated toilet tissue (eg Lantex, Savet etc, ie not dry paper tissues/handkerchiefs).

623   Toilet paper.

624   Other toilet requisites.

Shaving soap/cream, toothpaste, toothbrushes, face flannel, all paper handkerchiefs/tissues (excluding those at 622), toilet bag, Cosmetic bag etc. (limit £2), nailbrushes, hairbrushes, combs, steradent, hairgrips, rubber gloves, lightweight plastic gloves, razors, blades, hair nets, hot water bottles, shampoos, hair clippers, Interdens, bath scrubber, toilet sponges, head rest, pumice stone, holder for tissues, make-up mirror, shaving mirror, wig stand, nail files, emery boards, manicure sets, tweezers, hair rollers.

625   NHS Prescription charges and payments for NHS medical appliances.

NHS elastic stockings. Exclude contraceptive pills (621). NHS Wigs and hairpieces.

631   Games, Toys and Pastimes other than equipment for hobbies (634) or Sports (641).

Playing cards, card games, chess, draughts, darts, dominoes, child's paint box, fireworks, crackers, balloons, Xmas stocking containing toys/sweets.

632   Photographic and optical goods excluding spectacles.

Cameras, light meters, flash bulbs, tripods, films and charges for developing and printing, developing and printing equipment, photographic album, projector, school photographic material, magnifying glasses, opera glasses, binoculars, telescopes, microscopes, all sunglasses except those stated to be NHS.

634   Hobbies

Stamp collecting, stamp albums, artists' materials, all items bought for hobbies, scraper board, stamp albums, coins/medals other than precious metals (see 643).

641   Sports goods (not clothes).

Tennis, squash and badminton racquets, footballs, cricket equipment, golf clubs/balls, cartridges, pellets, bait, life-belt/jacket, tents, Girl Guide's whistle, sleeping bags, camp bed, camping equipment, canvas beach huts, camping stoves,

Item Codes 1979	Description of items	Additional Examples
641 (continued)		Handice, Freezella, fishing equipment, echo sounder and battery, handwarmer, golf gloves. Exercise Kit (body trimmers, trim wheels, 'slimming aids' which could be used as exercise machines).
642	Leather and travel goods.	Suitcases, trunks, brief cases, handbags, wallets, baby basket, shooting sticks, walking sticks, umbrellas, shopping baskets, sewing case, vanity case, school haversack/satchel/bag, baby bouncers/walkers, baby carrying harness, shopping bag-on-wheels, shopping bags (not carrier), jewel case, Spectacle case.
643	Jewellery, watches, clocks, barometers and silverware.	Cuff links, electric clock, thermometers, silver flasks, silver scent bottle, spectacle chain, telephone timer, compacts without powder, coins and medals made from gold or platinum.
644	Smokers' requisites and decorative fancy goods.	Pipes, pouches, lighters, cigarette cases, ashtrays, lighter fuel, cigar boxes. Ornaments, vases, reproductions, pictures and picture frames, original works of art, mirrors, plastic flower pot holder, artificial flowers, fancy china bowl/flower pot, bird baths, joss sticks, posters, optic lights.
655	Stationery and other paper goods.	Writing paper/envelopes, charity stamps/cards, paper napkins/doyleys, jampot covers, calendars, greaseproof paper, paper decorations, bin liners, binders for mags, cardboard folders, football card photos, scrap book, kitchen rolls, pens, ink, pencils, rulers, string, polythene bags, drinking straws, lighter types of glue, gloy, glucine, typewriter ribbons, cocktail sticks, bin liners (plastic). Aluminium foil, tinsel, artificial Christmas tree, 'Stretch & Seal', carrier bags, decorative candles (including birthday cake candles).
721	Books (not library subscriptions), including school and text books.	Learned journals, book tokens, programmes, maps, diaries, time-tables, catalogues, book club, horoscope (book form only), cookery cards, sheet music, music tutors, painting books, patterns in books, address books, autograph albums, telephone book.
722	Newspapers.	Including delivery charge.
723	Magazines/Periodicals.	Knitting or needlework patterns in magazines.
731	Food for animals and pets, not normally for human consumption.	Trill budgie food, Lassie, horsemeat, lights, fish-heads.
732	Other expenditure on animals and pets.	Purchase of pets and equipment, medicine, sand, rent for horse field, nosebag for horse, Kennel Club, Vet's fees, Registration of animals.
733	Seeds, plants, flowers.	Include gardening clubs, rents for allotment, manure, flower-pots, gardening stakes, week-killer.
741	Matches.	
745	Toilet soap.	Infacare.
746	Other soap and soap products.	Stergene, Dirty Paws, Swarfega.
749	Other cleaning materials.	Soda, polishes, ammonia, disinfectants, starch, insecticide, abrasive powders, dyes, steel-wood, methylated spirits, Brillo pads, sulphur candle, shoe-

Item Codes 1979	Description of items	Additional Examples
749 (continued)		cleaning materials, Domestos, turpentine, record cleaning cloth, spectacle cleaning cloth, Nappisan, fabric conditioner (eg Comfort).
750	Miscellaneous expenditure on goods not assigned to any other code.	Include collective presents where goods not known. Cigarette coupons (buying), Masonic regalia, headstone, gift vouchers (purpose not specified), Beach hut (*if canvas* 641), Globe map (unless antique), Ice for freezer.

Services

Item Codes 1979	Description of items	Additional Examples
751	Postage, including parcel post and poundage.	Giro charges.
752	Telephone (not telephone accounts), telegrams.	
756	Hotels and boarding houses, (including deposits) for holidays in the United Kingdom.	Holiday camps, hostel charges, money for board to relatives.
757	Advance payments, (including deposits) for holidays abroad, in Channel Islands or Isle of Man and other payments during holiday period (total for record keeping period only).	Holiday insurance, international driving licence, green card (car), Commission on purchase of travellers' cheques and foreign currency should be coded, but the value of the cheques and money should not be coded. Money invested eg purchase of a holiday bungalow should not be coded.
759	Holiday expenses not allocated elsewhere.	Holiday savings money for children's holidays arranged by school (if place known then code 756—757 as appropriate), hire of accommodation eg caravan for self catering holidays, camping site fees.
761	Cinemas.	
762	Dances (admission).	Discotheque.
763	Theatres, concerts, circus.	Amateur shows, theatre agent's fee, Folk Group.
764	Participant sports and specialised pastimes — subscriptions, ad hoc admission and similar charges.	Golf clubs, sports clubs, billiards, fishing, darts clubs, fishing licences and permits, swimming clubs, subs to pigeon/greyhound clubs and racing. Rent for part of river. Bridge club, jazz club (sub), band levy, fee for model, showing animals. Skating, golf, tennis (eg fee to play tennis on public court), swimming, boating charges, weight lifting, fishing trip, jazz club (entrance), hiring boat, weight training club, post.
766	Football matches (admission)	Rugby
767	Other spectator sports (admission)	Cricket/tennis matches, horse, dog and speedway racing, and stockcar racing. Boxing, swimming, wrestling, school sports.
768	TV/Radio rental — slot meter payments.	
769	Miscellaneous entertainment not assignable to specific item codes.	Whist drives, fun fairs, exhibitions, museums, castles, country houses, flower shows, horse shows, zoos, visit to Father Xmas, social ticket, beetle drive, spectator at airport, horoscopes, fashion show, night club, trip round the bay, Juke box, amusement machines, Youth Club entrance fee. Holiday school play scheme.
770	Stamp duties to Central Authorities.	Passport, driving test fee, birth certificate Import duty, search fee St. Catherine's House.
771	Domestic Services.	Baby sitter, NI contribution paid for domestics by employer, private and local authority nurseries for children, gardener.
773	NHS payments to dentists and for other services (except the supply of spectacles).	Amenity hospital bed.

Item Codes 1979	Description of items	Additional Examples
775	Private medical, dental, optician, etc fees, excluding non-NHS spectacles. Including items undefined as to NHS or other.	Chiropodist, nursing home and convalescent fees, family planning clinic, repairs to spectacles, artificial teeth, ears pierced, Medical certificate fee.
781	Sweeps and window cleaners.	
782	Repairs to footwear and materials for home repairs.	Staining footwear.
784	Repairs and maintenance to tape recorder, radio television and musical instruments.	TV Insurance maintenance contract, tuning piano, re-charging battery.
785	Repairs and maintenance to central heating systems including insurance premiums (only applies when central heating is mentioned in D book beside the entry.)	
786	Repairs and maintenance to other gas electric and oil appliances (not account).	Servicing.
788	Repairs to personal goods (excluding medical repairs) and repairs not codable elsewhere.	Jewellery, watches, clocks, fountain pens, cigarette lighter, umbrella, scissors, clothing, skates sharpened. Teapot resilvered. Lawn mowers (not electric) furniture recovering, eiderdown recovering, mattress repairs.
790	Cleaning and Dyeing	Cleaning fur coat, dyeing footwear.
791	Laundry, launderette and hire of washing machine.	Self service dry cleaning, Bagwash, deductions from pay for washing overalls.
793	Hairdressing, manicure, beauty treatment.	Hairdressing club, diathermy, Hair pieces and wigs. (Not NHS).
795	Subscriptions to Friendly Societies.	Sick clubs, Burial Clubs, HSA, Oddfellows, Death Levy, Mutual Aid. Firemen's benevolent fund. Docks distress fund. Penny in the £ hospital fund, Crematorium Fund, Benevolent fund unless states charity.

NOTE Widows and orphans fund for police and firemen, to be coded 196 Life Insurance, at Q.37 A schedule.

Item Codes 1979	Description of items	Additional Examples
796	Subscriptions to trade union, professional, associations, etc.	Contributions to strike funds.
797	Other subscriptions.	Youth/ social/ welfare/ working men's/ masonic/ Buffaloes/ Scouts/ guides/ cubs. Ratepayers Association. Conference fee, choir fund, Weight Watching Club, Veterans motor club, National Trust.
798	Charitable gifts	Church collections, charitable organisations, (including donations), pew rent, benevolent funds. Bob-a-job. Entrance to Bazaar, entrance to Jumble Sale. School fund.
799	Miscellaneous expenditure on services not assignable to any other code. Inc. rent on property prior to moving away from present home.	Library subscriptions and fines, left luggage charges, undertaking, emptying cess pit, cloak-room charges, newspaper adverts, public baths (not swimming), turfing grave, payment to house agent/architect, hire of deck chair, legal charges, visa, storage, parked motor vehicle towed away by police, platform ticket. Do-it-yourself job with a friend's help, wired TV and radio, piped TV, bill paying services (eg Safe Homes), rental (eg holiday TV, vacuum/carpet cleaner), Banns, Legal aid (Q.43 if HP).

Item Codes 1979	Description of items	Additional Examples

Miscellaneous

801	Children's pocket money, the expenditure of which cannot be assigned to a particular code.	
802	Cash gifts (not donations) and tips not allocated elsewhere	Include collective money presents (collective money presents, where goods known should be assigned to appropriate item code), maintenance of children/-parents outside household. Money gift to friends or relatives. Jubilee donations (regardless of type of celebration or form of collection.
803	Savings	Savings/Slate/Holiday/Christmas/Office/clubs. Tontine, loan club/Co-op Savings Stamps, Savings seals, Savings certificates, premium saving bonds, defence bonds, savings stamps, deposits in savings banks, investments in building societies, school bank, stocks and shares, unit trusts, Save as You Earn, Deposit Accounts.
811	Stakes—football pools	Football pools run by charities
812	Bookmakers, betting shops, totalisator	
813	Lotteries	
814	Other betting	Bingo, including admission charge, sweepstakes, raffles, fruit machines, pontoon, office 'tote'.

Food bought and consumed away from home

856	Potato crisps and similar products. Chips alone.	
860	Apples and Pears. Oranges and bananas	
863	Dried fruit and nuts. Fruit juice (canned or in glass)	
875	Non-alcoholic drinks other than soft drinks.	Cups of tea, coffee, milk, Horlicks, including 'tea clubs'.
877	Meals out in workplace, canteen etc. of educational establishment (spender classified under SIC minimum list heading 872) (exclude students)	'Meals out' lunch, dinner, etc., carton of soup. Meals that include one or more prepared dishes not specifically covered in the series 850-899. When such a dish is part of a meal, the whole meal should be coded 877/878/879 (eg all items in a meal described as bacon and egg, bun, cup of tea). Do not apply 'drink test' except in case of fish and chips.
878	Meals out in workplace, canteen etc. other than places covered by code 877 inc: students' meals at education institutes.	
879	Other meals out, bought and consumed elsewhere away from home other than State School meals.	'Weekly tea fund at work', tea club code 875.
883	Ice cream	
884	Soft drinks (whether in can, bottle or glass)	
885	Sweets and chocolates.	
886	Biscuits, shortbread, Chocolate coated biscuits, wafers, etc.	
887	Cakes, buns, currant bread, fruit pies, pastries, scones, etc.	
889	Cooked meat and meat products, provided not sandwiches.	
894	Snacks, unspecified.	Snacks costing more than 75p code as meal 877/8/9 as appropriate.
896	Sandwiches, rolls with filling.	Toasted sandwiches.
897	Take-away meals (excluding fish and chips, code 138) Other items in Meals out sections 1 and 2 not prepared by catering which cannot be coded 850-899.	Meals on wheels, packet of prawns, whelks, mussels, 'Tuck shop', other fruits not codable 860.

Codes on page 18 of Record Book

Q.2.   *Written answers should be coded as follows:*

821	Football pools
822	Bookmaker, Betting shop, totalisator
823	Lotteries
824	Other betting, sweepstake, etc.

Q.3   *Expenditure made on behalf of another person:*

271	Rent, unfurnished dwelling, local authority
272	Rent, unfurnished dwelling, other
273	Rent, furnished dwelling
274	Rates, unfurnished dwelling, local authority
275	Rates, unfurnished dwelling, other
276	Rates, furnished dwelling
277	Rates, rent-free dwelling
278	Rates, dwelling in process of purchase
279	Rates, dwelling owned outright
280	Water rate, unfurnished dwelling, local authority
281	Water rate, unfurnished dwelling, other
282	Water rate, furnished dwelling
283	Water rate, rent-free dwelling
284	Water rate, dwelling in process of purchase
285	Water rate, owned outright
286	Gas account
287	Electricity account
288	Telephone account
289	Television licence
290	Television rental
291	Any other

Appendix C Household Schedule (A)—Detailed Notes

C1 Note on contents and layout

This schedule is taken first at the main interview. Information for most of the questions is obtained from the head of household or housewife, but certain questions of a more individual character (Qs 34A—47) are put to every member aged 16 or over. Information on rateable value and rate poundage (Qs 48—50) is obtained by the interviewer from the appropriate local authority. The questionnaire is used to obtain details about the household, the sex and age of each member, and also details about the type and size of the household accommodation. The main part of the questionnaire relates to expenditure both of a household and individual nature, but the questions are mainly confined to expenses of a recurring nature. On the household side the expenditure questions cover:

	Questions
Housing costs	15B-24
Payments to Gas and Electricity Boards	26-28
Telephone charges	29,30
Licences and television rental	31,32

On the individual side the expenditure questions cover:

Motor vehicles	34A,B,35
Season tickets for transport	36
Life and accident insurances	37
Payments through a bank	38,39
Instalment payments	40-43
Welfare foods	45
Educational grants and fees	46,47

Schedule A consists of three sections:

Page 1—Details of each household member are entered on a separate line, and each line is punched.

Pages 2 to 18, 20 to 22 — The text of the questions is on the left of the page and the information to be punched appears in the two right-hand columns.

Page 19 — The information relating to an agreement is recorded in a vertical column, and each column is then punched.

It may also be useful to give some further explanation about the use of the layout on the main part of the schedule. Of the two columns on the right the first, or amount column, contains the amount of expenditure, or in some cases a number, and this is followed in the last column by an identifying three-digit code which is usually pre-printed. Where the three-digit code is preceded by a capital A the entry on the left usually consists of an indicative code in the £ column. In all other cases the three-digit code identifies an amount in the £ p column, and on the right the three-digit code is followed by a period code inserted by the SSD Primary Analysis Branch (PAB) when this period code is not pre-printed. The latter code (see Section B1) enables the amount to be converted to its equivalent weekly rate at the computer stage. Wherever possible the form has been designed in such a way that the answer to a question is recorded by the interviewer directly in the £ p column in order to avoid unnecessary clerical work. Usually this is indicated by an arrow followed by a dotted line in the £ p column. In cases where the answer obtained by the interviewer has to be converted into a numeral code by the PAB or is subject to substantial editing, the interviewer records the amount to the left of the vertical columns, and the edited amount is entered on the right by the PAB.

C2 Household Schedule (A) 1979

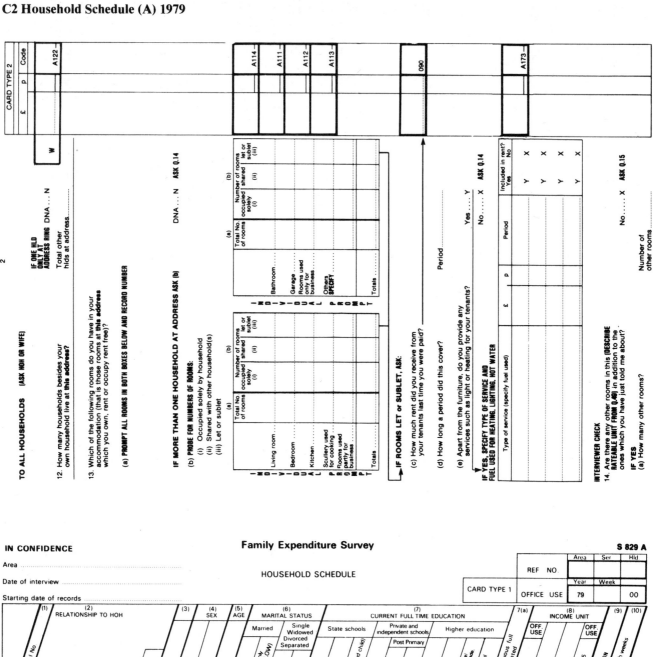

3

TO ALL HOUSEHOLDS (ASK HOH OR WIFE)

15A. Is your accommodation connected to a mains sewerage?
Yes .... Y
No X   NOW ASK Q.15B

TO ALL HOUSEHOLDS | ASK ALL SPENDERS |

15B (a) Do (any of) you have a garage (anywhere) which is:
INCLUDE GARAGE(S) AT Q.13

	No	IF YES How many?	
owned?	X		ASK (b)
rented?	X		ASK (a1)
rent free?	X		ASK (b)

IF NO GARAGE ASK Q.16A or 16B

IF RENTED
(a1) Is the rent included in any rent you pay a landlord for your accommodation .... R ASK (b)
or is it paid separately? .... S (i) - (ii)

IF PAID SEPARATELY
(i) How much rent did you pay last time? £ .... ASK (b)
(ii) How long a period did this cover? Period ....

TO ALL WITH A GARAGE
(b) Do you pay a separate rate and/or ground rent for the garage?

	Rates	Ground rent	
Yes	Y	Y	ASK (ii) - (iii)
No	X	X	[c]
	£	£	ASK (c)

IF YES
(i) How much did you pay last time? £
(ii) How long a period did this cover? Period ....

(c) Is the garage:
used solely by this household 0   ASK Q.16A or 16B
shared with others, but not let or sub-let X   [c1] - [c2]
let or sub-let? .... Y

IF LET OR SUB-LET
(c1) How much did you receive from your tenant for the garage the last time you were paid? £   SEE [c3]

IF ROOM ALSO SUB-LET at Q.13
(c2) How long a period did this cover? Period ....
(c3) Has this rent from the garage been included in the rent you mentioned you received from letting the rooms?
Yes .... Y   ASK Q.16A or 16B
No X

IF ANOTHER GARAGE, CODE ON RIGHT

IF HOUSEHOLD OCCUPIES A CARAVAN OR HOUSEBOAT, ASK Q.16B ON NEXT PAGE

ALL OTHER HOUSEHOLDS (ASK HOH or WIFE)
16A. Do you rent or do you own this accommodation?
Rents ... 0   ASK [a]
Owns X   ASK [b]
Neither . Y   ASK [c]

IF RENTS (CODED O at Q.16A)
(a) Do you rent your accommodation
RUNNING PROMPT
from a Council or New Town Corporation 1
from someone else, unfurnished 2
or furnished 3   ASK [d]

IF OWNS (CODED X at Q.16A)
(b) Do you own your accommodation
RUNNING PROMPT
with a mortgage 4   ASK Q.20
or outright 5

IF NEITHER (CODED Y at Q.16A)
(c) Do you receive your accommodation rent free?
Yes 6   PROBE TO MAKE CERTAIN NOT CODES 1 - 5 THEN SEE [d]
No ..... Z

SPECIFY DETAILS

HOUSEHOLDS CODED 0 or Y at Q.16A
(d) Is your tenancy dependent on your job?
Yes 1
No X   SEE Q.17

Codes: A115, 189, A116, A117, A118, 100, A120, A110

4

TO ALL LIVING IN CARAVAN OR HOUSEBOAT (ASK HOH or WIFE)
16B. (a) Do you pay site rent?
No X   ASK (b)
IF YES
(a1) How much site rent did you pay last time?
(a2) What period did this cover? Period ....

(b) Is your caravan/houseboat........
RING ONE
Rented? 3   ASK Q.17
Owned outright? 5   ASK Q20
Being bought on HP or loan? 5   INCLUDE at Q.40 AND ASK Q.20
Other? 6   SPECIFY ON LEFT AND ASK Q.19

TO ALL WITH RENTED ACCOMMODATION (ASK HOH or WIFE)
(CODED 1, 2 or 3 at Q.16A(a) or 3 at Q.16B)
17. (a) How much rent did you pay last time (including any rooms you sublet)?

(b) How long a period did this cover? Period ....   No X   ASK (d)

(c) Do you have a rent holiday?
IF YES
(i) For how many weeks of the year? Weeks ....   No X   ASK (e)

(d) Did you receive a rent rebate or allowance from the Council in connection with your **last rent payment**?
IF YES
(i) Was the rent rebate/allowance
deducted from the last rent repayment? .... D
or returned direct to you in a lump sum, that is by cash, cheque or giro? L

(ii) How much was the rent rebate or allowance?

(iii) How long a period did this cover? Period ....

(iv) Is the amount for rent you mentioned earlier before or after deduction of the rebate or allowance?
Before .. X
After ... Y

(e) Does the rent you mentioned include any services such as:
PROMPT lighting   cleaning
heating   lift
hot water porter
or any other services?
Yes .... Y   SPECIFY BELOW
No X   ASK (f)

Type of service (specify fuel for heating, lighting, hot water)

Codes: 120, A120, 010, 230, 024, 025, 026, 027, 020, A156

TO ALL WITH RENTED ACCOMMODATION (ASK HOH OR WIFE)

Q.17 (continued)

(f) Are there any (other) regular payments which you make in connection with this accommodation which are not included in the rent?

Yes.... Y ASK (i) - (iii)
No..... X ASK Q.18(a)

IF YES
(i) What is the payment for?
(ii) How much is the payment?
(iii) What period does the payment cover?

Items	f(ii) £	p	f(iii) Period
f(i)			

060

18. (a) Does the rent include rates?

Yes.... Y ASK (b)

IF NO
(a1) How many times a year do you pay rates? No. of times
(a2) How much did you actually pay last time in rates?

030

(b) Was a rates rebate deducted from your last rent/rates payment?

Yes.... Y ASK (b1) - (b3)
No..... X ASK (b4)

IF YES
(b1) How much was deducted?

040

(b2) What period did this rebate cover? Period........ DK........ 0
(b3) Was the amount for rates you mentioned earlier before or after deduction of the rebate?

Before... X
After... Y

A148

IF NO
(b4) In the last 12 months, that is since ...... have you had any rates rebates refunded by the Council direct to you, that is by a lump sum in cash, cheque or Giro?

Yes.... Y ASK (i) - (iii)
No..... X ASK (c)

IF YES
(i) How much was/were the amount(s) refunded?
(ii) What period(s) did the rebate(s) cover?
(iii) In which month(s) and year(s) did you receive it/them?

ENTER DETAILS BELOW

Amount refunded	Period	DK	Month	Year	DK
£		0			0
£		0			0

047 8
014
A127

(c) Do you pay a separate water rate?

No..... X ASK (d)

IF YES
(c1) What was your last payment of water rates?
(c2) How long a period did this cover? Period

050

(d) Do you pay a separate land drainage rate?

Yes.... Y ASK (d1) - (d2)
No..... X ASK Q.24

IF YES
(d1) How much was your last payment? £
(d2) How long a period did this cover? Period

NOW ASK Q.24

INTERVIEWER TO CODE	RATES DOCUMENTS:	seen by interviewer	1
		consulted by informant	2
		not consulted	3
	SPECIFY		

TO ALL WITH RENT FREE ACCOMMODATION (CODED 6 at Q.16A(c)) and OTHERS (CODED Z at Q.16A(c) or CODED 6 at Q.16B)

19. (a) Does anyone outside your household pay rent on this accommodation on your behalf?

No..... X ASK (b)

IF YES
(a1) How much rent did they pay last time? £
(a2) How long a period did this cover? Period

030

(b) Do you pay rates on this accommodation?

Yes.... Y ASK (b1) - (b3)
No..... X ASK (c)

IF YES
(b1) How many times a year do you pay rates? No. of times
(b2) How much did you actually pay last time in rates?

040

(b3) Was a rates rebate deducted from your last rates payment?

Yes.... Y ASK (1) - (3)
No..... X ASK (4)

(1) How much was deducted?

A148

(2) What period did this rebate cover? Period........ DK........ 0
(3) Was the amount for rates you mentioned earlier before or after deduction of the rebate?

Before... X
After... Y

047 8

IF NO
(4) In the last 12 months, that is since ...... have you had any rates rebate(s) refunded direct to you, that is a lump sum in cash, cheque or Giro?

Yes.... Y ASK (i) - (iii)
No..... X ASK (c)
DK... 0

014

IF YES
(i) How much was/were the amount(s) refunded?
(ii) What period(s) did the rebate(s) cover?
(iii) In which month(s) and year(s) did you receive it/them?

ENTER DETAILS BELOW

A127

Amount refunded	Period	DK	Month	Year	DK
£		0			0
£		0			0

NOW ASK (c)

(c) Do you pay a separate water rate?

No..... X ASK (d)

IF YES
(c1) What was your last payment of water rates?
(c2) How long a period did this cover? Period

050

(d) Are there any (other) regular payments which you make in connection with this accommodation?

Yes.... Y SPECIFY
No..... X ASK (e)

SPECIFY ITEMS, AMOUNTS AND PERIODS

060

(e) Do you pay a separate land drainage rate?

Yes.... Y ASK (e1) - (e2)
No..... X ASK Q.24

IF YES
(e1) How much was your last payment? £
(e2) How long a period did this cover? Period

NOW ASK Q.24

INTERVIEWER TO CODE	RATES DOCUMENTS:	seen by interviewer	1
		consulted by informant	2
		not consulted	3
	SPECIFY		

7

TO ALL WHO OWN (CODED X at Q.16A or CODED 5 at Q.16B)   (ASK HOH OR WIFE)

20. (a) How many times a year do you pay rates? .... No. of times ....

(b) How much did you actually pay last time in rates?

(c) Was a rates rebate deducted from your last rates payment?   Yes ..... Y ASK (c1)-(c3)   No ..... X ASK (c4)

IF YES
(c1) How much was deducted?

(c2) What period did this rebate cover?   Period ....   DK 0

(c3) Was the amount for rates you mentioned earlier before or after deduction of the rebate?   Before .. X   After .... Y

IF NO
(c4) In the last 12 months, that is since ..... have you had any rates rebate(s) refunded direct to you, that is a lump sum in cash, cheque or Giro?   Yes .... Y ASK (d1)-(iii)   No ..... X ASK (d)

IF YES
(i) How much was/were the amount(s) refunded?

(ii) What period(s) did the rebate(s) refunded?

(iii) In which month(s) and year(s) did you receive it/them?

ENTER DETAILS BELOW

Amount refunded	Period	DK	Month	Year	DK
£		0			0
£		0			0

(d) Do you pay a separate water rate?   Yes ..... Y ASK (d1)-(d2)   No ..... X ASK (e)

IF YES
(d1) What was your last payment of water rates?

(d2) How long a period did this cover?   Period

(e) Do you pay a separate land drainage rate?   Yes ..... Y ASK (e1)-(e2)   No ..... X ASK (f)

IF YES
(e1) How much was your last payment? .... £

(e2) How long a period did this cover?   Period

(f) Do you pay ground rent, feu duty (Scotland), chief rent, service charge and/or compulsory or regular maintenance charges? [EXCLUDE SITE RENT FOR CARAVAN OWNERS]   Yes .... Y ASK (f1)-(f2)   No ..... X SEE Q.21

IF YES
(f1) How much was your last payment?   Period

INTERVIEWER TO CODE   RATES DOCUMENTS: seen by interviewer 1   consulted by informant 2   not consulted 3
SPECIFY ....   NOW SEE Q.21

TO ALL WHO OWN WITH MORTGAGE   (CODED 4 at Q.16A (b))   DNA ..... N ASK Q.24

21. (a) Did you get the loan or mortgage to purchase your accommodation from a ....
RUNNING PROMPT: Building Society 1   Local Authority 2   Bank 3   Insurance company 4   Other source 5   SPECIFY ON LEFT

(b) Is the mortgage an option mortgage? ....   Yes 1   No X

(c) Are you paying ....   PROMPT   interest only? .... 8 ASK Q.22   interest and principal?.. 9 ASK Q. 23.

Code column: 030, 040, A148, 047 8, 014, A127, 050, 060, A119, A121

TO THOSE WITH MORTGAGES WHERE PAYMENTS COVER INTEREST ONLY   (CODED 8 at Q.21(c))   (ASK HOH OR WIFE)

22. (a) How much did you pay last time as interest on the mortgage (loan)?

(b) How long a period did your last payment cover?   Period ....

(c) Is there an endowment policy covering the repayment of the principal of the mortgage?   No X   £ | p   SPECIFY AT LEFT HOW PRINCIPAL COVERED

IF YES
(c1) How much was your last insurance premium on the endowment policy covering the principal?

(c2) How long a period did this cover?   Period ....

(c3) Has this insurance premium been included in the amount of interest you mentioned earlier?   Yes ..... Y   No X

(d) Did the amount of interest you have just told me about include other amounts such as insurance on the structure of your accommodation or a mortgage protection policy?   No ..... X ASK Q.24

IF YES, ENTER SEPARATE DETAILS BELOW
(d1) How much of your last interest payment was for:

	None	Amount	Period
Insurance on structure?	X	£	
Mortgage protection policy?	X	£	
Other, SPECIFY	X	£	

INTERVIEWER TO CODE   DOCUMENTS: seen by interviewer 1   consulted by informant 2   not consulted 3
SPECIFY ....   ASK Q.24

TO THOSE WITH MORTGAGES WHERE PAYMENTS COVER INTEREST AND PRINCIPAL   (CODED 9 at Q.21(c))   (ASK HOH OR WIFE)

23. (a) How much was your last instalment on the loan or mortgage?

(b) How long a period did this cover?   Period ....

(c) Did this instalment include any other amounts such as insurance on the structure of your accommodation or a mortgage protection policy?   No ..... X ASK (d)

IF YES, ENTER SEPARATE DETAILS BELOW
(c1) How much of your last interest payment was for:

	None	Amount	Period
Insurance on structure?	X	£	
Mortgage protection policy?	X	£	
Other, SPECIFY	X	£	

(d) How much interest did you pay over the last year for which you have figures?   GIVE DATES: From .... to ....

INTERVIEWER TO CODE   DOCUMENTS: seen by interviewer 1   consulted by informant 2   not consulted 3
SPECIFY ....   ASK Q.24

Code column: 130, 200, 150 8, A158, A159

Page 9

£	p	Code

TO ALL HOUSEHOLDS (ASK HOH or WIFE)

24. (a) Do you pay an insurance premium on the **structure** of this accommodation?

No ..... X **ASK (b)**

(This is compulsory for owners with mortgages from building societies (coded 1 at Q.21(a))

INCLUDE: POLICIES FOR DAMAGE TO ROOF BY TV AERIAL

IF YES
(a1) How much was the last premium? — Code **110**

(a2) What period did this cover? Period

IF PREMIUM COVERS BOTH STRUCTURE AND CONTENTS AND CANNOT BE SEPARATED ASK:

Total premium £ .... Period of payment

Insured value of house £ ....

Insured value of contents £ ....

ASK ALL SPENDERS

(b) Do (any of) you pay an insurance premium on the **furniture and contents** of your accommodation?

No ..... X **ASK (c)**

IF YES
(b1) How much was the last premium on the contents? — Code **166**

(b2) How long a period did this cover? Period

(c) Do (any of) you pay an (additional) insurance premium on any kind of **personal possessions**?

No ..... X **ASK Q.26**

INCLUDE:
JEWELLERY, FURS
CAMERAS, BOATS
CARAVANS (IF NOT SAMPLED ADDRESS)
TV (EXCLUDING MAINTENANCE CONTRACTS)

EXCLUDE:
CARS
MAINTENANCE CONTRACTS

IF YES
(c1) How much was the last premium? — Code **168**

(c2) How long a period did this cover? Period

THERE IS NO Q.25

10

Page 10

£	p	Code

TO ALL HOUSEHOLDS (ASK HOH OR WIFE)

26. Do you have gas, electricity or both supplied to your (part of this) accommodation?

CODE ONE
Gas only .... 5 ⎤
Electricity only .... 6 ⎟ ASK (a)
Both .... 7 ⎦
Neither .... 8 — ASK Q.29 — A103

CODE ALL THAT APPLY

	Gas	Elec.	
(a) Do you pay for your gas/electricity by Slot meter*	1	1	ASK Q.27A
Account	2	2	ASK Q.28 (a)-(d)
Board Budgeting scheme	3	3	ASK Q.27B AND THEN Q.28 (b)-(d)
Or by some other method	4	4	SPECIFY AT LEFT AND ASK Q.28(b)-(d)
No	X	X	ASK Q.(b)

A128 A130

*INCLUDE METER OWNED BY LANDLORD, BUT EXCLUDE METER WITH OWN KEY

TO THOSE PAYING BY SLOT METER (CODE 1 at 26(a))

27A. (a) In the last 12 months, that is, since .... have you received a rebate?

No ..... X **SEE 27B**

IF YES
(i) How much was the last rebate?
Gas **173**
Electricity **178**

(ii) How long a period did it cover?
Gas
Electricity

(b) Do you make any other **regular** payments to the Gas/Electricity Board (eg for rent of appliances or maintenance)?

No ..... X **SEE 27B**

IF YES, ENTER DETAILS BELOW
EXCLUDE HIRE PURCHASE OR LOAN (ENTER AT 0.40)

Type of payment	RING	Amount paid last time £ p	Period covered	Was payment made from rebate or separately — Reb	Sep	Was the rebate mentioned earlier the full rebate or after payment was deducted for — Before	After	Code
	G E			R	S	Y	X	197
	G E			R	S	Y	X	198
	G E			R	S	Y	X	237
	G E			R	S	Y	X	238

TO THOSE PAYING BY BOARD BUDGETING SCHEME (CODED 3 at 26(a))

27B. (a) How much was your last payment under this scheme?
Gas **221**

(b) What period does this cover?
Period
Electricity **222**
Period

(c) How much was the amount of your last account/advice, including standing charge and meter rent?
EXCLUDE RENTAL OF APPLIANCES, HIRE PURCHASE, LOANS, MAINTENANCE CHARGE.
Gas **223**

(d) How long a period did it cover?
Electricity **224**
Period

NOW ASK Q.28 (b)-(d)

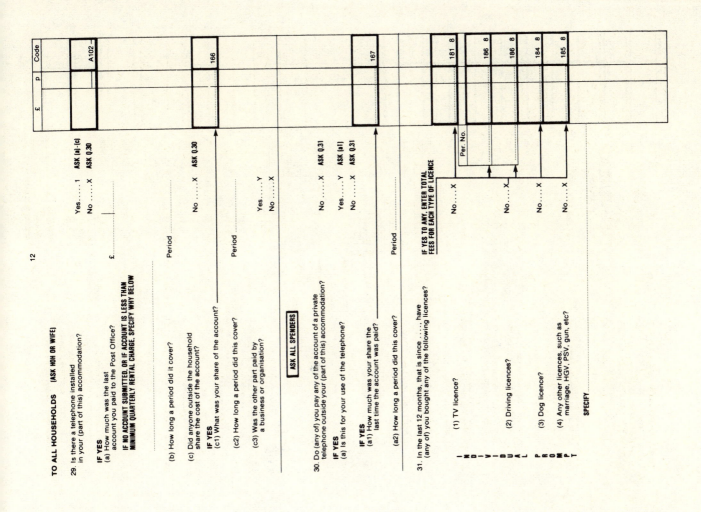

TO ALL HOUSEHOLDS (ASK HOH OR WIFE)

29. Is there a telephone installed in your (part of this) accommodation?
Yes.....1   ASK (a)-(c)
No......X   ASK Q.30   Code A102-

IF YES
(a) How much was the last account you paid to the Post Office? £
IF NO ACCOUNT SUBMITTED, OR IF ACCOUNT IS LESS THAN MINIMUM QUARTERLY RENTAL CHARGE, SPECIFY WHY BELOW

(b) How long a period did it cover?   Period
No X   ASK Q.30   166

(c) Did anyone outside the household share the cost of the account?
IF YES
(c1) What was your share of the account?   Period
(c2) How long a period did this cover?   Period
(c3) Was the other part paid by a business or organisation?   Yes.....Y   No X   167

ASK ALL SPENDERS

30. Do (any of) you pay any of the account of a private telephone outside your (part of this) accommodation?
No X   ASK Q.31
IF YES
(a) Is this for your use of the telephone?   Yes.....Y   ASK (a1)   No X   ASK Q.31
IF YES
(a1) How much was your share the last time the account was paid? £
(a2) How long a period did this cover?   Period

31. In the last 12 months, that is since ...... have (any of) you bought any of the following licences?
IF YES TO ANY, ENTER TOTAL FEES FOR EACH TYPE OF LICENCE   Per. No.

(1) TV licence?   No....X   181   8
(2) Driving licences?   No....X   186   8
(3) Dog licence?   No....X   186   8
(4) Any other licences, such as marriage, HGV, PSV, gun, etc?   No....X   184   8
SPECIFY   185   8

(margin: INDIVIDUAL PROMPT)

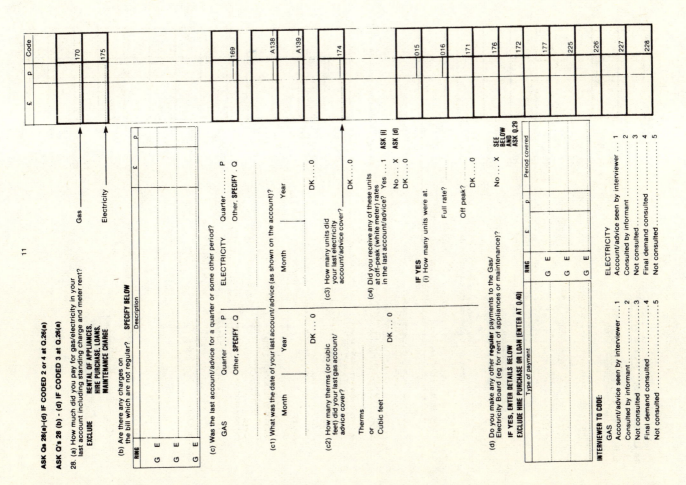

ASK Qs 28(a)-(d) IF CODED 2 or 4 at Q.26(a)
ASK Q's 28 (b) - (d) IF CODED 3 at Q.26(a)

28. (a) How much did you pay for gas/electricity in your last account including standing charge and meter rent?
EXCLUDE   RENTAL OF APPLIANCES. HIRE PURCHASE, LOANS, MAINTENANCE CHARGE

Gas   170
Electricity   175

(b) Are there any charges on the bill which are not regular?   SPECIFY BELOW

RING	Description	£	p
G E			
G E			169
G E			

(c) Was the last account/advice for a quarter or some other period?
GAS   Quarter ..... P   Other, **SPECIFY** . Q   A138
ELECTRICITY   Quarter .... P   Other, **SPECIFY** . Q   A139

(c1) What was the date of your last account/advice (as shown on the account)?
Month   Year   DK....0
Month   Year   DK....0

(c2) How many therms (or cubic feet) did your last gas account/advice cover?
Therms or Cubic feet   DK ... 0   174

(c3) How many units did your last electricity account/advice cover?   DK.....0

(c4) Did you receive any of these units at off-peak (white meter) rates in the last account/advice?   Yes 1   ASK (i)   No X   ASK (d)   DK 0   015

IF YES
(i) How many units were at:
Full rate?   DK....0   016
Off peak?   DK....0   171

(d) Do you make any other **regular** payments to the Gas/Electricity Board (eg for rent of appliances or maintenance)?   No ... X   SEE BELOW AND ASK Q.29   176

IF YES, ENTER DETAILS BELOW
EXCLUDE HIRE PURCHASE OR LOAN (ENTER AT Q.40)

Type of payment	RING	£	p	Period covered
	G E				172
	G E				177
	G E				225 226 227 228

INTERVIEWER TO CODE:

GAS
Account/advice seen by interviewer 1
Consulted by informant.................2
Not consulted 3
Final demand consulted 4
Not consulted 5

ELECTRICITY
Account/advice seen by interviewer ... 1
Consulted by informant 2
Not consulted 3
Final demand consulted 4
Not consulted 5

TO ALL HOUSEHOLDS [ASK ALL SPENDERS]

34A (i) Do (any of) you **at present** own or have the continuous use of any cars, vans motorcycles, mopeds or any other motor vehicles?

Yes ... Y   ASK (b)-(h) THEN ASK Q.34A (II) — A124

No X   ASK Q.34A (II)

ASK (b)-(h) FOR EACH VEHICLE AT Q.34(I) AND 34(II) AND ENTER DETAILS IN BOX BELOW

(a) INTERVIEWER TO CODE — A160

(b) What type of vehicle is/was it? — A161

(c) Do/did you own the vehicle or do/did you have continuous use of it? — A162

(d) How much did you (each) pay in vehicle licence(s) (Road Fund Tax) during the last 12 months (for each vehicle)? — A163

(e) How long a period(s) did the amount(s) cover (eg year, four months)? — 187 8

(f) When was the vehicle licence last renewed?

(g) How much did you (each) pay in vehicle insurance during the last 12 months? — 187 8

(h) How long a period(s) did the amount(s) cover (eg year, 3 months, month)? — 188 8 / 188 8

(a) Per No.	Has vehicle now Yes / No	(b) Vehicle type Car Van M/c Other	(c) Vehicle owned use only	(d) Vehicle licence Amount £ p	(e) Period	(f) Date renewed Mth. Yr.	(g) Insurance Amount £ p	(h) Period
	Y X	1 2 3	P U					
	Y X	1 2 3	P U					
	Y X	1 2 3	P U					
	Y X	1 2 3	P U					

34A (ii) (Apart from the vehicles already mentioned) have (any of) you owned or had the continuous use of any other cars, vans, motorcycles, mopeds or other motor vehicles at any time **during the last 12 months, that is since ....?**

Yes ... Y   ASK (b)-(h)

No X   ASK Q.34B

ASK (b)-(h) FOR EACH VEHICLE AND ENTER DETAILS IN BOX ABOVE

TO ALL HOUSEHOLDS [ASK ALL SPENDERS]

32. Do (any of) you have a television set in your (part of this) accommodation?

Yes ... 1 ASK (a) — A105

No .... X ASK Q.33

IF YES

(a) Do you rent it?

Yes ... 1 ASK (I) — A106

No .... X ASK Q.33

IF YES

(a1) Do you pay for the TV set - by slot meter or by regular payments to the rental company?

Slot .... 1 ASK (I)

Regular payments .. 2 ASK Q.(II)-(III)

Other .... 3 SPECIFY AND ASK (II)-(III)

IF SLOT (CODED 1 at (a1))

(i) Did you get a rebate when the meter was last cleared?

No .... X ASK (a2)

IF YES

(1) How much was the rebate before any deductions for hire purchase or credit purchase? — 194

(2) How long a period did this cover? Period — 195

IF CODED 2 or 3 at (a1)

(ii) How much did you pay last time?

(iii) How long a period did this cover? Period

No X

(a2) Are there any other rented TV sets in your household?

IF ANOTHER RENTED TV SET, ASK ALL RELEVANT QUESTIONS AND NOTE ON LEFT

33. (a) Are any of these items owned or continuously available for use in this accommodation?

INCLUDE ITEMS OWNED, RENTED OR SUPPLIED BY EMPLOYER

	No	Yes	
Washing machine	X	1	A108
Refrigerator with freezer unit attached (with separate door for freezer unit)	X	1	A164
Separate refrigerator	X	1	A165
Separate deep freeze	X	1	A166

Full or partial central heating by:

[P R O M P T]

	No	Yes	
electricity INCLUDE STORAGE HEATER	X	1	A150
gas?	X	1	A151
oil?	X	1 ASK (b)	A152
solid fuel? ..	X	1	A153
D.K. fuel		1	A154

TO ALL WITH OIL CENTRAL HEATING

(b) have you purchased any oil for the central heating in the last 12 months?

Yes ... 1 ASK (ii)

No .... X ASK Q.34A(II)

DK .... 0 — 017 8

IF YES

(i) What was the total expenditure on oil in the last 12 months?

15

TO ALL HOUSEHOLDS | ASK ALL SPENDERS |

34B. Have you received any refund(s) of vehicle licence during the last 12 months?
Yes ... Y   **ASK (a)**
No X   **SEE Q.35**

IF YES
(a) How much was (were) the refund(s)? ———
(b) What period did it (they) cover?   Period ....

	£	p	Code	
			179	8

TO ALL WHO OWN OR HAVE OWNED VEHICLE (CODED P at Q.34A(I) and (II) (c))

35. Did you buy the vehicle **outright** during the last 12 months, that is with cash or by loan from a friend or relative?
No.....X   **ASK Q.36**
Yes ... Y   **ENTER BELOW**

EXCLUDE: LOAN FROM ORGANISATION, BANK FINANCE HOUSE OR H.P. (ENTER AT Q.40)

Per. No.	Vehicle (eg car, van, motor cycle)	New / 2nd hand	Acquired Mth / Yr	Total cost of vehicle £ p	Deduction for trade-in £ p	Net cost of vehicle* (defined below) £ p	Code	
		X Y					244	8
		X Y					245	8
		X Y					246	8
		X Y					247	8

*NET COST = TOTAL COST OF VEHICLE **LESS** ROAD TAX, INSURANCE AND TRADE-IN (IF INCLUDED IN TOTAL COST)

TO ALL HOUSEHOLDS | ASK ALL SPENDERS |

36. Do (any of) you hold a current **weekly** or season ticket for any form of transport for which you yourself paid, including any you have bought for a child?
No ... X   **ASK Q.37**

IF YES ENTER DETAILS BELOW

Per. No	Mode of transport	Period	£	p	Code
					191
					192
					193
					219
					258
					255
					256
					257

WHERE SEASON TICKET IS FOR COMBINED MODES, SPECIFY MODES. eg BUS/TUBE, BUS/RAIL, etc.

TO ALL HOUSEHOLDS | ASK ALL SPENDERS |

37. (a) Do (any of) you pay premiums on any life assurance policies?
Yes ... Y   **GIVE DETAILS**
No ... X   **ASK (b)**

INCLUDE: Self employed pension policies; Premiums on all endowment policies, annuities and education; also insurance policies in connection with house mortgages. Death and Burial policies.
EXCLUDE: National Insurance

Per. No.	RING ONE — House purchase endowment	Other life assurance	Name of insurance company	Period covered by premium (eg month, year)	£	p	Code
	X	Y					196
	X	Y					196
	X	Y					196
	X	Y					196
	X	Y					196
	X	Y					196
	X	Y					196
	X	Y					196
	X	Y					199

(b) Do (any of) you have any other policies on which you regularly pay premiums?
Yes ... Y   **GIVE DETAILS**
No ... X   **ASK Q.38**

INCLUDE: Personal accident and miscellaneous, Private medical insurance schemes, eg BUPA
EXCLUDE: Car, motor cycle, house, contents or personal possessions insurance

Per. No.	Purpose of policy	Insurance company	Period covered by premium (eg month, year)	£	p	Code
						229
						206
						206
						206
						206
						206

TO ALL HOUSEHOLDS [ASK ALL SPENDERS]

38 Do (any of) you have any **current** or **budget** accounts, on which you can draw cheques?

Yes ..... Y ASK (a)-(b)
No ...... X ASK Q.39

IF YES TO ANY ASK (a)-(b) FOR EACH ACCOUNT

(a) With which (type of) bank do you have a current (or budget) account?

PROMPT: National (Post Office) Giro   Trustee Savings Bank
Commercial bank   Co-op
Other banks **SPECIFY:**

(b) Do (any of) you pay any bank charges?

IF YES
(b1) About how much were your bank charges, **excluding** interest on a loan or overdraft in the last 12 months, that is since .....?

(b2) Was any part of this amount for business purposes?

IF YES
(i) About what proportion would be for business?

Per. No.	(a) Type of bank				(b) Bank charges Yes No	Other SPECIFY	(b1) Amount paid £ p	(b2) Business Yes No	(b2)(i) Business propn.
	PO Giro	Bank	Trustee Savings	Co-op					
	1	2	3	4	Y X			Y X	X
	1	2	3	4	Y X			Y X	X
	1	2	3	4	Y X			Y X	X
	1	2	3	4	Y X			Y X	X

39 Do (any of) you pay for anything by means of a standing order or direct debit through a bank or through a National (Post Office) Giro account or by bank budget account?

Yes ... Y ASK FOR DETAILS
No ... X ASK Q.40

FOR LOANS GIVE PURPOSE AND SOURCE OF LOAN (ENTER ALSO AT Qs. 40-43)

EXCLUDE CREDIT TRANSFERS

Per. No.	Purpose (Mortgage, life assurance, car loan. Automobile Association membership, etc)	Period covered by payment

---

18

TO ALL HOUSEHOLDS   [ASK ALL SPENDERS]

CODE ALL THAT APPLY USING SEPARATE COLUMN FOR EACH ARRANGEMENT

ENTER PER NO.

USE SEPARATE COLUMN FOR EACH ARRANGEMENT

40. (a) Do you have a loan for a particular item (or service) from a:

	Code	No	Yes	Yes	Yes	Yes	Yes
Bank	A168	X	1	1	1	1	1
Finance house	A169	X	2	2	2	2	2
Organisation granting second mortgages	A170	X	3	3	3	3	3

ASK Q.41 THEN Q.42

(b) Do you have an HP or Credit Sale agreement? **INCLUDE GAS OR ELECTRICITY BOARD OR CO-OP**

	Code	No	Yes	Yes	Yes	Yes	Yes
Hire purchase	A171	X	4	4	4	4	4
Credit sale	A172	X	5	5	5	5	5

(c) Are (any of) you **at present** making regular payments and/or paying instalments to any of the following:

	Code	No	Yes	Yes	Yes	Yes	Yes
A budget or option account at a shop or store? [EXCLUDE BANK BUDGET ACCOUNTS]	180 8	X	6	6	6	6	6
A Co-op club? [EXCLUDE HP AND LOANS]		X	7	7	7	7	7
Any other shop running a club?		X	8	8	8	8	8
A Mail Order club as an agent or through a friend or relative?		X	9	9	9	9	9
Any other Mail Order organisation?		X	10	10	10	10	10
A Credit Trader calling regularly on customers?		X	11	11	11	11	11
A Check Trader?		X	12	12	12	12	12
Or any other arrangements? [ENTER CREDIT CARD BELOW AT (d)] SPECIFY ARRANGEMENTS FOR REPAYMENT BELOW		X	13	13	13	13	13

ASK Q.41 THEN Q.43

(d) Do (any of) you **at present** have a credit card account*?
* ACCESS, BARCLAYCARD, DINERS CLUB, AMERICAN EXPRESS, etc.

	No	Yes	Yes	Yes	Yes	Yes
	X	14	14	14	14	14

DETAILS ON 829C

RE-PROMPT Qs. 40 (a)-(c) FOR TYPE OF ARRANGEMENT

		Y	Y	Y	Y	Y

SEE BELOW

	X	X	X	X	X	X

41. Have you acquired anything by **formal agreement** on which you have made a down payment but on which you have not yet paid an instalment?

Yes...
No ...

CHECK BACK TO Qs. 40 (a)-(b) TO SEE IF Q.42 APPLIES

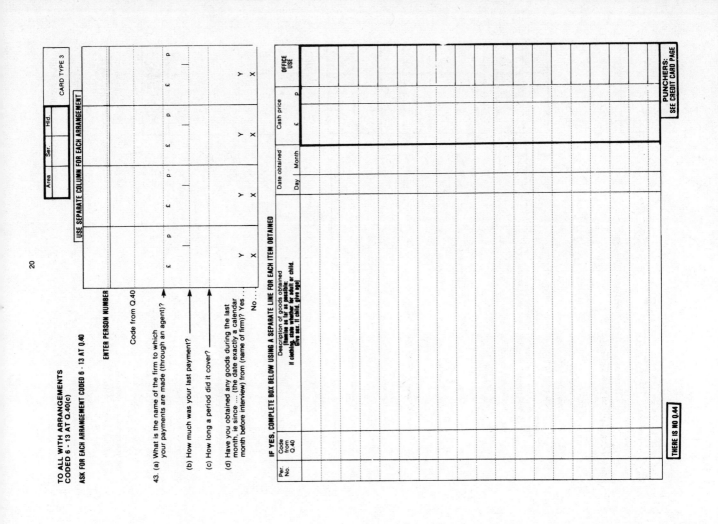

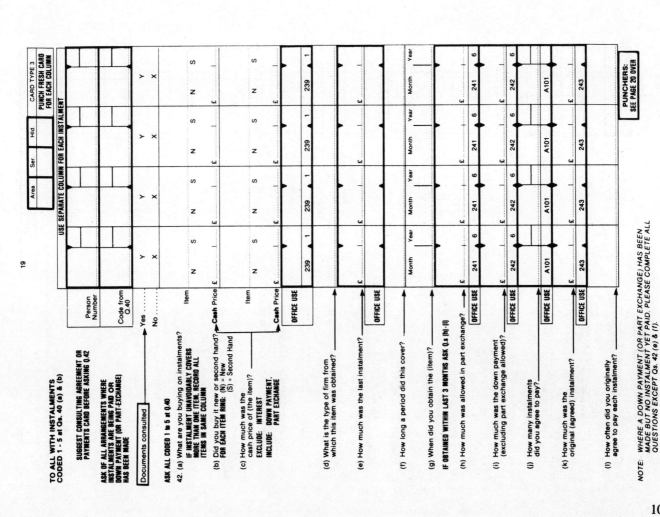

21

TO ALL HOUSEHOLDS   (ASK MAN OR WIFE)

45 Has any member of your household had any of the
following **during the past 7 days ending yesterday:**

PROMPT	Quantity	Per. No receiving benefit	IF FREE RING	If not free amount paid £ p
WELFARE MILK				
Free liquid milk	pints			
	pints			
	pints			
Free Dried milk	tins			
	tins			
	tins			
DNA...N **SCHOOL MEALS/MILK**				
(No school School meals	No	7		
children) (children at State schools)	No	7		
	No	7		
Free school milk	pints			
	pints			
None to all ... X				

ASK ALL SPENDERS

46 Have (any of) you (or your children under 16)
received any education grants, maintenance grants or
scholarships during the last 12 months, that is since .....?

No .... X ASK Q.47

IF YES ENTER DETAILS BELOW

Person receiving grant	Type of grant or scholarship	Source of grant or scholarship	Annual value £ p	Received by Cash/cheque Yes No	Still receiving grant Yes No
				Y X	Y X
				Y X	Y X
				Y X	Y X
				Y X	Y X

47 In the last 12 months, that is since ......
have (any of) you paid any of the following:

PROMPT (a) Any school fees?   No ... X

(b) fees for private tuition,
eg music, dancing or driving lessons?   No ... X

(c) fees for any other kinds of education
such as technical or commercial college,
university, art school, evening classes or WEA?   No ... X

(d) Parental contribution for full-time
education, including maintenance payments?   No ... X

IF YES TO ANY, GIVE DETAILS BELOW

Person receiving education	Subject being studied (eg maths, degree)	Type of institution running course (eg WEA, university)	Amounts paid in last 12 months		
			Fees £ p	Board & lodging £ p	Total £ p

Give further details if child or adult is not a member of the household
eg grandson at commercial college

CHECK THAT Q.50 IS COMPLETED

CARD TYPE 2

£	p	Code
		267
		268
		263 1
		265 1
		260 1
		261 1
		259 1
		248
		249
		250
		251
		252
		253
		156
		157
		207 8
		209 8
		210 8
		211 8
		212 8
		213 8
		214 8
		215 8
		216 8
		217 8
		218 8
		220 8

22

**ALL INFORMATION ON THIS PAGE, EXCEPT Q.50,
SHOULD BE OBTAINED FROM RATING OFFICE OF THE LOCAL AUTHORITY**

48 (a) **Yearly** domestic rate poundage for (address of household)   .... in the £
EXCLUDE WATER RATE, SEWERAGE AND ENVIRONMENTAL SERVICES POUNDAGES

NOTE: A different system of rate poundage is
used in Scotland: see Interviewer's Instructions

(b) Water rates for (address of household) are:

collected by local authority.................1

collected by water authority or water company 2

IF CODED 1

(i) **Yearly** water rate poundage for (address)   .... in the £
EXCLUDE SEWERAGE AND ENVIRONMENTAL SERVICES POUNDAGES

(ii) **Yearly** water supply standing (fixed) charge

(c) Sewerage and/or environmental services
charges for (address) are:

collected by local authority..................1 **ASK (i)-(iii)**

collected by water authority or water company ......2 **GO TO Q.49**

IF CODED 1

(i) **Yearly** sewerage charge (rate) poundage for (address)   .... in the £

(ii) **Yearly** sewerage standing (fixed) charge

(iii) **Yearly** environmental services
charge (poundage) for (address)   .... in the £

49 (a) Gross Value of rateable unit(s) covering the household   £

(b) Net Rateable Value of rateable unit(s) covering the household

COPY FROM VALUATION LISTS

Description (Flat, Shop with flat, house with garage, etc)	Location in building

50 Does the description and Rateable Value
agree with the informant's rate demand?

Yes.................Y

No.................X   **SEE (a)**

Rates demand not seen 2

IF NO
(a) SPECIFY DIFFERENCES _____

FINAL CHECK AT END OF RECORDING PERIOD

Are there two completed D books for each spender?

Yes....Y

No....X

IF YES code column 10, page 1

IF NO note reasons below

Has page 18 been completed in each D book?

Yes....Y

No....Y

IF NO note reasons below

NOW SEE NEXT PAGE

£	p	Code
		080 1
		231 1
		234 8
		A155
		232 1
		235 8
		233 1
00	070 8	
		A174

Social Survey Division, OPCS,
St Catherines House,
10 Kingsway,
London, WC2B 6JP

23

SPECIAL CIRCUMSTANCES

ASK HOM or WIFE

Were there any special circumstances, such as visitors
staying with you or temporary absences of members
of your household during the past two weeks?

SPECIFY:

W1511 OPCS 1/78

Appendix D Income Schedule (B) — Detailed Notes

D1 Note on contents and layout

A questionnaire contains two sets of columns on the right to enable data for two household members aged 16 or over to be entered on the same form. Apart from page 1, the questionnaire is concerned with income, national insurance contributions and income tax. Income of a child under 16 is obtained from one or other of his parents and entered on the parent's questionnaire. The interview schedule is made up as follows:

	Questions
Working status and recent absences from work	1-4
Earnings of an employee	5-26
Self-employed earnings	27,28
National Insurance contributions	29
Pensions and other regular allowances	30-40
Occasional benefits—social security benefits and other types	41-50
Investment income	51-58
Miscellaneous allowances	59A-60C
Miscellaneous earnings of a 'once-only' character	64
Tax and NI contribution paid directly to Inland Revenue or refunded	65-68
Miscellaneous windfalls	69-71
Income of a child under 16	72

The questionnaire is designed on similar lines to the main part of schedule A; that is, the text is on the left and the data to be punched appears in the two sets of columns on the right, each set being used for the household member identified by the Per. No. at the head of the column; each set consists of two sub-columns. As in the A schedule, wherever possible the amount is entered directly by the interviewer in the first of the two sub-columns. This is followed by an identifying three-digit code, with a fourth digit indicating the frequency of the payment. Where this period code is not pre-printed it is inserted by the SSD Primary Analysis Branch from the answer on the left. A three-digit code preceded by an A indicates either a descriptive code or a number.

D2 Income Schedule (B) 1979

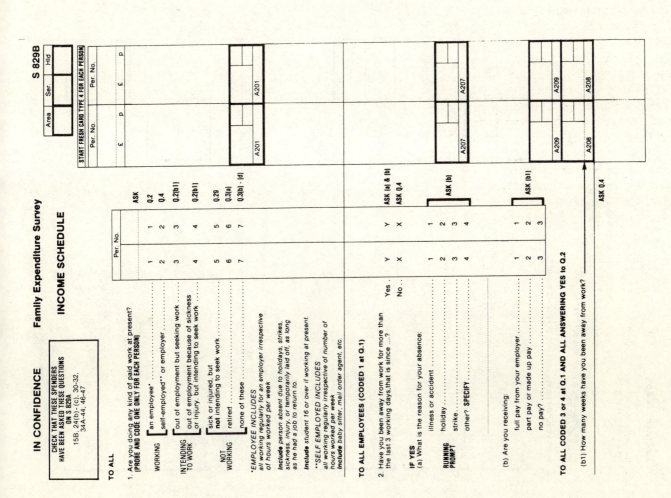

Family Expenditure Survey

INCOME SCHEDULE

IN CONFIDENCE

Area	Ser.	Hld

CHECK THAT THESE SPENDERS
HAVE BEEN ASKED THESE QUESTIONS
ON S 829A

15B, 24(b)–(c), 30–32,
34A–44, 46–47

TO ALL

1. Are you doing any kind of paid work at present?
(PROBE AND CODE ONLY FOR EACH PERSON)

				ASK
WORKING	an employee*	1		0.2
	self-employed** or employer	2		0.4
INTENDING TO WORK	out of employment but seeking work	3		0.2[b1]
	out of employment because of sickness or injury, but intending to seek work	4		0.2[b1]
NOT WORKING	sick or injured, but not intending to seek work	5		0.29
	retired	6		0.3[a]
	none of these	7		0.3[b] - [d]

*EMPLOYEE INCLUDES
all working regularly for an employer irrespective
of hours worked per week

Include person absent due to holidays, strikes,
sickness, injury, or temporarily laid off, as long
as he has a job to return to.

Include student 16 or over if working at present.

**SELF EMPLOYED INCLUDES
all working regularly irrespective of number of
hours worked per week
Include baby sitter, mail order agent, etc.

TO ALL EMPLOYEES (CODED 1 at Q.1)

2. Have you been away from work for more than
the last 3 working days, that is since ....?

			ASK (a) & (b)
Yes	Y		ASK Q.4
No	X		

IF YES
(a) What is the reason for your absence:

			ASK (b)
illness or accident	1		
RUNNING PROMPT holiday	2		
strike	3		
other? SPECIFY	4		

(b) Are you receiving:

			ASK (b1)
full pay from your employer	1		
part pay or made up pay	2		
no pay?	3		

TO ALL CODED 3 or 4 at Q.1 AND ALL ANSWERING YES to Q.2

(b1) How many weeks have you been away from work?

ASK Q.4

START FRESH CARD TYPE 4 FOR EACH PERSON

Per. No.	£	p		Per. No.	£	p
		A201				A201
		A207				A207
	A209	A208			A209	A208

ASK Q.4

TO ALL CODED 6 (RETIRED) AT Q1

3. (a) In what year did you retire? _____ Year

IF LESS THAN 2 YEARS AGO
(i) What was the exact date of your retirement? ____ IF LESS THAN 2 YEARS AGO ASK (i)–(iii) IF 2 YEARS OR MORE ASK Q.29

(ii) How much did you earn from your job (before tax) in the 12 months just before you retired? £ ____ ASK Q.29

TO ALL CODED 7 (NONE OF THESE) at Q.1

3. (b) Have you done any paid work during the last 12 months, that is, since ....?

		Per. No.		
Yes	Y	Y		ASK (i)
No	X	X		ASK Q.3(c)

IF YES
(i) For how many weeks did you work? ____ ASK Q.3(c)

(c) Are you prevented from seeking work because you are looking after a sick or aged relative?

Yes	1	1	ASK Q.29
No	2	2	ASK Q.3(d)

(d) (As far as you know) are you permanently unable to work?

Yes	1	1	ASK (ii)
No	2	2	ASK Q.29

IF YES
(i) Could you tell me why you are permanently unable to work?

REASON _____

NOW ASK Q.29

Per. No.		Per. No.	
£	p	£	p
A206	8	A206	8
302	8	302	8
A215		A215	
A217		A217	
A221		A221	
410	1	410	1
411	1	411	1
412	1	412	1
413	1	413	1
414	1	414	1

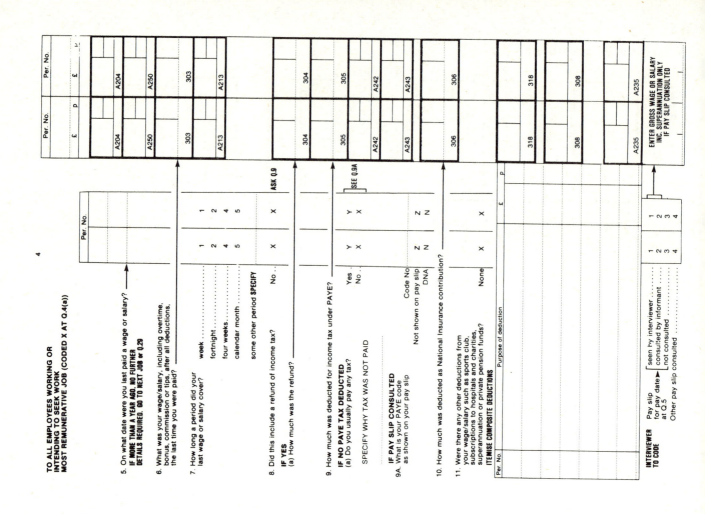

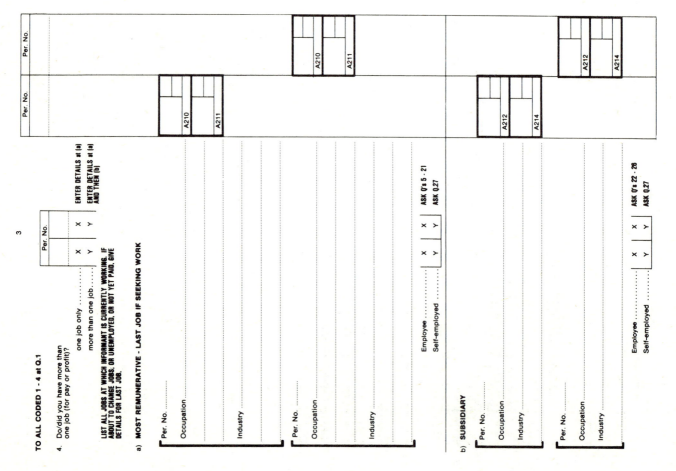

Page 4 section

TO ALL EMPLOYEES WORKING OR INTENDING TO SEEK WORK MOST REMUNERATIVE JOB (CODED X AT Q.4(a))

5. On what date were you last paid a wage or salary? **IF MORE THAN A YEAR AGO, NO FURTHER DETAILS REQUIRED. GO TO NEXT JOB or Q.29**

6. What was your wage/salary, including overtime, bonus, commission or tips, after all deductions, the last time you were paid?

7. How long a period did your last wage or salary cover?
   - week 1
   - fortnight 2
   - four weeks 4
   - calendar month 5
   - some other period **SPECIFY**

8. Did this include a refund of income tax? No .... X — **ASK Q.9**
   IF YES
   (a) How much was the refund?

9. How much was deducted for income tax under PAYE? Yes .... Y / No .... X — **SEE Q.9A**
   IF NO PAYE TAX DEDUCTED
   (a) Do you usually pay any tax?
   SPECIFY WHY TAX WAS NOT PAID
   IF PAY SLIP CONSULTED
   9A. What is your PAYE code as shown on your pay slip
   - Code No.
   - Not shown on pay slip .... N
   - DNA .... N

10. How much was deducted as National Insurance contribution? None X

11. Were there any other deductions from your wage/salary such as sports club, subscriptions to hospitals and charities, superannuation or private pension funds?
    ITEMISE COMPOSITE DEDUCTIONS

    Per. No. | Purpose of deduction | £ | p

    INTERVIEWER TO CODE
    Pay slip for pay date — seen by interviewer .... 1 / consulted by informant .... 2 / not consulted .... 3 / Other pay slip consulted 4
    at Q.5

    ENTER GROSS WAGE OR SALARY INC. SUPERANNUATION ONLY IF PAY SLIP CONSULTED

Codes column: A204, A250, 303, A213, 304, 305, A242, A243, 306, 318, 308, A235

Page 3 section

TO ALL CODED 1 - 4 at Q.1

4. Do/did you have more than one job (for pay or profit)?
   - one job only .... X — **ENTER DETAILS at (a)**
   - more than one job .... Y — **ENTER DETAILS at (a) AND THEN (b)**

LIST ALL JOBS AT WHICH INFORMANT IS CURRENTLY WORKING, IF ABOUT TO CHANGE JOBS, OR UNEMPLOYED, OR NOT YET PAID, GIVE DETAILS FOR LAST JOB.

a) **MOST REMUNERATIVE - LAST JOB IF SEEKING WORK**

Per. No. ....
Occupation ....
Industry ....
Codes: A210, A211

Per. No. ....
Occupation ....
Industry ....

Employee .... X — **ASK Q's 5 - 21**
Self-employed .... Y — **ASK Q.27**

b) **SUBSIDIARY**

Per. No. ....
Occupation ....
Industry ....
Codes: A212, A214

Per. No. ....
Occupation ....
Industry ....

Employee .... X — **ASK Q's 22 - 26**
Self-employed .... Y — **ASK Q.27**

EMPLOYEES - MOST REMUNERATIVE JOB (continued)

ASK WEEKLY PAID ONLY (CODED 1 at Q.7)

12. For how many **actual** hours' work (excluding meal intervals, but including paid overtime) were you paid in the weekly pay you quoted before?

NOW ASK Q.14(a) - (c) → A216

ASK ALL OTHER PAY PERIODS (CODED 2 - 5 and OTHER at Q.7)

13. How many hours a week (excluding meal intervals, but including paid overtime) did you work during the [GIVE PERIOD at Q.7] for which you have given me the details of your pay?

NOW ASK Q.14(a) - (c) → A218

ASK ALL PAY PERIODS

14. (a) How many hours paid overtime a week were included in the hours you have just mentioned?

NOW ASK (b)-(c) → A219

(b) How many hours a week do you **usually** work, excluding meal breaks and overtime? → A220

(c) On average, how many hours paid overtime do you actually work in a week? → A244

IF Q.14 CANNOT BE ANSWERED BECAUSE OF THE IRREGULAR NATURE OF THE JOB, GIVE REASON:
→ A234 / A254

ASK ALL

15. Your last wage/salary was £.... (see Q.6). Is this the amount you usually receive?
Yes ... 1 — ASK Q.16
No ... 2 — ASK (a)-(b)

IF NO

(a) What do you usually receive each time you are paid
after all deductions? → 329
AND
before all deductions? → 315

IF UNABLE TO GIVE USUAL PAY BECAUSE IT VARIES CONSIDERABLY GIVE AVERAGE PAY RECEIVED (NOT BASIC)

(b) How often are you usually paid?
week 1
fortnight 2
four weeks 4
calendar month 5
some other period ... 0 (SPECIFY AT LEFT)
No ... X — ASK Q.17

16. Do you ever get an occasional addition to pay such as Christmas or quarterly bonus or an occasional commission?
No ... X

IF YES

(a) What payments of this kind have you had in the last 12 months? PLEASE ITEMISE BELOW

Per. No.	Description	Total amount in last 12 months £	Is this amount: Before tax	After tax	DK	IF NO AT Q.15 ASK: Did you include the bonus you just mentioned in your usual/average pay? Yes - how much was included? £ p	No
			1	2	3		X
			1	2	3		X
			1	2	3		X
			1	2	3		X
			1	2	3		X
			1	2	3		X

Per. No.		£ p	Per. No.		£ p
	355	1		355	1
	316	1		316	1
	317	1		317	1
	320	5		320	5
	370	8		370	8

EMPLOYEES - MOST REMUNERATIVE JOB (continued)

DO NOT ASK Qs. 17-19 OF THOSE UNEMPLOYED FOR LONGER THAN 13 WEEKS

17. Do you receive any of the following benefits from this employer?
PROMPT EACH

(a) Luncheon vouchers? No ... X
Yes - number received in last 7 days
value of each voucher
number used in last 7 days

(b) Meals supplied free? No ... X
Yes - meals in last 7 days

(c) Any other food supplied free eg milk, potatoes, in the last month? No ... X
IF YES, SPECIFY WITH QUANTITIES RECEIVED

18. Has Inland Revenue allowed you, or will you be claiming, tax relief or expenses, incurred as a result of your employment, such as overalls, clothing, tools, subscriptions to professional societies? No ... X
IF YES, SPECIFY BELOW

Per. No.	Description of expenses claimed as tax relief	Period	Amount on which tax relief allowed £

19. Do you have (have you had) any of these items of household expenditure, which you have mentioned, refunded by your employer? **SEE PROMPT CARD**
FOR EACH ITEM REFUNDED ASK (a) - (b1)
(a) How much of the £.... you mentioned did you have refunded?
(b) Was any of the refund for this item included in your pay received on .... (see Q.5)?
IF YES
(b1) How much was included?

PROMPT AMOUNTS FROM S 829A

	No Per. No.	(a) Refunded £ p	(b) Included in pay No	(b1) £ p
Rent (Q.17)	X		X	
Rates (Q.18, 19, or 20)	X		X	
Water charges (Q.18, 19 or 20)	X		X	
Mortgage on structure (Q.22, 23)	X		X	
Insurance on structure (Q.24(a))	X		X	
Gas (Q.27B(c) or Q.28(a))	X		X	
Electricity (Q.27B(c) or Q.28(a))	X		X	
Telephone (Q.29, 30)	X		X	
Road Fund tax (Q.34A(d))	X		X	
Vehicle insurance (Q.34A(g))	X		X	
Vehicle purchase (Q.35, Q.42)	X		X	
Other SPECIFY			X	
No refunds	X			

Page 7

EMPLOYEES – MOST REMUNERATIVE JOB (continued)

DO NOT ASK Qs 20A-20B-21 OF THOSE UNEMPLOYED FOR LONGER THAN 13 WEEKS

			Per. No.			Per. No.		
			£	p		£	p	

20A. Have you used a vehicle for business/work purposes in the last three months?

Yes ..... Y | X | **ASK (a)**
No ..... Y | X | **ASK Q.21**

IF YES
(a) Was the vehicle your own or your employer's?

Own ..... 1 | 1 | **ASK (b)**
Employer's ..... 2 | 2 |

(b) Have you received a fixed allowance or mileage allowance from your present employer for business motoring in the last 3 months?

Yes ..... 1 | 1 | **ASK (b1)**
No ..... 2 | 2 | **ASK Q20B**

IF YES
(b1) How much have you received on average in a week/month?

(b2) How long a period does this cover?

(b3) Was any allowance for expenses included in the pay that you received on ..... (see Q.5)?

Yes ..... Y | Y | **ASK (I)**
No ..... X | X | **ASK Q.20B**

IF YES
(1) How much was included?

20B. (In addition to the fixed/particular business mileage allowance) have you received any refund of particular business motoring expenses in the last three months?

Yes ..... Y | Y | **ASK (a) & (b)**
No ..... X | X | **ASK Q.21**

IF YES
(a) For which of the following expenses have you received refunds:

	Yes	No	DK	Yes	No	DK	
PROMPT Petrol	Y	X	0	Y	X	0	
Maintenance	Y	X	0	Y	X	0	
Repairs	Y	X	0	Y	X	0	
Other **SPECIFY**	Y			Y			

(b) Was/were there any refund(s) for expenses included in the pay of £..... that you received on ..... (Q.5)?

Yes ..... Y | Y | **ASK (i)**
No ..... X | X | **ASK Q.21**

IF YES
(i) How much was included?

21. Have you received any other refunds or allowances from this employer for business expenses in the last three months?

No ..... X | X | **GO TO NEXT JOB OR Q.29**

IF YES
(a) What do these allowances cover?

FOR EACH REFUND OR ALLOWANCE
(b) How much have you received on average in a week/month?

(c) Was any of this allowance included in the pay that you received on ..... (see Q.5)?

IF YES
(c1) How much was included?

(d) Was this included in your usual pay (see Q.15a)?

IF YES
(d1) How much was included?

Per. No.	(a) Covered by refund/allowance	(b) Period	(c1) Included in pay £ p	No	(d1) Included in usual pay £ p	No	DK
				X		X	0
				X		X	0
				X		X	0
				X		X	0
				X		X	0

GO TO NEXT JOB OR Q.29

Page 8

DETAILS OF JOB FOR SUBSIDIARY EMPLOYMENT AS EMPLOYEE (CODED X AT Q.4(b))

	Per. No.			Per. No.		
	£	p		£	p	

22. On what date were you last paid a wage or salary?

23. What was your wage or salary, including overtime, bonus, commission or tips after all deductions the last time you were paid? | A255 | | | A255 |

24. How long a period did this cover? | 309 | | | 309 |

25. Were any deductions made from this pay before you received it? | 310 | | | 310 |

IF YES, SPECIFY BELOW

Per. No.	Purpose of deduction		£	p	No.		£	p	No.
			311		X		311		X
			319		X		319		X
			314				314		

ENTER GROSS WAGE OR SALARY INC. SUPER-ANNUATION ONLY IF PAY SLIP CONSULTED

GO TO NEXT JOB OR Q.29

26. Have you received any refunds or allowances for business expenditure from your present employer in the last three months?

No. ..... X | X

IF YES
(a) What did these refunds/allowances cover?

FOR EACH REFUND OR ALLOWANCE ASK
(b) How much have you received on average in a week/month/year?

(c) Was any of this allowance included in the pay that you received on ..... (see Q.22)?

IF YES
(c1) How much was included?

Per. No.	(a) Covered by refund/allowance	Refunded £	p	(b) Period	(c) Included in pay No	£	p
					X		
					X		
					X		

GO TO NEXT JOB OR Q.29

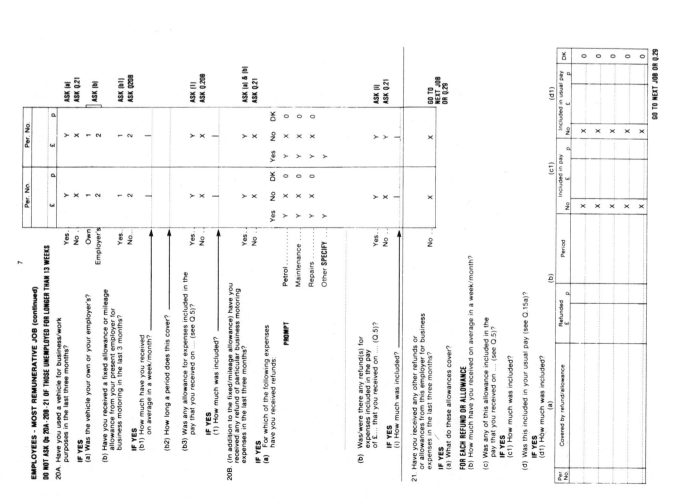

TO ALL SELF EMPLOYED - continued

27. (d) Apart from meal breaks do you usually work:

RUNNING PROMPT — more than 30 hours a week? 1

30 hours a week or less? 2

SEE PROMPT CARD

28. What proportion of your expenditure which you have already told me about have you claimed/will you be claiming as a business expense for tax purposes?

PROMPT AMOUNTS FROM S 829A

	None		Per. No.	
Vehicle expenses (Qs 34A, 35, 42)	X		1	1
Rent (Q.17)	X		2	2
Mortgage payments on structure (Qs 22, 23)	X			
Rates (Qs 18, 19, 20)	X			
Water charges (Qs 18, 19, 20)	X			
Insurance on structure (Q 24a)	X			
Gas (Q.27B(c) or Q.28(a))	X			
Electricity (Q.27B(c) or Q.28(a))	X			
Telephone (Q.29, 30)	X			
Other SPECIFY	X			
No expenditure claimed	X			

RELATING TO THIS ACCOMMODATION ONLY

IF SUBSIDIARY JOB AS EMPLOYEE GO BACK TO Q.22

IF SUBSIDIARY JOB AS SELF-EMPLOYED ASK Q27 USING MARGIN AT LEFT FOR ANSWERS

TO ALL

(NOTE: FOR MOST EMPLOYEES ANSWER IS AVAILABLE AT Q.s 10 & 25)

29. Do you pay a National Insurance contribution? Yes ... Y Ask(a)-(b)
  No ... X ASK Q.30

IF YES
(a) How much was the last contribution you paid?

(b) How long a period did this cover? Period

Per. No.		Per. No.	
		336	
336			

A203 — A203

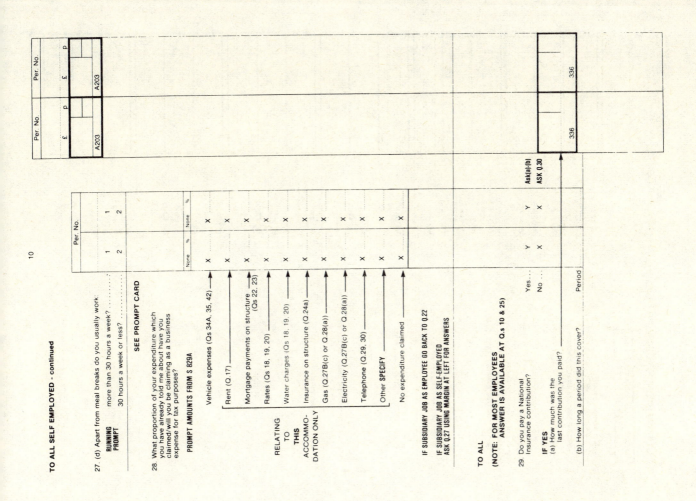

TO ALL SELF EMPLOYED - DETAILS OF JOB(s) CODED Y at Q.4(a) and Q.4(b)

27. (a) How much net profit (or loss) did you receive in the last 12 months from your business or profession? That is, after deducting all expenses and wages BUT BEFORE DEDUCTING INCOME TAX, N.I. CONTRIBUTIONS OR MONEY DRAWN FOR YOUR OWN USE?

	Per. No.		Per. No.	
Profit	£		£	ASK (i)
Loss	£		£	ASK (b)
DK ...	0	0	0	0
(i) Dates of most recent 12 months for which figures are available - BEGINNING - Month ...				ASK (a1)
Year ...				
ENDING - Month ...				ASK Q.27(d)
Year ...				
DK ...	0	0	0	0 £

**ALTERNATIVE WORDING FOR Q.27(a)
FOR REGULAR JOBS, SUCH AS MAIL ORDER AGENT, BABYSITTER, ETC.
ASK. How much did you earn in the last 12 months?**

IF NET PROFIT OR LOSS GIVEN at (a) ASK:
(a1) Are you the sole owner of your business or are you in partnership with someone else?

Sole owner ... | X | ASK (d) | X | ASK (d)
In partnership ... | Y | ASK (i) | Y | ASK (i)

IF IN PARTNERSHIP ASK:
(i) Have your partner's shares been included in the net profit (or loss) you gave me?

No ... | X | ASK (d) | X | ASK (d)

IF YES
(1) How much was included? ... ASK (d)

IF DK TO (a) ASK:
(b) Do you draw sums of money regularly from the business for your own use?

No ... | X | ASK (c) | X | ASK (c)

IF YES
(b1) How much on average do you usually take out?

DK ... | 0 | ASK (c) | 0 | ASK (c)

(b2) How often is this? Period

(b3) After deducting the amount you withdrew and other expenses, how much profit (or loss) before tax did your share of the business yield in the most recent 12 months for which you have figures?

Profit | ASK (i)
Loss
DK ... | 0 | ASK (c) | 0 | ASK (c)

	Per. No.		Per. No.	
326	8		8	326	8
307	8		8	307	8
327	2		2	327	2
328	8		8	328	8
313	8		8	313	8
A226				A226	
A227				A227	
364				364	

(i) Dates of most recent 12 months for which figures are available

BEGINNING - Month ...
Year ...
ENDING - Month ...
Year ...
DK ... | 0 | ASK (c) | 0 | ASK (c)

IF NO to (b) or DK to (b1) or (b3) ASK:
(c) What was the total turnover of the business during the most recent 12 month period for which you have figures?

(i) Dates of most recent 12 months for which figures are available

BEGINNING - Month ...
Year ...
ENDING - Month ...
Year ...
DK ... | 0 | ASK (d) | 0 | ASK (d)

11

TO ALL

Are you **at present** receiving any of the following State benefits?

CODE Yes...Y FOR EACH BENEFIT CURRENTLY BEING RECEIVED

EXCLUDE SUPPLEMENTARY BENEFIT FROM Q.31 to Q.34

PROMPT EACH

							Per. No.	£	p	Per. No.	£	p
30. Child benefit INCLUDE CHILD BENEFIT INCREASE	Yes.. Y	No.. X	IF YES Weekly rate					337			337	
31. N.I. retirement pension [INCLUDE ADDITIONAL PENSION] Old Person's pension	Yes.. Y Yes.. Y	No.. X	IF YES Weekly rate					338			338	
32. N.I. Widow's benefits [INCLUDE EARNINGS - RELATED SUPPLEMENT] ENTER WAR WIDOW'S BENEFIT AT Q.42	Yes.. Y	No.. X	IF YES Weekly rate					339			339	
33. War disability pension Related State allowance SPECIFY	Yes.. Y Yes.. Y	No... Y	IF YES Weekly rate					340			340	
34. (a) Mobility allowance	Yes.. Y	No.. X	IF YES Weekly rate					417			417	
(b) Non contributory invalidity pension	Yes.. Y	No.. X	IF YES Weekly rate					418			418	
(c) Housewives' non-contributory invalidity pension	Yes.. Y	No.. X	IF YES Weekly rate					419			419	
(d) Invalid care allowance	Yes.. Y	No.. X	IF YES Weekly rate					420			420	
(e) Attendance allowance	Yes.. Y	No.. X	IF YES Weekly rate					421			421	

TO ALL   SHOW PROMPT CARD (Q.s 35 - 45)

In the last 12 months, that is since ...., have you received any of the following State benefits shown on this card?

CODE Yes...Y FOR EACH BENEFIT RECEIVED IN LAST 12 MONTHS

EXCLUDE SUPPLEMENTARY BENEFIT FROM Q.35

						Per. No.	£	p	Per. No.	£	p
35. Contributory invalidity pension [INCLUDE ADDITIONAL PENSION] Invalidity allowance	Yes.. Y Yes.. Y	No.. X	IF YES (a) Total number of weeks received					A258			A258
			AND (b) Last full weekly payment					369			369
(c) Are you receiving benefit at present?	Yes.. 1	No.. X	AND ASK (c)					A259			A259

12

TO ALL

EXCLUDE SUPPLEMENTARY BENEFIT FROM Q's.36A, 36B, 37 and 39

						Per. No.	£	p	Per. No.	£	p
36A. N.I. sickness benefit Industrial injury benefit [INCLUDE EARNINGS RELATED BENEFIT]	Yes. Y Yes. Y	No.. X	IF YES (a) Total number of weeks received					A224			A224
			AND (b) Last full weekly payment					363			363
(c) Are you receiving benefit at present?	Yes. 1	No.. X	AND ASK (c)					A225			A225
36B. Industrial injury disablement pension [ENTER INDUSTRIAL WIDOW'S PENSION at Q.42]	Yes. Y	No.. X	IF YES (a) Total number of weeks received					A205			A205
			AND (b) Last full weekly payment					325			325
(c) Are you receiving benefit at present?	Yes. 1	No.. X	AND ASK (c)					A238			A238
37. N.I. unemployment benefit [INCLUDE EARNINGS-RELATED SUPPLEMENT]	Yes. Y	No.. X	IF YES (a) Total number of weeks received					A222			A222
			AND (b) Last full weekly payment					362			362
(c) Are you receiving benefit at present?	Yes. 1	No.. X	AND ASK (c)					A223			A223
38. Family income supplement	Yes. Y	No.. X	IF YES (a) Total number of weeks received					A256			A256
			AND (b) Last full weekly payment					368			368
(c) Are you receiving benefit at present?	Yes. 1	No.. X	AND ASK (c)					A257			A257
39. Maternity allowance	Yes. Y	No.. X	IF YES (a) Total number of weeks received					A239			A239
			AND (b) Last full weekly payment					341			341
(c) Are you receiving benefit at present?	Yes. 1	No.. X	AND ASK (c)					A240			A240
40. Supplementary benefit [INCLUDING SUPPLEMENTARY PENSION AND SUPPLEMENTARY ALLOWANCE]	Yes. Y	No.. X	IF YES (a) Total number of weeks received					A228			A228
			AND (b) Last full weekly payment					365			365
(c) Are you receiving benefit at present?	Yes. 1	No.. X	AND ASK (c)					A229			A229

TO ALL

PRIVATE PENSIONS — INCLUDE ONLY IF BY VIRTUE OF OWN (OR SPOUSE'S) FORMER EMPLOYMENT
EXCLUDE LUMP SUM GRATUITIES

	Per.	IF NO RING	Own pension	Spouse's	Last payment £ p	Period	NO	IF YES How much? £ p	Was last payment before tax?	after tax?	Per. No. £ p	Per. No. £ p

Are you at present receiving:
Pension from:

46.(a) Central or Local Govt. or Armed Forces — X 3 4 ... X ... Y X — 342 / 342
(b) or Nationalised Industry? — X 3 4 ... X ... Y X — 343 / 343
— A236 / A236

47. Other previous employers? SPECIFY INDUSTRY FULLY
I N D U S T R I A L O U A L P R O M P T
— X 3 4 ... X ... Y X — 344 / 344
— 345 / 345
— A237 / A237

48. Annuity — X ... X ... Y X — 346 / 346
— X ... X ... Y X — 347 / 347

49. Payment from trust or covenant? — X ... X ... Y X — 348 / 348
— X ... X ... Y X — 349 / 349

50. In the last 12 months, that is since ..... have you received a pension as a member of a Trade Union or pension from a Friendly Society?
No .... X X — 350 / 350
IF YES
(a) How much was the last payment?
(b) How long a period did it cover?

TO ALL

	Per. No. £ p	Per. No. £ p

41A. N.I. Maternity grant — Yes.. Y No... X
41B. N.I. Death grant — Yes.. Y No... X
IF YES 12 months total — 406 8 / 406 8
IF YES 12 months total — 407 8 / 407 8

42. Any N.I. or State benefit not mentioned earlier? — Yes.. Y No... X
IF YES
(a) SPECIFY
IF YES (b) Total number of weeks received — A232 / A232
AND
(c) Last full weekly payment — 367 1 / 367 1
AND ASK (d)
(d) Are you receiving benefit at present? — Yes.. 1 No... X — A233 / A233

43. Redundancy payment under Redundancy Payments Act? — Yes.. Y No... X
IF YES 12 months total — 356 8 / 356 8
AND ASK (b)
(b) How many years were you working with the firm? — 357 8 / 357 8

44. (a) Any other lump sum payment from the State?
ENTER: £5 ELECTRICITY DISCOUNT
£10 CHRISTMAS BONUS — Yes.. Y No... X
IF YES
(a) SPECIFY — 354 8 / 354 8
*BASIC DISCOUNT — 398 8 / 398 8
(b) 12 months total

45. Trade union sick pay or strike pay, Friendly Society benefits, benefits under private sickness scheme, accident insurance, hospital savings scheme? [EXCLUDE LUMP SUM BENEFITS] — Yes.. Y No... X
IF YES
(a) Total number of weeks received — A230 / A230
AND
(b) Last full weekly payment — 366 1 / 366 1
AND ASK (c)
(c) Are you receiving benefits at present? — Yes.. 1 No... X — A231 / A231

TO ALL WITH BENEFITS AT Qs 30–42 AND THOSE WITH RATES/RENT REBATES AND RENT ALLOWANCES

TO THOSE PAYING ELECTRICITY (GAS) BY SLOT METER (code 1 at Q.26(a) Schedule A)
DNA ... N
45D. Did you receive a discount under the Electricity (Gas) Discount Scheme following the last time your meter was cleared?
Yes.. Y ASK (a) - (b) THEN Q.45F
No ... X ASK Q.46
IF YES
(a) How much was the discount? — 394 8 / 394 8
Electricity — 393 8 / 393 8
(b) What period did the discount cover? (Gas) Period — 332 / 332
Period — 333 / 333

TO THOSE PAYING ELECTRICITY (GAS) BY ACCOUNT (code 2 or 3 at Q.26(a), Schedule A)
45E. Did you receive a discount under the Electricity (Gas) Discount Scheme on the electricity (gas) bill you mentioned?
Yes.. Y ASK (a) THEN Q.45F
No ... X ASK Q.46
IF YES
(a) How much was the discount?
Electricity — 358 / 358
(Gas) — 359 / 359

TO THOSE ANSWERING YES to Q's 45D and 45E
45F. Was the amount for electricity (gas) which you mentioned earlier* before or after deduction of this discount
Before. X
After .. Y   NOW ASK Q.46
* See A Schd. Q.27B(c) and Q.28(a)

15

TO ALL   SHOW PROMPT CARD (Q's 51 - 55)

Do you have now, or have you had in the last 12 months, private savings accounts with any of the banks or societies shown on this card:

		Per. No.	

51. National Savings Bank (Post Office)
(a) Ordinary Savings Account(s)?   Yes.. 1   No.. X
(b) Investment Account(s)?   Yes.. 2   No.. X
(c) Giro Deposit Acount(s)?   Yes.. 3   No.. X

52. Trustee Savings Bank?
(a) Ordinary Savings Account(s)?   Yes.. 4   No.. X
(b) Investment Deposit Account(s)?   Yes.. 5   No.. X

53. Co-operative Society?   Yes.. 6   No.. X

54. Building Society?   Yes.. 7   No.. X

55. (a) Bank Deposit Account(s)?   Yes.. 8   No.. X
(b) Bank Savings Account(s)?   Yes.. 9   No.. X
(c) Any other savings banks or societies?   Yes.. 10   No.. X

SPECIFY
IF YES, ASK (a) FOR EACH TYPE OF SAVINGS

USE SEPARATE COLUMN FOR EACH TYPE OF SAVINGS

DO NOT SPLIT JOINT ACCOUNTS

Per. No. Code from Q's 51-55

(a) How much interest/ Co-op divident have you received or been credited with from all your account(s) past and present with the ..... over the last 12 months?

Documents consulted?   Yes.. Y   No.. X

PLEASE RING

		Per. No.					Per. No.	
£	p			£	p			
373	8			373	8			
371	8			371	8			
375	8			375	8			
376	8			376	8			
374	8			374	8			

16

TO ALL   SHOW PROMPT CARD (Q's 56-58)

In the last 12 months, that is since ....., have you received or been credited with any of the following:
Interest on:
56. (a) British Savings Bonds?   Yes.. Y   No.. X   — IF YES TO ANY ENTER 12 MONTHS TOTAL

(b) War loan?   Yes.. Y   No.. X   — ASK Q.56(b)   408, 8

Interest and dividends on:
57. (a) Unit trusts?   Yes.. Y   No.. X   — ASK Q.57(a)   409, 8

(b) Local Authority Securities   Documents consulted?   Yes.. Y   No.. X   — ASK Q.57(b)   415, 8
Documents consulted?   Yes.. Y   No.. X

(c) Stocks, shares, bonds, debentures or any other securities after deduction of tax at source?   Yes.. Y   No.. X   — ASK Q.57(c)   416, 8
Documents consulted?   Yes.. Y   No.. X

58. In the last 12 months, that is, since ..... have you received rent from property (excluding the part of your accommodation you sub-let which you told me about earlier)?   Yes.. Y   No.. X   — ASK Q.58   378, 8

IF YES
(a) How much did you receive in the last 12 months before deducting income tax but after deducting all allowable expenses?   — ASK (a)   ASK Q.59A

TO ALL   SHOW PROMPT CARD (Qs 59A - 59C)

In the last 12 months, that is since ..... have you received any of the following allowances shown on this card?

59A. Allowances from someone in the Armed Forces or Merchant Navy?   No.. X   360, 8
EXCLUDE SPOUSE TEMPORARILY NOT A MEMBER OF HOUSEHOLD
IF YES
(a) How much was the last payment?
(b) How long a period did it cover?

59B. Regular allowance from a friend or relative outside the household or from an organisation; or alimony or separation allowance?   No.. X
IF YES
(a) How much was the last payment?
(b) How long a period did it cover?   351   — SEE Q.60A

59C. An allowance for a foster child?   No.. X   352
IF YES
(a1) Local Authority grant: last payment   353
(a2) How long a period did it cover?
(b1) Other source: last payment   352
(b2) How long a period did it cover?   — SEE Q.60A

TO ALL

61. In the last 12 months, that is, since ...... have you received any coal or coke from your present (or former) employer?

No .. X   **ASK Q.63**

Per. No.

IF YES GIVE DETAILS BELOW

Per. No.	Quantity received in last 12 months (tons or cwt)	Brand of coke or smokeless fuel	Free	Reduced price	Amount paid if not free including haulage costs £ p
Coal			X	Y	
			X	Y	
Coke			X	Y	
			X	Y	

THERE IS NO Q.62

63. Do you have any expenses refunded by an organisation for which you do unpaid work eg a club, council or charitable organisation?

No .. X   **ASK Q.64**

IF YES, ASK FOR EACH ALLOWANCE
(a) What does the allowance cover?

(b) What type of organisation gives the allowance?

(c) How much do you receive on average in a week/month/year?

Per. No.	(a) Covered by allowance	Type of organisation	(b) Amount received £ p	(c) Period

64. During the last 12 months, that is since ...... have you received any money for odd jobs or any occasional fees for work or professional advice which we have not yet covered?

No .. X   **ASK Q.65**

Per. No.	Description of work or advice	Dates when job took place From Month Year	To Month Year	Total amount of fee £ p	Period covered by fee

IF JOB IS A REGULAR COMMITMENT, REGARDLESS OF HOURS, AND IS CURRENTLY HELD, GO BACK TO EMPLOYEE OR SELF-EMPLOYED QUESTIONS

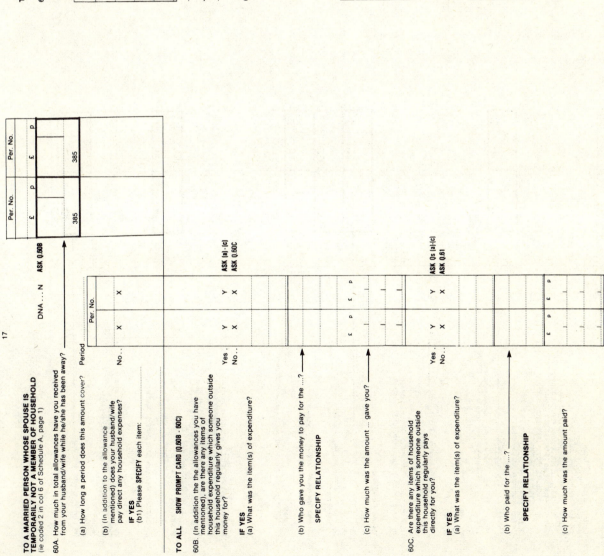

Per. No. £	p	Per. No. £	p
A247		A247	
321	8	321	8
322	8	322	8
A248		A248	
323	8	323	8
324	8	324	8
392	8	392	8
384	8	384	8
381	8	381	8

TO A MARRIED PERSON WHOSE SPOUSE IS TEMPORARILY NOT A MEMBER OF HOUSEHOLD
(ie coded 2 in col 6 of Schedule A, page 1)

DNA ... N   **ASK Q.60B**

60A. How much in total allowances have you received from your husband/wife while he/she has been away?

(a) How long a period does this amount cover?   Period

(b) (In addition to the allowance mentioned) does your husband/wife pay direct any household expenses?   No .. X

IF YES
(b1) Please **SPECIFY** each item:

TO ALL   SHOW PROMPT CARD (Q.60B - 60C)

60B. (In addition the the allowances you have mentioned), are there any items of household expenditure which someone outside this household regularly gives you money for?

Yes . Y   **ASK (a)-(c)**
No .. X   **ASK Q.60C**

IF YES
(a) What was the item(s) of expenditure?

(b) Who gave you the money to pay for the ....?

SPECIFY RELATIONSHIP

(c) How much was the amount ... gave you?

60C. Are there any items of household expenditure which someone outside this household regularly pays directly for you?

Yes . Y   **ASK Qs (a)-(c)**
No .. X   **ASK Q.61**

IF YES
(a) What was the item(s) of expenditure?

(b) Who paid for the ....?

SPECIFY RELATIONSHIP

(c) How much was the amount paid?

Per. No. £	p	Per. No. £	p
385		385	

19

TO ALL

65. During the last 12 months, that is since ...... have you paid any tax direct to Inland Revenue?

EXCLUDE: NATIONAL INSURANCE CONTRIBUTIONS: TAX COLLECTED THROUGH PAYE DEDUCTIONS FROM WAGES OR SALARY OR DEDUCTED AT SOURCE FROM INCOME ON INVESTMENTS PENSIONS AND ANNUITIES.

No .... X X ASK Q.66

IF YES
(a) How much did you pay direct in:
PROMPT (a1) income tax?
(a2) What was the source of income on which you were taxed? SPECIFY:
Per. No.
Per. No.
(a3) capital gains tax?

66. Have you had any income tax refunded directly by Inland Revenue during the last 12 months?

Yes ... Y Y ASK (a)-(c)
No ... X X ASK Q.67

EXCLUDE N.I. REFUNDS

IF YES
(a) How much was refunded?
(b) Was this a refund of tax deducted under PAYE?
No ... X X ASK Q.67 (c1)
Yes ... Y Y ASK Q.67
(c) Was this refund received in respect of either unemployment or redundancy?
No ... X X ASK (c1)

IF NO
(c1) What was the reason for the refund? SPECIFY:
Per. No.
Per. No.

67. Have you paid any N.I. Contributions direct to Inland Revenue or Department of Health and Social Security during the last 12 months?

No ... X X ASK Q.68

EXCLUDE: DEDUCTIONS FROM WAGE OR SALARY, OR SELF-EMPLOYED, NON-EMPLOYED CONTRIBUTIONS NORMALLY SHOWN AT Q.29

IF YES
(a) How much did you pay?
SPECIFY REASON FOR DIRECT PAYMENT

68. Have you had any N.I. contributions refunded directly by Inland Revenue or Department of Health and Social Security during the last 12 months?

No ... X X ASK Q.69

IF YES
(a) How much was refunded?

Box codes: 387, 390, A241, 391, 386, 388

20

TO ALL

69. In the last 12 months, that is since ...... have you sold any cars belonging to you (excluding the trade-in you mentioned earlier)?

No .... X X ASK Q.70

IF YES
(a) How many? — Number
(b) When did you sell the car? — Month / Year
(c) Was the car used for: Private use only ... O O ASK (d)
Business use only ... X X ASK Q.70 (d)
Private and business use ... Y Y ASK (d)
(d) Did you receive payment by cash, cheque or giro?
Yes ... Y Y ASK (d1)
No ... X X ASK Q.70

IF YES
(d1) How much did you receive?

During the last 12 months have you received a lump sum payment (ie cash, cheque or giro) from:

70. An Endowment Assurance Policy?
No ... X X ASK Q.71

IF YES
(a) How much did you receive?

71. A Life Assurance Policy?
No ... X X SEE Q.72

IF YES
(a) How much did you receive?
NOW SEE Q.72

ASK ABOUT EACH DEPENDANT UNDER 16   DNA ... N

72. Have any of your children received an income from any source such as earnings from a spare time job, interest on child's bank account, or income from a trust fund within the past 12 months?
PROMPT FOR EACH CHILD

Person number of each child
(a) No income received ... X
(b) What kind of job or income?
(c) Has he had this income throughout the past 12 months? Yes ... Y
IF NO
For how many weeks has he had it?
(d) How much did he get last time?
(e) How often does he get it?
(f) Does he usually ....
dispose of (or save) it all himself ... O
partly dispose of (or save) it and give the rest to you ... X
give it all to you? ... Y

FRESH CARD FOR EACH PERSON
Per. No.

Box codes: 331, 334, 335, A245, 400, 401, 402, 403, 404, 395, 396, 397

Social Survey Division, OPCS
St Catherines House
10 Kingsway
LONDON WC2B 6JP

Family Expenditure Survey IS 829II
INCOME SCHEDULE
W15(2) OPCS 9-78

Appendix E Credit card account payments

E1 Note on contents

The Credit Card Account Payment sheet is a double sided page on which informants record details related to credit card accounts paid during the fourteen days record-keeping period. On the front of the sheet the amount paid plus details of outstanding balances, interest and final amount outstanding are recorded. The back of the form is similar in layout to the Diary Record and details of acquired items shown on the paid account are recorded.

SSD Primary Analysis Branch proportion the account payment across the cash value of the acquired items plus balance brought forward from a previous account period. This ensures that the expenditure nature of the survey is adhered to. The proportional amounts are given a three digit item code (see Section B8).

E2 Credit card payment sheet

CREDIT CARD PAGE

W 1539 OPCS 8/78

Area	Ser	Hld	Card type
			3

Please write below the description and cash price of the goods or services covered by this credit card account (eg. Petrol £5).

Description of items bought* If clothing please give sex of wearer, and if child the age	Cash price of item £ p	PLEASE LEAVE BLANK	

* If you cannot remember the goods purchased please enter type of firm from which they were acquired eg garage, chemist, department store.

Should you have any problems filling in this form please let the interviewer know.

Interviewer	
P	NP

FAMILY EXPENDITURE SURVEY-1979

S 829 C

Person No.			Week No.	1	2

CREDIT CARD ACCOUNT PAYMENTS

A payment made to a credit card company (e.g. Access or Barclaycard) is a different type of payment to the other payments recorded by you in the weekly personal spending diary.

As you know, the payment normally covers several items and can also include an amount towards an outstanding balance plus interest.

To give a clear picture of just what your payment covers, we would like you to copy the following details from your account, **if you pay part or all of your account during the 7 days of record keeping.**

1. Name of Credit card company

As on account

2. Balance from previous statement (if any) £...........*

3. Previous payment made £...........

4. Balance brought forward (if shown on the statement) £...........

5. Interest £...........

6. Present / New } balance outstanding £...........*

* If you have a credit balance shown on your account please write CR next to the amount when you copy it onto this form.

7. Payment made to credit card company **during the week** £...........

8. Date of payment ....

PLEASE TURN OVER

120

Appendix F Diary Record (D) — detailed notes

F1 Note on content and layout

Content

Each record book covers seven days. Each household member aged 16 or over is given a booklet at the end of the main interview and asked to complete it day by day. A second booklet covering a second seven-day period is left by the interviewer about five days after the start of the first diary. The first set of completed books is collected by the interviewer a few days later or, if that is not possible, with the completed second set of books after the end of the 14-day period. Each record-keeper is asked to record all payments made during the 14 days. A payment basis is used instead of an acquisition basis, partly for simplicity because this makes it easier to explain that every item of expenditure, whether on account of goods or services, should be recorded. It is also explained that every payment should be included irrespective of how the payment is made, whether by cash, cheque, postal order, money order, or by some other means. Shop-keepers and farmers, should they obtain food or other goods from their own businesses, are asked to record such items whether they pay for them or not. In the latter case, informants are asked to note the items concerned. No account is taken of food produced entirely for home consumption unless it is part of food produced on a commercial basis.

Layout

The record book is reproduced in Appendix F2.

The main part of the record book consists of seven pairs of pages, a pair for each day. These are preceded by a page of notes explaining some of the more important points which it is desirable that record-keepers should bear in mind when completing the diary. At the end of the booklet there are three questions for the informant to complete; one deals with amounts recorded in the diary, which will subsequently be repaid by an employer or charged as a business expense by an informant who is self-employed; the second with gambling winnings, and the third relates to bills paid on behalf of another household.

Finally, the booklet contains a list of items partly in order to emphasize the comprehensiveness of the inquiry, and partly to encourage the record-keeper to describe each entry precisely. Each of the seven pairs of pages is identical apart from the date; this is entered by the interviewer before the diary is left with the household member. Each pair of pages is also divided into sections corresponding to broad expenditure categories. This sub-division is of some use in coding, but informants are advised to ignore the section headings whenever the number of items is too great to be fitted in to the appropriate section. This applies particularly to a housewife who has bought a large number of food items.

Editing and coding

The information for punching is taken from the last two right-hand columns. The expenditure amount has normally been entered by the informant, and to the right of this the SSD Primary Analysis Branch enters a three-digit code corresponding to the informant's description of the item (see Section B8). However, before the main coding stage is reached extensive comparisons are made between the data in these diaries and the information recorded by the interviewer on schedules A and B. The expenditure categories involved are the following:

> Rent of accommodation
> Rent of garage
> Rates
> Water rates
> Ground rent, feu duty, chief rent
> Mortgage instalment
> Insurance on structure and contents
> Gas and electricity accounts
> Telephone account
> Licences
> Television payments
> Road tax
> Vehicle insurance
> Outright purchase of motor vehicle
> Driving licence
> Season ticket
> Life assurance and other insurance premiums
> Payments by bankers' standing order
> Payments into clothing clubs, commodity clubs of all kinds
> Instalments and down payments for goods being purchased by instalments
> School meals
> Milk under National Milk Scheme, liquid and dried
> Education fees.

When the checking stage is completed entries in the record books within the sectors listed above are deleted in order to avoid duplication, irrespective of whether there is a corresponding entry in the interview schedules. There are many other points concerned with the records on which some action has to be taken at the editing stage and prior to the main work of coding the separate items. Some of these are listed below.

(a) Business expenses re-paid by an employer or claimed by a self-employed person as expenses for tax purposes are deleted. This adjustment is made on the basis of Q1 on page 18 in the record booklet and Qs 19—21, 26, 28B schedule.

(b) Some information reported at the interview is transferred to these records. It mainly concerns payments included with rent and deductions from wages and salaries other than income tax and national insurance contributions.

(c) Money set aside for payment of future bills, and payments to other household members are also discarded, with two exceptions: (i) Wages paid to a resident domestic servant or paid housekeeper are retained and coded 771. (ii) Pocket money to a child member under 16 — if the items on which the child spent the pocket money are known the separate amounts are classified with the appropriate codes; if not, the amount is coded 801. Cash gifts to persons outside the household are coded 802. The latter includes donations towards a present for someone outside the household, unless the amount is a substantial proportion of the cost of the gift, when the amount is coded according to the type of gift.

(d) The purchase of a postal order is treated as though it were another form of currency, so such entries are deleted except for the poundage, which is coded 751. If a postal order is used to pay for something during the 14 days of record keeping it is classified according to the item or service involved.

(e) Informants are asked to itemize all expenditure incurred within the United Kingdom, and, the separate items are coded accordingly. This instruction applies whether the informant was at home or on holiday within the United Kingdom; holidays abroad are not itemized, but the total expenditure abroad within the 14 days, if known, is coded into 757.

(f) Sometimes when groceries are paid for on a monthly basis there is difficulty over itemizing the bill. Interviewers are instructed to try to discover in advance whether a housewife pays for groceries on a monthly basis, and if so, whether she expects to pay such an account during the 14 days. She is then asked if she will itemize the bill, and if it appears that this is not possible, she is also asked to record acquisitions from the same retail outlet during the 14 days. This additional information is used by the coders to pro rata any unitemized monthly account paid by the same housewife.

(g) Purchases by means of a credit card are deleted from the diaries.

S829D

FAMILY EXPENDITURE SURVEY – 1979

7-day period
1
2

Ref. No.

Area	Ser.	Hld.	Per.
CARD TYPE 5			

IN CONFIDENCE

All the particulars you give on this form will be treated in STRICT CONFIDENCE.
Please do not put your name or address on it.

The interviewer will call again on:

DAY	DATE	TIME

INTERVIEWER	
P 3 – 17	
P 18	

Social Survey Division, OPCS,
St Catherines House,
10 Kingsway,
London, WC2B 6JP

HOW TO FILL UP THIS BOOKLET

1. This booklet should contain a complete record of everything which **you yourself** pay for; other members of your household are being provided with separate booklets.

2. Please include **everything** that you pay for during the seven days, whether it is paid for out of your own money, housekeeping, meal vouchers, money from a loan or any other source, and whether payment is by cash, cheque, postal order, Giro cheque, credit card or other means of payment.

3. Write down the actual payments you make during the seven days, even if the goods were obtained previously, or are going to be delivered later. Any goods ordered or delivered but **not** paid for during the seven days should not be included. If you buy anything by part exchange, please give the amount paid **after** deducting the amount allowed in part exchange.

4. Show each item, however small, **on a separate line** and the amount spent on it. Do not, for example, write 'vegetables' but show separately how much you spent on potatoes, cabbages, tinned peas and so on.

5. If you ask another member of your household or a neighbour to buy things for you, and you pay for them, details of the purchases should be included in your own record book.

6. **Look through the list shown at the end of this booklet in case it reminds you of items which you may have forgotten to record.**

7. **Hire Purchase.** If you **start** buying anything by instalments on any of the seven days, write down the amount and state that it is the first instalment, down payment, etc.

   If during the seven days you pay instalments on any goods which you are buying by instalments, write down what the article is and how much you pay.

8. **Budget Accounts, Clothing Clubs, Mail Order Clubs, etc.** If you pay anything **into** a budget account, clothing club, etc. during the seven days, please write each payment down with a description of the account or club into which it is paid. There is no need to record any goods you **obtain** from these clubs.

9. **Credit Cards.** If you have a bank credit card, or similar credit card, eg Access, American Express, Barclaycard, Diners Club (exclude bankers cheque cards), please write 'credit card' against any item which you obtain with the credit card during the seven days. Please see separate sheet regarding payment of credit card accounts.

10. **Meals out, snacks out, liquid refreshments out.** Include any food or liquid refreshment **bought and consumed outside the home.** Please include breakfast, lunch, snacks, dinner, cups of tea or coffee if these are bought and consumed away from home. Meals or snacks or liquid refreshments bought at a workplace should be recorded separately from other meals etc. bought and consumed elsewhere away from home. Please try to give cost of alcoholic drinks separately.

11. **Take-away meals.** Regardless of where consumed these should be recorded separately in the space provided.

12. **Postal Orders.** If you buy a postal order on one of the seven days, please record it on that day, noting its value and poundage on separate lines. Note beside the postal order the purpose for which it is to be used and the date it will be posted. If a postal order is recorded in either of the two booklets, but will not be paid by the end of the 14 days covered by the two booklets, please add a note to this effect.

13. **Holiday Expenses.** Please say whether holiday is in this country or abroad. (a) If in England, Wales, Scotland or Northern Ireland give payments during the 7 days covered by this record in as much detail as possible; if it is impossible to give each item separately, a single heading (eg hotel bill) will do. (b) If in the Channel Islands, the Isle of Man, the Irish Republic or abroad please do not itemise the expenses, but give the total spent in the days covered by this booklet and the country where the holiday is spent.

14. **Gifts and Presents.** Please say what is bought, and record it on the day of purchase. If money is given, say that it is a present of money and who received it, for example: 'Present of money to niece'. 'Pocket money to son', or 'Money to daughter away at university'.

15. **Clothing.** For any clothing or footwear, including gifts to people outside your household, please say for whom the item is bought, also the sex and age, eg shoes for grand-daughter, aged 6.

16. **Betting.** If you make any bets during the seven days, please state what they are (sweepstake, bookmaker, totalisator, Bingo, lottery, etc.) and give the amounts. If you receive any winnings during the seven days please give details in question 2 on page 18.

17. **Shopkeepers, Farmers.** If your household obtains any food or other goods from its own shop or farm, please write down what is obtained each day with its approximate value. If these goods were not paid for at the time also write 'own shop' or 'own farm' against each item.

18. **Expenditure on behalf of a person not in your household.** (If, during the seven days, you pay a bill on behalf of a person outside your household and this money is not to be repaid, please enter details on page 18 of this booklet (eg daughter pays rent for her mother who lives in a separate household).

3

HOW TO ENTER AMOUNTS

	Amount paid		Please leave blank
	£	p	
FOOD (except take-away meals, meals out, snacks out, etc)			
Lamb	-	85	
Peas (tinned)	-	17½	
Peaches (fresh)	-	32	
Fish (fingers)	-	59½	
Apple pie	-	25	
Any other payments made today, with full details			
Postal order - football pools - posted 15 August			
Poundage	-	50	
Shoes - for self	-	8	
Present - toy for grandchild	8	99	
Jacket for self (credit card)	-	78	
	30	00	

NOTES

Please use the space below for any explanation of your purchases you may wish to make.

FIRST DAY (continued)

Please write each item on a separate line

	Amount paid		Please leave blank
	£	p	

Meals out, snacks out, liquid refreshments out (including tips):

(1) bought at workplace, canteen, staff dining room, etc

(2) bought and consumed elsewhere away from home, eg cafe, restaurant, hotel, cinema, park, etc

Take-away meals, eg fish and chips, take-away Chinese food, Meals on Wheels, etc

Fuel and Light (including payments into slot meters), Household goods, cleaning materials, Furniture

Cigarettes, Tobacco, Beer, Wines, Spirits and Soft drinks

Travel by rail, bus, air, taxi, Motor vehicles (purchase, running costs and repairs), Cycles, etc

Newspapers, Magazines, Books, Postage, Laundry, Hairdressing, Domestic help, Cinema, etc

Any other payments made to-day, with full details

If any of **today's expenses** are to be claimed as business expenses, or will be refunded, please add 'to be claimed or refunded'

RECORD OF EXPENDITURE - FIRST DAY

Day of week............ Date............

Please write each item on a separate line

	Amount paid		Please leave blank
	£	p	

FOOD (except take-away meals, meals out, snacks out, etc)

Clothing, Clothing materials and Footwear

If any of **to-day's expenses** are to be claimed as business expenses, or will be refunded, please add 'to be claimed or refunded'

RECORD OF EXPENDITURE — SECOND DAY

6

Day of week .... Date ....

Please write each item on a separate line

	Amount paid.		Please leave blank
	£	p	

FOOD (except take-away meals, meals out, snacks out, etc)

Clothing, Clothing materials and Footwear

If any of **to-day's expenses** are to be claimed as business expenses, or will be refunded, please add 'to be claimed or refunded'

SECOND DAY (continued)

Please write each item on a separate line

	Amount paid		Please leave blank
	£	p	

Meals out, snacks out, liquid refreshments out (including tips):

(1) bought at workplace, canteen, staff dining room, etc

(2) bought and consumed elsewhere away from home, eg cafe, restaurant, hotel, cinema, park, etc

Take-away meals, eg fish and chips, take-away Chinese food, Meals on Wheels, etc

Fuel and Light (including payments into slot meters), Household goods, cleaning materials, Furniture

Cigarettes, Tobacco, Beer, Wines, Spirits and Soft drinks

Travel by rail, bus, air, taxi. Motor vehicles (purchase, running costs and repairs). Cycles, etc

Newspapers, Magazines, Books, Postage, Laundry, Hairdressing, Domestic help, Cinema, etc

Any other payments made to-day, with full details

If any of **today's expenses** are to be claimed as business expenses, or will be refunded, please add 'to be claimed or refunded'

RECORD OF EXPENDITURE — THIRD DAY

Day of week .... Date ....

Please write each item on a separate line

	Amount paid		Please leave blank
	£	p	

FOOD (except take-away meals, meals out, snacks out, etc)

Clothing, Clothing materials and Footwear

If any of **to-day's expenses** are to be claimed as business expenses, or will be refunded, please add 'to be claimed or refunded'

9

THIRD DAY *(continued)*

Please write each item on a separate line

	Amount paid		Please leave blank
	£	p	

Meals out, snacks out, liquid refreshments out (including tips):

(1) bought at workplace, canteen, staff dining room, etc

(2) bought and consumed elsewhere away from home. eg cafe, restaurant, hotel, cinema, park, etc

Take-away meals, eg fish and chips, take-away Chinese food. Meals on Wheels, etc

Fuel and Light (including payments into slot meters), Household goods, cleaning materials, Furniture

Cigarettes, Tobacco. Beer, Wines. Spirits and Soft drinks

Travel by rail, bus, air, taxi. Motor vehicles (purchase, running costs and repairs), Cycles, etc

Newspapers, Magazines, Books, Postage. Laundry. Hairdressing. Domestic help, Cinema, etc

Any other payments made to-day, with full details

If any of **today's expenses** are to be claimed as business expenses, or will be refunded, please add 'to be claimed or refunded'

RECORD OF EXPENDITURE — FOURTH DAY

10

Day of week................ Date................

	Amount paid		Please leave blank
Please write each item on a separate line	£	p	

FOOD (except take-away meals, meals out, snacks out, etc)

Clothing, Clothing materials and Footwear

If any of **to-day's expenses** are to be claimed as business expenses, or will be refunded, please add 'to be claimed or refunded'

FOURTH DAY *(continued)*

11

	Amount paid		Please leave blank
Please write each item on a separate line	£	p	

Meals out, snacks out, liquid refreshments out (including tips):

(1) bought at workplace, canteen, staff dining room, etc

(2) bought and consumed elsewhere away from home. eg cafe, restaurant, hotel, cinema, park, etc

Take-away meals, eg fish and chips, take-away Chinese food. Meals on Wheels, etc

Fuel and Light (including payments into slot meters), Household goods, cleaning materials, Furniture

Cigarettes, Tobacco, Beer, Wines, Spirits and Soft drinks

Travel by rail, bus, air, taxi, Motor vehicles (purchase, running costs and repairs), Cycles, etc

Newspapers, Magazines, Books, Postage, Laundry, Hairdressing, Domestic help, Cinema, etc

Any other payments made to-day, with full details

If any of **today's expenses** are to be claimed as business expenses, or will be refunded, please add 'to be claimed or refunded'

FIFTH DAY (continued)

Please write each item on a separate line

	Amount paid		Please leave blank
	£	p	

Meals out, snacks out, liquid refreshments out (including tips):

(1) bought at workplace, canteen, staff dining room, etc

....

(2) bought and consumed elsewhere away from home, eg cafe, restaurant, hotel, cinema, park, etc

....

Take-away meals, eg fish and chips, take-away Chinese food, Meals on Wheels, etc

....

Fuel and Light (including payments into slot meters), Household goods, cleaning materials, Furniture

....

Cigarettes, Tobacco, Beer, Wines, Spirits and Soft drinks

....

Travel by rail, bus, air, taxi, Motor vehicles (purchase, running costs and repairs), Cycles, etc

....

Newspapers, Magazines, Books, Postage, Laundry, Hairdressing, Domestic help, Cinema, etc

....

Any other payments made to-day, with full details

....

If any of **today's expenses** are to be claimed as business expenses, or will be refunded, please add 'to be claimed or refunded'

RECORD OF EXPENDITURE — FIFTH DAY

Day of week .... Date ....

Please write each item on a separate line

	Amount paid		Please leave blank
	£	p	

FOOD (except take-away meals, meals out, snacks out, etc)

....

Clothing, Clothing materials and Footwear

....

If any of **to-day's expenses** are to be claimed as business expenses, or will be refunded, please add 'to be claimed or refunded'

RECORD OF EXPENDITURE — SIXTH DAY

14

Day of week	Amount paid		Please leave
Date	£	p	blank
Please write each item on a separate line			

FOOD (except take-away meals, meals out, snacks out, etc)

Clothing, Clothing materials and Footwear

If any of to-day's expenses are to be claimed as business expenses, or will be refunded, please add 'to be claimed or refunded'

SIXTH DAY (continued)

15

	Amount paid		Please leave
Please write each item on a separate line	£	p	blank

Meals out, snacks out, liquid refreshments out (including tips):

(1) bought at workplace, canteen, staff dining room, etc

(2) bought and consumed elsewhere away from home, eg cafe, restaurant, hotel, cinema, park, etc

Take-away meals, eg fish and chips, take-away Chinese food, Meals on Wheels, etc

Fuel and Light (including payments into slot meters), Household goods, cleaning materials, Furniture

Cigarettes, Tobacco, Beer, Wines, Spirits and Soft drinks

Travel by rail, bus, air, taxi, Motor vehicles (purchase, running costs and repairs), Cycles, etc

Newspapers, Magazines, Books, Postage, Laundry, Hairdressing, Domestic help, Cinema, etc

Any other payments made to-day, with full details

If any of **today's expenses** are to be claimed as business expenses, or will be refunded, please add 'to be claimed or refunded'

16

RECORD OF EXPENDITURE — SEVENTH DAY

Day of week........... Date...........

Please write each item on a separate line

	Amount paid		Please leave blank
	£	p	

FOOD (except take-away meals, meals out, snacks out, etc)

Clothing, Clothing materials and Footwear

If any of to-day's expenses are to be claimed as business expenses, or will be refunded, please add 'to be claimed or refunded'

131

SEVENTH DAY (continued)

	Amount paid		Please leave blank
	£	p	

Please write each item on a separate line

Meals out, snacks out, liquid refreshments out (including tips):

(1) bought at workplace, canteen, staff dining room, etc

(2) bought and consumed elsewhere away from home, eg cafe, restaurant, hotel, cinema, park, etc

Take-away meals, eg fish and chips, take-away Chinese food, Meals on Wheels, etc

Fuel and Light (including payments into slot meters), Household goods, cleaning materials, Furniture

Cigarettes, Tobacco, Beer, Wines, Spirits and Soft drinks

Travel by rail, bus, air, taxi, Motor vehicles (purchase, running costs and repairs), Cycles, etc

Newspapers, Magazines, Books, Postage, Laundry, Hairdressing, Domestic help, Cinema, etc

Any other payments made to-day, with full details

NOW SEE p.18

If any of today's expenses are to be claimed as business expenses, or will be refunded, please add 'to be claimed or refunded'

1. Expenses refunded or claimed

Please give particulars below of any expenditure (eg motor car, travelling, hotel expenses) shown in **this booklet** which:

(a) have already been refunded by a business or organisation; **or**

(b) have already been claimed as expenses from a business or organisation; **or**

(c) will definitely be claimed by you in the future as expenses from a business or organisation; **or**

(d) will be entered as expenses in making your income tax return.

Description of business expense refunded or claimed or to be claimed from business or organisation	Amount refunded or claimed £ p

2. Football pools and other betting.

Please give details of any winnings you have received during the 7 days coverd by this booklet.

	Winnings in last seven days £ p	Please leave blank
Football pools		821
Bookmaker, betting shop, totalisator		822
Lotteries		823
Other betting (Bingo, sweepstake, etc)		824

3.

Please give details of any expenditure which you have made on behalf of a person living in another household during the seven days covered by this booklet.
(N.B. Paid out of your own money and will not be repaid.)

Description of expenditure made on behalf of another person	Relationship to you	Amount paid £ p	Please leave blank

REFERENCE LIST OF IMPORTANT ITEMS OF EXPENDITURE

Of the hundreds of different things which it is possible to buy, the following is only a list of examples. Please look through this list in case it reminds you of any purchase which you have forgotten to record.

Food (consumed at home):-
Bread, cakes, buns, biscuits, chocolate biscuits, flour.
Breakfast cereals, tapioca, rice, custard powder.
Beef, veal, mutton, lamb, pork, bacon, ham, offal, rabbit, poultry, sausages, tinned meat.
Fresh or smoked cod, haddock, plaice, herrings, tinned salmon, sardines.
Milk (fresh, dried, condensed)
Margarine, lard, suet, cooking fat.
Eggs, butter, cheese.
Tea, coffee, instant coffee, cocoa.
Sugar, syrup, jam, marmalade, honey, lemon curd.
Fresh, dried, frozen or tinned potatoes, chips, crisps, tomatoes, peas, beans, carrots.
Fresh, dried, frozen or tinned apples, oranges, plums, pears, peaches, pineapples, apricots.
Bottled or tinned tomato juice, grapefruit juice, orange juice.
Pickles, sauces, soups, jellies, salt, pepper.
Mustard, vinegar, spices.
Orangeade, lemon squash, fruit cordials, soda water.
Food for animals and pets.

Clothing, Clothing materials, Footwear:-
Overcoats, raincoats, suits costumes, skirts, sports coats, trousers, blazers, pullovers, overalls, aprons, dresses, blouses, hats, gloves.
Vests, pants, pyjamas, shirts, knickers, slips, corsets, brassieres, nightdresses, socks, stockings, tights.
Dress material, knitting wool, thread, braces, ribbons, scarves, patterns, handkerchiefs.
Boots, shoes, slippers, sandals.
Payments to clothing clubs.

Meals out, Snacks out, Liquid refreshments out:-
Tea, coffee, snacks, sandwiches and meals bought and consumed at work, in restaurants, cafes, hotels, in parks, in cinemas.
Alcoholic drinks with meals out
Sweets, chocolate, ice-cream, soft drinks.

Take-away meals:-
Fish and chips, Chinese food, Indian food, Fried chicken, Meals on wheels.

Fuel and light, Household goods, Cleaning materials, Furniture:-
Coal, coke, gas, electricity, paraffin and other fuel oil, firewood, candles, nightlights, matches.
Soap, soda, cleaning powders, detergents, polishes.
Paint, distemper, wallpaper.
Dustbins, pails, brushes, brooms, tools, screws, nails.
China, glass, bowls, kettles, saucepans.
Suites or separate articles of furniture.
Radios, television sets or parts, hi-fi, cassettes, pianos, music.
Mattresses, pillows, sheets, blankets, tablecloths, towels, curtains, teacloths.
Carpets, rugs, linoleum, mats, floor covering.
Fires, cookers, vacuum cleaners, refrigerators, wringers, washing machines, spin-driers, sewing machines, irons, electric lamps, bulbs and fittings.
Clocks, watches, jewellery, cutlery, suit-cases, handbags, sports goods.
Repairs to furniture, radio, TV and watches.

Tobacco and drink:-
Cigarettes, tobacco, cigarette papers, cigars, pipes, pouches, lighters, lighter fuel, cigarette cases.
Beer, ale, stout, wines, spirits, cider.

Travel:-
Journeys by rail, bus, air, taxi, including fares to and from work.
Purchase, repairs and running costs of cars, motor cycles, cycles, perambulators.

Newspapers, Magazines, Books, Entertainment, Toiletries, etc:-
Cinemas, theatres, concerts, football, cricket, dog-racing, dances.
Books, newspapers, magazines, stationery, toilet paper.
Stamps, postal orders, telegrams, telephone calls.
Lipstick, face powder, face cream, mascara, perfumes, talc, shampoos, sanitary towels, deodorant.
Shaving cream, after shave, hair cream, razors and blades.
Hairdressing (including tips), sponges, face cloths, nail brushes.

Other payments:-
Cameras, photographic materials, developing and printing of films.
Flowers, seeds, plants, garden tools, lawnmowers.
Animals and pets.
Toys, games, playing cards.
Shoe repairs, laundry, dyeing and cleaning, domestic help.
Football pools and other betting, Bingo, lotteries etc.
Children's pocket money, birthday presents, money given to charities, raffle tickets.
Payments to chemists, doctors, dentists, opticians, chiropodists.
Holiday expenses.
Purchase of Savings Certificates, Premium Bonds, etc.
House purchase and repairs.

Appendix G Other documents used in the field in 1979

G1   Address list

G2   Purpose leaflet

G3   Regular commitments questions sheet

G4   Consistency checks sheet

G5   Wage/salary check and schedule B final check sheet

G6   Form E, record of identity of cooperating household members

G7   Form F, record of outcome at each non-cooperating address/household

G8   Form H, weekly progress return

G9   Form J, despatch note

G10   Calls and contact sheet

G11   Pre-sampled multi-household selection sheet

G12   Concealed multi-household selection sheet

G1 Address List

SS BEGINNING [ ]

SAMPLING AREA CODE [ ]

(Sample from Electoral Register)

Interviewer's Name ....

Sheet No. ....

Total No. of Sheets ....

Serial No.	Elector's No.	Surnames of People Registered at address in current Electoral Register	Nos. Registered		Address	Ward or Parish	
			M	F			

FAMILY EXPENDITURE SURVEY

WHAT THE SURVEY IS ABOUT

This survey is one of the principal sources of information on how people spend their money and on their sources of income. It shows how spending patterns differ from one household to another, and from one part of the country to another. It is carried out continuously to ensure that it is always up-to-date and that it accurately reflects changes in prices and other circumstances that affect the cost of living. The survey provides information on the amounts spent on food, clothing, household and other goods, travel, entertainment and services, and shows how these amounts vary from household to household.

WHY WE WANT THE INFORMATION

One of the most important uses of this information is to keep up-to-date the Index of Retail Prices which is compiled each month by the Department of Employment. In addition to the main Index, the survey provides data for two special pensioner indices, the retail price indices for one-person and two-person pensioner households. Because the survey collects both income and expenditure of households and because it is collected on a continuous basis, the survey is of considerable importance to other government departments in the formulation of policies. For example, the survey is used to assess the economic and social effects of changes in benefits and taxes on different types of households; it is also used to show the take-up of benefits, as well as to consider changes in the benefits system or changes in taxes on expenditure. It is used to study the relationship between income and expenditure on particular goods and services, such as different forms of transport and fuel. There are also numerous users outside Central Government.

HOW YOU HAVE BEEN SELECTED AND WHAT YOU ARE ASKED TO DO

The Social Survey Division of the Office of Population Censuses and Surveys is responsible for carrying out the Family Expenditure Survey on behalf of the Department of Employment. The Social Survey selects addresses at random in different parts of the country, and arranges for

interviewers to call on people aged 16 or over who live at these addresses to ask for their help in the survey. This involves keeping a record of all payments made during 14 days, answering some questions about payments over longer periods, and also giving details of income and of other money coming into the household. The survey covers people living on their own as well as families and others forming parts of larger households. Approximately 7,000 households take part in this survey over a period of 12 months.

PAYMENT FOR HELPING

The Family Expenditure Survey has been running continuously since 1957 and depends on voluntary cooperation for the information it obtains. In appreciation of the help given a payment of £2 is made to each person who takes part, provided that all other members of the same household also co-operate.

WHAT HAPPENS TO THE INFORMATION

We ensure that information given by individual households and members is kept confidential. Names and addresses of people who cooperate in the survey are removed from the original documents on which data is recorded and are known only by OPCS. They are never passed on to any other government department, nor to members of the public or Press.

Access to questionnaires on which data is recorded is restricted to the staff in the Social Survey Division of OPCS who collect and code the data and to the staff of the Department of Employment who process the data and retain the documents. Data collected during the survey are sent to other Government Departments only in such a form that no individual can be identified from them.

In published reports the identity of an individual is never revealed either directly or by implication from the details of results released.

As in all our surveys we rely on people's voluntary co-operation which is essential if our work is to be successful. We hope that this leaflet shows you how the information collected can benefit everybody and that no one could suffer in any way at all from contributing to the survey's success. Your co-operation is very much appreciated.

Office of Population Censuses and Surveys
Social Survey Division
St Catherines House
10 Kingsway
London WC2B 6JP
Telephone 01-242 0262

S829

W29 OPCS 10/78

G3 Regular commitments questions sheet

FAMILY EXPENDITURE SURVEY – 1979

REGULAR COMMITMENTS QUESTIONS

Area	Ser.	Hld.

<table>
<tr><td>INITIAL INTERVIEW</td></tr>
</table>

ALL EXPLANATORY NOTES AND ADDITIONAL INFORMATION
SHOULD BE INSERTED AT THE RELEVANT QUESTION/ITEM
IN THE A, B OR D SCHEDULES: <u>NOT</u> ON THIS SHEET

ASK ALL SPENDERS Q'S A-D DURING 'D' BOOK
INTRODUCTION

A. Are (any of) you likely to buy any Postal Orders or Money Orders in the next two weeks?

YES Y Enter Per. No.
NO   X ask B

	INDICATE BY (✓) WHEN ITEM APPEARS IN D RECORDS FOR:		
	Per. No.	1st week	2nd week
	....	....	....
	....	....	....
	....	....	....

POINTS TO EXPLAIN WHEN <u>SHOWING</u> D RECORD:

WHEN SPENT PURPOSE OF POSTAL ORDER/MONEY ORDER SHOULD BE GIVEN. POUNDAGE SHOULD BE RECORDED ON A SEPARATE LINE.

TO INTERVIEWER.

B. Do any spenders have a credit card (Q40d)?

IF YES, EXPLAIN CREDIT SHEET

C. Do (any of) you make any other regular payments to the:

NO

	Person Number	How often do you pay the ....?			INDICATE BY (✓) WHEN ITEM APPEARS IN D RECORDS FOR:	
		Weekly	Fort-nightly	Other (CHECK D BELOW)	1st week	2nd week
	....					
	....					
Milkman? X	....	1	2	3	....	....
Newsagent? X	....	1	2	3	....	....
Football Pools? X	....	1	2	3	....	....
or Any Others? (specify below) X						
DO NOT INCLUDE COMMITMENTS COVERED BY Q's ON A SCHEDULE	....	1	2	3	....	....
	....	1	2	3	....	....
	....	1	2	3 CHECK D BELOW	....	....

SEPARATE AMOUNT PAID FOR

Milk, cream etc.*

Newspapers, comics etc.*

(*At checking call: confirm and <u>note</u> eg milk only)

IF YES at D

GROCERY & MEAT ACCOUNTS: Check that bill can be itemised on day paid; if not ask informant to record total bill and all items acquired on the account during record period.

IF FREQUENCY AT C IS CODED 3 ASK:

D. Will you be paying your .... bill/account within the next fourteen days?

Yes Y Specify in box
No   X

....
....

Jan 1979

W1505 OPCS

136

G4 Consistency checks sheet

FAMILY EXPENDITURE SURVEY

CONSISTENCY CHECKS-1979

The following should be completed directly after interview

Area	Ser.	Hld.

FIRST CHECK AT HOME

NB MISSING OR DISCREPANT INFORMATION SHOULD BE QUERIED WITH HLD. ON RECALL, & AMENDMENTS AND NOTES SHOULD BE MADE ON INTERVIEW SCHEDULES, NOT ON THIS SCHEDULE.

A Schedule

Front Page

Col.(2) Are there children under the age of 19 who are taking full time education (or under school age)?   Yes .... Y   No X

IF YES
1) Child Benefit should appear at Q.30 of mother's B Schedule for all children.

Col.(5) Are there any children under the age of 1 year?   Yes .... Y

IF YES
1) N.I. Maternity Allowance and/or Grant should appear at Q.39 and/or Q.41A on mother's B Schedule

Col.(6) Is HOH a married woman whose husband is temporarily away?   Yes .... Y   No X

IF YES
1) Check whether husband is a member of household.
   a) If household member. Enter him in household box and ask wife for details of husband's income on a 'B' schedule.
   b) If not household member Exclude from household box. Enter details of husband's allowance at Q.60A of wife's 'B' schedule, and annotate any household items paid by husband.

Col.(7) Are there any children attending Private School? (codes 4-6)   Yes .... Y   No X

IF YES
1) School fees should appear at Q.47 of A Schedule

Page 2

Q.13 Is there a garage shown at this question?   Yes .... Y   No X

IF YES
1) Is there a garage shown at Q.15 B?   Yes .... Y   No .... X PROBE

Page 13

Q.32 (a1)(1) Is the rebate being used for the purchase of goods?   Yes .... Y   No X
(1)

IF YES
Enter details of goods bought on this form of credit at Q.40, and the full rebate (including the credit payment at Q.32)

Page 14

Q.34 A(1) & Has any informant had a motor vehicle in the last 12 months?   Yes .... Y   No X
(11)/B

IF YES
1) If no road tax paid, enter nil and note reason and who pays it eg. employer.

Q.35 Has a vehicle been bought outright within the last 12 months?   Yes .... Y   No X

Check Q.42 to ensure no duplication with vehicle on HP or loan there.

IF YES
1) Make sure that for all vehicles entered, total expenditure on road tax and vehicle insurance is excluded from cost of vehicle but noted at Q34 A (1)(11)

Jan 1979

Page 16

Q.39 Does any informant use Standing orders or direct debit at a bank/bank budget account?   Yes .... Y   No X

IF YES
i) Look out for items that should also appear at other Q's on A schedule and check that amounts agree (eg. HP should also appear at Q.40 etc) Do not copy amounts.
ii) Describe standing order fully, eg. house structure insurance, gas budget account.

B Schedule

Q.6-11 Has any spender just started a new job?   Yes .... Y   No X

IF YES
1) Details of earning should be entered about new job and not for the last job. If not known, accept estimate or recall when first payslip available. If unable to obtain this information write details of pay received from last job in margin.

Is informant not working but waiting to take up a job already obtained?   Yes .... Y

IF YES
1) Enter details of job and what he expects to earn in his new job.

Q.12-15 (1) If hours vary, check that pay varies accordingly. If there is no variation in pay, probe for reason.

(2) If pay varies, check that hours vary accordingly. If there is no variation in hours, probe for reason.

Q.19-21 Items shown here as being refunded should also appear in the relevant D Schedules
26, 28, 63 if they occur during the 14 day record keeping period.

A & B SCHEDULES

Documents consulted   Check that Documents consulted codes have been ringed appropriately at:
A SCH Q's 18, 19, 20, 22, 23, 28, 50
B SCH Q's 11

DK codes   Check that DK codes have been ringed appropriately at :
A SCH Q's 18, 19, 20, 28
B SCH Q's 27,

W1513 OPCS

G5 Wage/salary check and schedule B final check sheet.

ALL NOTES SHOULD BE MADE ON THE RELEVANT INTERVIEW DOCUMENTS

FIRST CHECK AT HOME

			CHECK AT ADDRESS
			(✓) IF IN RECORD
		Week 1	Week 2

Is payment made by slot meter?

GAS Yes 1
      No 2

ELECT. Yes 1
        No 2

Has household a TELEPHONE?
    Yes 1
    No 2

PHONE CALLS

PROBE CASH/SET ASIDE

FIRST CHECK AT HOME / CHECK AT RECALL

Copy from A Schedule if paid weekly, fortnightly or monthly

REGULAR COMMITMENT	£	P	Period Per No.	(✓) IF IN RECORD Week 1	Week 2	DO A & D AMOUNTS & PERIODS TALLY? Yes	No	
Rent (garage)						8 8	8 8	PROBE
Site Rent (caravan)						8 8	8 8	&
Rent (accommodation)						8 8	8 8	ADJUST
Rates						8 8	8 8	OR
Mortgage payment						8 8	8 8	NOTE
T.V. Rental						8 8	8 8	REASON
Season Ticket						8 8	8 8	on
Ins. Co's (NAME)						8 8	8 8	D
						8 8	8 8	SCHEDULE
						8 8	8 8	
						8 8	8 8	
Instalments/Clubs						8 8	8 8	PROBE
						8 8	8 8	&
						8 8	8 8	ADJUST
						8 8	8 8	OR
						8 8	8 8	NOTE
Other items						8 8	8 8	REASON
						8 8	8 8	on
						8 8	8 8	D
						8 8	8 8	SCHEDULE

FINAL CALL ROUTINE

A Are there 2 COMPLETE RECORD BOOKS for each Spender? Yes No
(and full income details)

B Check if any REFUNDS, or WINNINGS or PAYMENTS on Page 18 of D.

C Ask SPECIAL CIRCUMSTANCES Question on A Schedule.

D Check (a) SURNAME/S   ) Explain that
     (b) INITIALS   ) this is for
     (c) FULL POSTAL ADDRESS) the postal
                          order

1 Code Column 10 on front page
2 Give reason on page 23, & explain payment may not be made

E Mention that the postal order will take 4-5 weeks to arrive.

F Warn that we may need to contact them either by letter or interviewer recall if there are any queries.

Jan 1979

FIRST CHECK AT HOME

Area	Ser.	Hd.

"B" SCHEDULE – 1979

COMPLETE FOR EACH HOUSEHOLD MEMBER WHO IS AN EMPLOYEE

Q.5 Does this date come within the period shown at Q.7 counting back from date of interview?
    Yes
    No

	Per	Per	Per ....
	Y	Y	Y
	X	X	X

IF NO Explain why. (refer back to Q.2 for possible inconsistency)

Page 4 Copy pay details for each applicable spender in box below, and calculate gross pay. If gross pay has been shown on schedule check with calculated gross. If difference ask for explanation. DO NOT COPY CALCULATED GROSS ON TO INCOME SCHEDULE (PAGE 4).

Q. No.	Per. No.	£	Per. No.	£	Per. No.	£
6	Net Pay		Net Pay		Net Pay	
9	Income tax paid		Income tax paid		Income tax paid	
10	N.I. Contribution		N.I. Contribution		N.I. Contribution	
11	Other Deductions		Other Deductions		Other Deductions	
11	Other Deductions		Other Deductions		Other Deductions	
11	Other Deductions		Other Deductions		Other Deductions	
11	Other Deductions		Other Deductions		Other Deductions	
	Total including refund		Total including refund		Total including refund	
8(a)	Less (−) tax refund if any		Less (−) tax refund if any		Less (−) tax refund if any	
	= Total Gross Pay		= Total Gross Pay		= Total Gross Pay	

INTERVIEWER'S NOTES:

W1504 OPCS

G6 Form E, record of identity of cooperating houshold members

FAMILY EXPENDITURE SURVEY   SS 829 E

COOPERATING HOUSEHOLDS

TWO COPIES - IN INK OR BALL-POINT PEN

	Area	Ser.	Hld.

Area .... Ref. No

Postal Address ....
(BLOCK CAPITALS)
....

.... No. of households at address ....

Date and time of first call made at address ....

Interviewer's signature .... Auth. No. ....

LIST OF PERSONS TO WHOM PAYMENT
IS TO BE MADE (ie SPENDERS)

PERSONS IN
HOUSEHOLD:

All inc. children: ....

No. of spenders: ....

Personal number	Surname *(BLOCK CAPITALS)*	Initials	Mr/Mrs/Miss
....			
....			
....			
....			
....			
....			
....			

OFFICE USE

Certified correct ....

NOTES ABOUT SPENDERS MUST NOT APPEAR ON THIS FORM

W134 OPCS 10/78

FAMILY EXPENDITURE SURVEY

SS 829 F

Area	Ser.	Hld.

NON-COOPERATING CASES

ONE COPY ONLY - IN INK OR BALL POINT PEN

Area............................. Interviewer..................... Auth. No.........

Address.. No. of households.............
BLOCK CAPITALS   at address

....

....

_____

i) Date and time of first call made at address ....

ii) Surnames of residents at address:

COPY SURNAMES FROM ADDRESS LIST	Is someone with this name resident here?		
	DK	YES	NO
....	O	Y	X
....	O	Y	X
....	O	Y	X
....	O	Y	X
....	O	Y	X
....	O	Y	X

RECORD NAMES OF ANY OTHER RESIDENTS VOLUNTEERED BY INFORMANT:

....

....

....

iii) REASONS FOR NON-COOPERATION

RING LETTER AND NUMBER

Exclusions 1
          Hotel ....a
          Public House ....b
          Other premises where business & private expenditure
.....................................cannot be split, eg Cafe SPECIFY ON LEFT c
          Guest house/commercial Boarding house ....d
.....................................Institution SPECIFY ON LEFT ....e
          Household contains USA serviceman ....f
          Household contains diplomat ....g

No sample selected at address 1A

No household at address 2
          House empty at first call ....g
          House demolished ....h
.........Other SPECIFY i

Household away and not expected to return until after placing month 3

Household about to leave district within three weeks of first contact 4

Any other case where no contact can be made with any member of household 5

Refusal (all cases of non-cooperation where at least one member
                    is seen, except codes 4 or 7) 6

Refusal after promising to coop. (coded Y, cooperating, on form H) 7

W133 OPCS 10/78

OFF. USE

G8 Form H, weekly progress return

FAMILY EXPENDITURE SURVEY   SS 829 H

WEEKLY PROGRESS RETURN

Interviewer's name .... Auth. No. .... Area ....

Date of despatch to Field Service Section .... Area No. ....

THIS RETURN RELATES TO PLACING WEEK:	RING	All months except Feb	February
	1	days 1 to 7 inclusive	1 to 7
	2	8 to 15	8 to 14
	3	16 to 23	15 to 21
	4	24 to end of month	22 to end

Serial number						
Household number						
Promised to begin records during this week	Y	Y	Y	Y	Y	Y
Excluded	1	1	1	1	1	1
No sample selected at address	1A	1A	1A	1A	1A	1A
No household at address	2	2	2	2	2	2
Away and not returning until after end of placing month	3	3	3	3	3	3
About to leave district	4	4	4	4	4	4
Other non-contact	5	5	5	5	5	5
Refusal	6	6	6	6	6	6
Ring if already returned to HQ	X	X	X	X	X	X

CONCEALED MULTI-HOUSEHOLDS

Serial number				
No. of households eligible for interview				

Total number covered
by all previous returns .... Number in table ....
*(If other than 4 give
reason overleaf)*

W135 OPCS 10/78

141

FAMILY EXPENDITURE SURVEY   SS 829 J

DESPATCH NOTE

Interviewer's name ....   Auth. No. ....

Date of despatch to Field Service Section ....   Area ....

Area No. ....

ENCLOSED ARE SCHEDULES FOR THE FOLLOWING:

Serial number					
Household number					
Completed documents for co-operating household	Y	Y	Y	Y	Y
Excluded	1	1	1	1	1
No sample selected at address	1A	1A	1A	1A	1A
No household at address	2	2	2	2	2
Away and not returning until after end of placing period	3	3	3	3	3
About to leave district	4	4	4	4	4
Other non-contact	5	5	5	5	5
Refusal					
Outright	6	6	6	6	6
At first promised co-operation and was coded Y on schedule H	7	7	7	7	7

No. of serial numbers for which schedules E or F returned herewith ....

W139 OPCS 10/78

G10 Calls and contact sheet

SS 830
FAMILY EXPENDITURE SURVEY
RECORD OF CALLS AND OUTCOME

INTERVIEWER'S NAME ....

IS THIS A CONTINUATION SHEET ?

AREA NO.   SERIAL   HSEHLD

AUTH. NO:

YES 1
NO 2

RING CALL NO:	1	2	3	4	5	6	7	8	9	10
Day										
Date Month										
Time: Hour										
use 24 hour clock Minute										
Any placing interviewing done	90	90	90	90	90	90	90	90	90	90
Checking call	C	C	C	C	C	C	C	C	C	C
Final collection	F	F	F	F	F	F	F	F	F	F
No reply	J	J	J	J	J	J	J	J	J	J
Appointment made	K	K	K	K	K	K	K	K	K	K
Interviewer withdraws	L	L	L	L	L	L	L	L	L	L

CODE FINAL OUTCOME:

FULLY CO-OPERATING HOUSEHOLD: [8]

EXCLUSION (INELIGIBLE) :   [1]
Hotel   a
Public house   b
Other premises where business
and private expenditure
cannot be split eg Cafe
SPECIFY...........   c
Guest House/Commercial
Boarding house   d
Institution SPECIFY
....   e
Household contains USA
servicemen   f
Household contains diplomat   g
NO SAMPLE AT SELECTED ADDRESS

NO HOUSEHOLD AT ADDRESS: [2]
H/H empty at first call   g
House demolished   h
Other (specify)   i

HOUSEHOLD AWAY AND NOT EXPECTED TO
RETURN UNTIL AFTER PLACING MONTH: [3]

H/H ABOUT TO LEAVE DISTRICT
WITHIN 3 WEEKS OF FIRST CONTACT: [4]

NON CONTACT:
Any other case where no
contact can be made   [5]

REFUSAL:
All cases of non co-operation
where at least one member is
seen, except codes 4 or 7   [6]

Refusal after promising to
co-operate, coded Y on
H form   [7]

FOR ALL INTERVIEWS (CODED 90 ABOVE)
SPECIFY TIME IN MINUTES SPENT
ON EACH CALL CODED 90, C or F ABOVE

ALL CODED 1-7: PLEASE TURN OVER

PLACING 90	CHECKING C	FINAL COLLECTION F

W 1515 OPCS 10/77

CODES 1-4   PLEASE DESCRIBE FULLY HOW YOU REACHED THIS CONCLUSION

CODE 5   PLEASE DESCRIBE FULLY ANY STEPS YOU TOOK TO TRY TO CONTACT THE HOUSEHOLD.

CODES 6-7   PLEASE DESCRIBE FULLY WHO YOU SAW, WHAT HAPPENED, AND WHAT WAS SAID AT
EACH STAGE OF CONTACT, AND COMPLETE BOX BELOW.

SEEN	H/H AT SELECTED ADDRESS.	SEX	EST.
YES NO	STATE BY RELATIONSHIP TO HOH	M F	AGE
Y N		M F	
Y N		M F	
Y N		M F	
Y N		M F	

GIVE YOUR JUDGED REASON FOR THE REFUSAL
(whether or not different from the informant's stated reason)

G11 Pre-sampled multi-household selection sheet

Selection Table

NUMBER OF H/HLDS FOUND AT THAT ADDRESS	INTERVIEW AT HOUSEHOLDS NUMBERED
2	1,2
3	1,2,3
4	1,3,4
5	2,4,5
6	3,5,6
7	2,5,7
8	1,4,7
9	2,4,9
10	1,5,9
11	1,6,11
12	2,3,8
13	1,3,10
14	6,7,11
15	4,5,7
16	1,2,12
17	3,4,7
18	8,10,17
19	3,5,9
20	4,8,14
21	3,6,17
22	12,15,19

W15425 OPCS 11/79

GHS/FES

PRE-SAMPLED MULTI-HOUSEHOLD SELECTION SHEET

TO BE RETURNED TO FIELD WITH CALLS & CONTACT/OUTCOME SHEET

Area	
Ser. No.	

List of Households

H/Hld No:	DESCRIPTION OF HOUSEHOLDS eg. Location and Surnames if available	OUTCOME CODE Transfer from C & C / C & O sheet
1		
2		
3		
4		
5		
6		
7		
8		
9		
10		
11		
12		
13		
14		
15		
16		
17		
18		
19		
20		
21		
22		

IF MORE THAN 22 HOUSEHOLDS CONTINUE ON SEPARATE SHEET

Procedure: Note down the households on the table above. This must be done
systematically. Consecutively numbered flats are put down in
order. If unnumbered start with the lowest floor and work in a
clockwise direction thus:-
1. GROUND FLOOR, FRONT, L.H. SIDE
2. GROUND FLOOR, BACK
3. GROUND FLOOR, FRONT, R.H. SIDE
4. FIRST FLOOR, FRONT, etc.
NB EXCLUDE empty flats

Turn the sheet over for table showing household(s) to be interviewed.
On the front of the sheet ring the number(s) of the selected household(s).
Finally transfer code from Calls and Contact/Outcome sheet to 'outcome' box.

G12 Concealed multi-household selection sheet

SELECTION TABLE (B)

NUMBER OF H/HLDS FOUND AT THAT ADDRESS	INTERVIEW AT HOUSEHOLD(S) NUMBERED
7 or less	No interview
8	6
9	9
10	7
11	2
12	11
13	7
14	3,7
15	9,8
16	7,11
17	9,14
18	13,8
19	18,1
20	3,8
21	13,18
22	12,11
23	12,11
24	7,13,14
25	16,3,17

If the number of households found is more than 25 please telephone Sampling for instructions: GHS 2353 FES 2335

GHS/FES

CONCEALED MULTI-HOUSEHOLD SELECTION SHEET

TO BE RETURNED TO FIELD WITH CALLS & CONTACT/OUTCOME SHEET

Area	
Ser. No.	

List of Households

H/Hld No.	DESCRIPTION OF HOUSEHOLDS eg. Location and Surnames if available	OUTCOME CODE Transfer from C&C/C&O sheet
1		
2		
3		
4		
5		
6		
7		
8		
9		
10		
11		
12		
13		
14		
15		
16		
17		
18		
19		
20		
21		
22		

V15420 OPCS 11/79

IF MORE THAN 22 HOUSEHOLDS RING SAMPLING   GHS 2353   FES 2335

Procedure

1. Note down the households on the table above. This must be done systematically. Start at the lowest floor and work in a clockwise direction.
2. Turn the sheet over for the table showing households to be interviewed. On the front of the sheet ring the numbers of the selected households.
3. Finally transfer code from Calls and Contact/Outcome sheet to 'outcome' box.

Appendix H Bibliography

Abel-Smith, B and Townsend, PB. *The poor and the poorest: a new analysis of the Ministry of Labour's Family Expenditure Surveys of 1953—54 and 1960. Occasional Papers on Social Administration No 17. Bell. London. 1965.*

Atkinson, J. *A Handbook for interviewers* — a manual for Government Social Survey interviewing staff, describing practices and procedures for structured interviewing. M 136. HMSO. 1967. (Currently being revised).

CSO. FES/Blue Book expenditure comparisons for 1970—75 (available on request from the Central Statistical Office).

CSO. The distribution of income in the United Kingdom 1976/77. *Economic Trends*, February 1979. HMSO.

CSO. The effects of taxes and benefits on household income 1977. *Economic Trends*, January 1979. HMSO. Claycamp, H J. *The composition of consumer savings portfolios.* Studies in Consumer Savings No.3. Consumer Savings Project, Inter-University Committee for Research on Consumer Behavior, Bureau of Economic and Business Research, University of Illinois, Urbana, Ill. 1963.

Department of Employment. *Family Expenditure Survey.* Annual reports. HMSO.

Department of Employment. *Family Expenditure Survey information pack.*

Department of Energy. *Energy tariffs and the poor.* Department of Energy Information Directorate. 1976; available from the Library, Department of Energy, Thames House South, Millbank, London SW1P 4QJ. Also available is The Family Expenditure Survey — Expenditure on fuels. 1979.

Department of Finance, Northern Ireland. *Northern Ireland Family Expenditure Survey.* Annual reports. HMSO Belfast.

Dight, S. *Scottish drinking habits.* HMSO. 1976.

Donnen, S and Haskey, J. Alcoholism and cirrhosis of the liver. *Population Trends 7.* HMSO. 1977.

Ferber, R. *The reliability of consumer reports of financial assets and debts.* Studies in Consumer Savings No.6. Consumer Savings Project, Inter-University Committee for Research on Consumer Behavior, Bureau of

Economic and Business Research, University of Illinois, Urbana, Ill. 1966.

Ferber, R and Frankel, M. *The collection, measurement and evaluation of savings account reports.* Report 1 under contract HEW-100-77-0112. HEW Office of Survey Development. Washington, DC. Survey Research Laboratory, University of Illinois, Urbana, Ill. 1978.

Giles, GE and Worsley, TE. Development of methods for forecasting car ownership and use. *Economic Trends*, August 1979. HMSO. pp99—108.

Harris, R. Differential response in the Family Expenditure Survey — the effect on estimates of the re-distribution of income. *Statistical News*, November 1977. HMSO. pp39.7—39.12.

Inter-week variation in the FES — February-March 1978. An unpublished paper obtainable from the authors.

Kemsley, WFF. *Some technical problems in planning budget surveys.* M 78. HMSO. 1952.

Kemsley, WFF. Designing a budget survey. *Applied Statistics*, Vol VIII No 2. 1959. pp114—123.

Kemsley, WFF. Interviewer variability and a budget survey. *Applied Statistics*, Vol IX No 2. 1960. pp112—8.

Kemsley, WFF. The Household Expenditure Survey of the Ministry of Labour — variability in the 1953—54 Enquiry. *Applied Statistics*, Vol X No 3. 1961. pp117—135.

Kemsley, WFF. Interviewer variability in expenditure surveys. *Journal of the Royal Statistical Society, Series A (General)*, Vol 128 Part 1. 1965. pp118—139.

Kemsley, WFF. Sampling errors in the Family Expenditure Survey. *Applied Statistics*, Vol XV No 1. 1966. pp1—3.

Kemsley, WFF. *Family Expenditure Survey — Handbook on the sample, fieldwork and coding procedures.* HMSO. 1969.

Kemsley, WFF. Family Expenditure Survey — A study of differential response based on a comparison of the 1971 sample with the Census. *Statistical News*, November 1975. HMSO. pp31.16—31.22.

Kemsley, WFF. Collecting data on economic flow variables using interviews and record keeping, in Moss, L and

Goldstein, H (Eds). *The recall method in social surveys*. Studies in Education 9. University of London, Institute of Education. 1979. pp115—141.

Kemsley, WFF and Nicholson, JL. Some experiments in methods of conducting Family Expenditure Surveys. *Journal of the Royal Statistical Society, Series A (General)*, Vol 123 Part 3. 1960. pp307—328.

Lansing, J B, Ginsburg, G P and Braaton, K. An investigation of response error. Studies in Consumer Savings No.2 Consumer Savings Project, Inter-University Committee for Research on Consumer Behavior, Bureau of Economics and Business Research,University of Illinois, Urbana. I11. 1961.

McClements, LD. The economics of social security. Heinemann. London. 1978.

Maurice, R (Ed). *National account statistics: sources and methods*. HMSO 1968.

Method of construction and calculation of the Index of Retail Prices. HMSO. 1967.

OPCS. *The General Household Survey 1978*. HMSO. 1980.

Pearl, R. *Methodology of consumer expenditure surveys*. Working Paper No 27. Bureau of the Census, Washington, DC. 1966.

Prais, SJ and Houthakker, HS. *The analysis of family budgets with an application to two British Surveys conducted in 1937—39 and their detailed results*. University of Cambridge Department of Applied Economics, Monograph 4. Cambridge University Press. Cambridge. 1955.

Report of the Cost of Living Advisory Committee. Cmnd 3677. HMSO. 1968.

Report of the Committee on Privacy (The Younger Committee). Cmnd 5012. HMSO. 1972.

Report of the Committee on Data Protection (The Lindop Committee). Cmnd 7341. HMSO. 1978.

Report of the Committee into Local Government Finance, Annex 19. Cmnd 6453. HMSO. 1976.

Stark, T. *The distribution of income in eight countries*. Background Paper No 4. Royal Commission on the Distribution of Income and Wealth. HMSO. 1977.

SOEC. *Methodology of surveys on family budgets, 1980*. EUROSTAT. 1980.

Sudman, S and Ferber, R. *Experiments in obtaining consumer expenditures of durable goods by recall procedures — A preliminary report*. Survey Research Laboratory, University of Illinois, Urbana, I11. 1970.

Sudman, S and Ferber, R. *Consumer Panels*. American Marketing Association, Chicago, I11. 1979.

Townsend, P (Ed). *The concept of poverty: Working Papers on methods of investigation and life-styles of the poor in different countries*. Heinemann. London. 1970. See particularly Chapter 5.

Townsend, P. *Poverty in the United Kingdom: a survey of household resources and standards of living*. Penguin Books. Harmondsworth. 1979.

Turner, R. Inter-week variations in expenditure recorded during a two-week survey of family expenditure. *Applied Statistics*, Vol IV No.3. 1961. pp136—146.

US Bureau of the Census. *US Consumer Expenditure Survey 1972—73 — A preliminary evaluation*. Technical Paper No 45. US Bureau of the Census. Washington, DC. 1978.

Wilson, P. *Drinking in England and Wales*. HMSO. 1980.

Printed in England for Her Majesty's Stationery Office
by Commercial Colour Press, London E.7.
Dd.0699243 K9 12/80